A Good Start

The Aussteier or Dowry

Jeannette Lasansky

An Oral Traditions Project

Library of Congress Cataloging-in-Publication Data

Lasansky, Jeannette.
A good start: the Aussteier or dowry / by Jeannette
    Lasansky. p. cm.
"An Oral Traditions Project."
Includes bibliographical references.
ISBN 0-917127-06-4
  1. Dowry—Pennsylvania—History.
2. Dowry—Pennsylvania—History—Sources.
3. Mennonites—Pennsylvania—History—Sources.
4. Amish—Pennsylvania—History—Sources. I. Oral Traditions
Project (Union County Historical Society) II. Title.
HQ1017.L37 1990
392'.5'09748—dc20   89-48999
                                                   CIP

Published by the Oral Traditions Project of the Union County Historical Society, Court House, S. Second Street, Lewisburg, Pennsylvania 17837

Copyright © 1990, Oral Traditions Project. All rights reserved.

Partial Funding: Pennsylvania Council on the Arts
Editors: Joseph G. Foster, Elsbeth Steffensen
Design: Karelis & Timm/Graphic Design
Photography: The Terry Wild Studio
Typography: Batsch Spectracomp, Inc.
Printing: Paulhamus Litho, Inc.

Cover: A male dowry grouping around the first quarter of the nineteenth century might include such items as illustrated here: a blanket chest which would later evolve into a desk for males. This Centre County example is marked "1817". Courtesy of a private collection. On the chest's top is period currency or broken banknotes from the 1830s and 1840s, courtesy of the Heritage Center of Lancaster County; a linen grain bag stenciled "Samuel Meyer / 1828/4", courtesy of Dr. and Mrs. Donald M. Herr; the Slear family Bible printed in German Gothic script in Philadelphia in 1829, courtesy of Gary W. and Donna M. Slear. At the base of the chest are oats and wheat, courtesy of Harold B. Walter, in a rye coil double-ended grain measure, courtesy of Mr. and Mrs. Richard Flanders Smith; forged iron hay knife, courtesy of the Hans Herr House, Lancaster; forged iron log chain, courtesy of Arthur L. Reist; potatoes in painted oak splint bushel stamped "MORRIS", courtesy of William and Jeannette Lasansky; and painted grain rake, courtesy of Gary W. and Donna M. Slear.

Inside cover: Caleb Johnson's account book covers the years 1766 to 1797. Courtesy of the Library of the Chester County Historical Society, West Chester, PA. Manuscript number 76509.

Contents: Pennsylvania-German sgraffito red earthenware dish from Frederick Township, Montgomery County. The German inscription around the rim translates to: "Susanna Grob. She who trusts in God will also become a bride. She who can wait will also get a husband. October 21, 1793", 2¼" h. x 12⅛" d. Courtesy of the Philadelphia Museum of Art, purchased by the Baugh-Barber Fund. Accession number '59-41-1.

ACKNOWLEDGEMENTS

We would like particularly to thank these people for their assistance on this project: Joel D. Alderfer at the Mennonite Historical Library in Lansdale who not only led us through their collections' important *aussteier* or dowry holdings but who also kept thinking of other family accounts located in private collections; Carolyn C. Wenger at the Lancaster Mennonite Historical Society, who initially had no manuscript material for us but a year later, when filing the newly-acquired Bomberger family materials, found family accounts books and wrote us; Holly K. Green of Boyertown who advised us of an early family book and who also helped us tie up some genealogical loose ends in Berks, Bucks, and Montgomery counties; Stanley A. Kaufman, director/curator at the German Culture Museum in Walnut Creek, Ohio, who was able to show us actual family furniture pieces that were noted in his grandfather's account book, and Don Yoder, who apprised us of a former student's paper on the dowry and specifically the Leiby court case which illustrated the inter-relationship of family books and wills.

As crucial to this project as the manuscript sources was the ability to interview Amish and Old Order Mennonites about their current *aussteier* practices. The following individuals helped me make those invaluable contacts: Donald Carpenter of Vicksburg, Trish Herr of Lancaster, John Hostetler of the Anabaptist Studies Center at Elizabethtown College, Sylvia King of Belleville, and Mary Koons of Mifflinburg. Elsbeth Steffensen and Laurene Lozoski were important in their notetaking and transcriptions of the conversations. I also thank all who gave of their time to talk, often at great lengths, with us.

Also of great help was Amos B. Hoover of Muddy Creek Farm Library in Denver; Alan G. Keyser of the Goschenhoppen Historians; David Dunn, curator of the Packwood House Museum; Marion Strode and Rosemary Phillips at the Chester County Historical Society's library; Laurie Rofin and Barbara Weir at the Chester County Archives; Tandy Hersh of Carlisle, and John J. Snyder, Jr. of Washington Borough.

Shirley Bingaman, Emily Blair, Laurene Lozoski, Martha Root, Nancy Ruhl, and Elsbeth Steffensen were my invaluable research assistants who read diaries, letters, account books, indentures, wills, estate inventories, and nineteenth-century periodicals at the Berks County Historical Society, the Chester County Historical Society, Swarthmore College, the Lancaster Mennonite Historical Society, the Lebanon County Historical Society, the Lehigh County Historical Society, Winterthur Museum and Library, the Lancaster County Historical Society, the Mennonite Historical Library, the Muddy Creek Farm Library, the Spruance Library at the Mercer Museum, the Schwenkfelder Library in Pennsburg, the Historical Society of York County, and the Pattee Library at Penn State.

Also, the exhibition planning sessions at the Heritage Center of Lancaster County in the spring and fall of 1989 made me articulate my discoveries and to make them a more cogent whole. My thanks to Pat Keller-Conner, director, and Susan Messimer, registrar, for their inquiring minds.

I would also like to thank my daughter, Diana, who is now away at school and is no longer part of our regular research team yet still provides steady encouragement and sends bibliographic references and ideas. She too got involved indirectly with a course paper on Italian dowries in the Renaissance with their economic and social ramifications.

Also, collectors such as Dr. Paul M. Corman, Don and Trish Herr, Forest R. Kauffman, Jane and John Ziegler, whose input was important in previous studies and who, after learning of our project, came through with important dowry finds this year. Such enthusiasm and follow-up are essential to our work and to a better understanding of things Pennsylvanian.

Jeannette Lasansky
May 1990

Contents

4 FOREWORD

6 DEFINITIONS/
DOWRY, AUSSTEIER, DOWER

14 A COMPLEX INHERITANCE SYSTEM/
INDENTURES, FAMILY BOOKS, WILLS

30 IT'S IN THE ACCOUNTS/
WRITTEN AND ORAL

72 INITIALED AND DATED OBJECTS

84 BIBLIOGRAPHY

88 INDEX

Foreword

Over the past thirteen years, the Oral Traditions Project has researched different aspects of Pennsylvania's material culture from the eighteenth, nineteenth, and early twentieth centuries. Starting with pottery—high-fired stoneware and its cousin earthenware, then basketry, forged iron and plain tinware, quilts, homewoven textiles—sheets, grain bags, blankets and bed coverlets, we have gained insight into a range of what was made in the rural areas and small urban settlements here, and we have come to a better understanding of the attitudes of traditional craftspeople and the needs of their local communities.

In the anticipation of and preparation for setting up a household, all of these craft skills were used as well as others—for instance, those of the cabinetmaker, clockmaker, wheelwright and harnessmaker. The "gifts from home" for young people, both male and female, was called the dowry by the Anglo-Saxon community, or *aussteier* by many Pennsylvania Germans. It was also called "outfitting" and "advancement" and was considered essential in helping children make the transition to becoming responsible adults and heads of households.

The dowry symbolized preparation for one of life's major rites of passage. In a predominantly rural and agricultural society it also provided the necessary economic foothold for successfully continuing the family business. For some, it might have allowed for social mobility as well. The counterpart in today's society is perhaps college education.

The dowry was also part of a complex inheritance system for it was the first apportioning of family goods, lands, and cash. Inherent in it were parental and community approval and control during the eighteenth century and much of the nineteenth century. It was a tradition central to rural life. In a more urban environment it appeared to lose its significance. However, it is still an important aspect in the lives of our more traditional farm groups such as the Amish and Old Order Mennonites. Vestiges of it appear in our more mainstream culture, as high school senior girls are still solicited about getting their Lane cedar chest.

This book will examine the dowry as it evolved over more than two centuries in Pennsylvania for our two earliest and largest settlement groups—the Pennsylvania Germans and their "English" or Anglo neighbors.

Some fine research and writing on different aspects of the dowry, particularly among the Pennsylvania Germans, has provided both a factual foundation and a conceptual framework for our study and we should mention the more prominent pieces. Much of our new research corroborates and then expands upon what was pointed out earlier.

For instance, Russell Wieder Gilbert's extensive work on Pennsylvania-German wills over a seventeen-county area was a crucial resource in illustrating the preservation of the dowry portion through the time of marriage to death. At times wills also reflected the widow's share, or *ausbehalt*. We are indebted to the Pennsylvania German Folklore Society for publishing his work as their fifteenth volume in 1951. Their foreword sums it up: "One can only wonder that this task has not been done before. Our forefathers have left no documentary evidence that reveals more clearly the length, breadth and depth of the character of the Pennsylvania-German people, all the more genuine because these wills were done under a compelling sense of earthly finality. Here is a rich storehouse for the philologist, the antiquarian, the economist and particularly the cultural historian." Amen. Gilbert also wrote a subsequent article called "Pennsylvania-German Wills in Berks County." (*Historical Review of Berks County,* Vol. XXI, No. 1, October-December, 1955)

Twenty years later, the Pennsylvania German Society began translating, editing, and publishing a series of important historical documents; the first in the series was *The Account Book of the Clemens Family of Lower Salford Township, Montgomery County, Pennsylvania 1749-1857.* Raymond E. Hollenbach did the translation of this family book which covers the business of three successive generations of Mennonite farmers in Lower Salford Township, Montgomery County from 1749 to 1857. This period was one of assimilation of "English" cultural values; hence some changes in life style in the Pennsylvania-German farmhouse, of transition from an era of scarcity of goods to one of abundance, of a switch to urban mass-produced goods from an earlier local craftsman orientation, as well as a change in giving less land but more goods (usually tools) for male children. Mr. Hollenbach initially discussed the *aussteier* in the Clemens book with a series of articles that appeared in the *Allentown Morning Call* from March 23 to April 6, 1968.

An interesting court case was Jacob Leiby's—where a family book with its advancements was interpreted as having no bearing on the disposition of the family's estate as reflected in the will. This late nineteenth-century Berks County litigation is particularly pertinent because it illustrates the conflict that can be present between a literal interpretation of the common law and a community's long-held cultural beliefs and customs. John Seidel in his unpublished paper "Dowry and Inheritance in Rural Pennsylvania German Society" sets the Leiby case within a sociological and anthropological context.

Scott Swank in *The Arts of the Pennsylvania Germans* (New York: W. W. Norton, 1983) takes the evidence one step further as he juxtaposes some historical *aussteier* manuscript sources, such as the Clemens accounts and those of furniture makers, with contemporary practice among a few Amish families. He found striking similarities and a window through which to view past traditions and objects.

Recent, solid historical work on the material goods of some "English" Chester countians by Lee Ellen Griffith as well as two detailed studies of Pennsylvania Quaker communities by Barry John Levy provided a foundation for some assumptions on their "outfitting" practices that would not have been possible otherwise. Ms. Griffith's work concentrated on eighteenth-century line-and-berry inlaid furniture in Chester County, much of which was marked with initials and dates. Her first published work dealt with one form exclusively (*The Pennsylvania Spice Box*, West Chester: Chester County Historical Society, 1986). This catalog was followed by her Ph.D. thesis in 1988 and an article, also on this regional furniture style, for *Antiques* in May, 1989. Mr. Levy's work appeared first in his Ph.D. thesis, "Light in the Valley," (1976), also for the University of Pennsylvania, and most recently in his book, *Quakers and the American Family/British Settlement in the Delaware Valley* (Oxford, England: Oxford University Press, 1988).

With these published works and unpublished theses in mind, our project proceeded on the assumption that if we could examine period manuscripts—family books, furniture maker accounts, inventories, wills, letters and diaries—well-established patterns of commonly-held customs would emerge. Research centers, known for an abundance of such documents like the Chester and Bucks County historical societies were visited immediately. The list grew to include among others the Mennonite Historical Society Library in Lansdale, the Lancaster County Mennonite Library as well as private libraries and collections like the Muddy Creek Farm Library.

These manuscripts, many from the nineteenth century, were then contrasted with what appeared in periodicals of the time. Their public dialogues about private concerns were numerous and thoughtful although couched in florid romantic prose. Musings as to what was deemed proper, necessary, or possible in making marriage choices and preparation were obviously changing for society's mainstream—an increasingly urbanized one.

Patterns not dissimilar to those of the agrarian past did emerge however when we talked about contemporary practices with Amish and Old Order Mennonites. Not satisfied with a few informants, we established a series of interviews in different areas of settlement within the state: Lancaster, Mifflin, Union, Centre, and Clinton counties as well as among different branches within these Plain sects. The visits with these farm families confirmed what we had already seen in the earlier written family accounts: the dowry or *aussteier* was integral to such a family life style and to their rite of passage to self-sufficient adulthood.

Pennsylvania's dowry practices have evolved and will continue to be enriched by more recent immigrants. The Italians, Slavs and now the Hmong are among those groups who have brought diverse manifestations to this age-old concern with giving children a good start.

Baskets appeared sporadically in marriage portions. The earliest specific references were made for bread baskets (rye coil) sometimes in sets of six. Later basket listings included ample work or storage baskets often further defined as "willow" or "splint." These rye coil examples are larger than the average simple bread raising basket. From top to bottom: 16" d. x 6" h., 12¾" w. x 19¼" l. x 7¾" h.; 15½" w. x 18½" l. x 12½" h. with attached lid. Private collections.

Definitions

DOWRY, AUSSTEIER, DOWER

What is "dowry"? Two recent articles in *The New York Times* raise the issue as they expose aspects of dowry today in two distinctly different cultures: India and Louisiana. They illustrate the one commonality in the public's perception of dowry as being associated with females: what they bring to marriage or pay to the prospective groom at the time of marriage. Both stories also illustrate aspects of male control of the dowry. Beyond that, the tales are quite different.

The first article, "Ancient Bequest Puts Some Profit in Wedding Vows" (September 7, 1987, p. 6), tells of an unusual source of a community's dowry fund—one which was founded on traditional attitudes but which is used for some non-traditional purchases by recent recipients:

> The Poydras Dowry is the creation of Julien de Lalande Poydras, a merchant, politician and poet who began as an itinerant French peddler and was one of the richest men in Louisiana when he died in 1824. . . . According to legend, Poydras once wanted to marry a woman who was too poor to provide the dowry needed for their marriage. Because of that, they never married and he died a bachelor. But in his will, along with other charitable bequests, he left a provision intended to save others from a similar fate.
>
> West Baton Rouge Parish and Pointe Coupee Parish each got $30,000 with the instructions that the interest be used annually to provide dowries for all needy women. Pointe Coupee, just northwest of Port Allen, Louisiana, later diverted the money to an educational fund but West Baton Rouge has left the dowry intact.
>
> Originally the money was distributed according to a complex formula based on family wealth, and it went only to those deemed in need of it. But the system changed in 1951 and now the total interest generated each year is divided among all the couples married in the parish. After the year ends, a check is issued to each groom. The only requirement is that the bride must have lived in the parish for at least five years and she can get the dowry only once . . .
>
> When the dowry began, it could literally create fortunes because of the paucity of marriageable residents and the availability of cheap land. In 1841 for example, three newlyweds each received $966.21 at a time when land was selling for about 50 cents an acre. But although the fund has grown to $80,000 through land added to the original grant, its conservative management has struggled to keep up with inflation. In addition, oil leases on the land no longer provide the return they did a few years back. That has left a much larger group of newlyweds dividing up a stagnant pie. Last year 73 couples divided the $4963.17 generated by the fund.
>
> Sharon DeJean Landry, who got married in 1985, used her husband's $114.06 to balance her overdrawn checking account. Kirk Badeaux, who got married last year cashed his check and isn't sure what he did with it. "I might have gone out and partied," he said. "I may have spent it on bills."

An article on Indian dowry was called "Studying Accidental Deaths of Hindu Wives." (January 15, 1989) Such "dowry deaths" were said to have reached 610 in 1982 alone, and many are not reported, (*India Today*, 1983). There, as in the Louisiana example, dowry is sex-linked to females and is associated with the ability to purchase goods:

> Most marriages are arranged by families, and a man who does not marry for love learns he can marry for possessions. For this man, and his family, a woman becomes the ticket to a few imported watches, a stereo, a refrigerator, a motorbike or a car through the system of dowry. A dowry, once a way a father could endow a Hindu daughter with material goods when she could not inherit property, has evolved into a reward paid to a man and his family to take a woman off her parents' hands.
>
> The dowry system, which has also degenerated into extortion that goes on long after marriage, is outlawed in India, but it thrives.
>
> "The number of things people desire to have in their own houses but cannot afford, they now believe they can use the opportunity of a son's marriage to get," Mrs. Dandavate [a former member of the Indian Parliament] said. "In marrying a son, they can fulfil all their unfulfilled ambitions. The woman has become a kind of a commodity," she said. "In her name people can get any number of things."
>
> The fatalities of recently married women are often collectively known as "dowry deaths"—where a husband kills a wife for failing to deliver on a request, or she kills herself to spare her father further hardship.

Growing up in the 1950s in suburban New York State, I was only aware of a remnant of dowry—the "hope chest." I did not have such a chest nor had my mother, but I was aware of its tradition and that some other adolescent girls had

Coverlets were the topmost bedcovering of choice here in Pennsylvania-German families well into the nineteenth century and even later in the more culturally conservative families. This multiple shaft overshot example in red and blue wool and white cotton was probably given to Anna Kurtz (b. 1820, d. 1899) by her parents prior to her marriage to Jacob Stoltzfus. It was her maiden initials "A + K" and the date "1836" sewn in red wool cross stitch. It measures 106½" x 105¾". Courtesy of Dr. and Mrs. Donald M. Herr.

a chest or bureau where they were accumulating textile items or flatware in anticipation of marriage. On the other hand, a friend of mine, Elsbeth Steffensen, who was born as I was during World War II, remembers dowry being an active and important concept for young women where she grew up in Hannover, Germany. It meant not just the purchase but the making and embellishment of *many* textile items for the bed and table and the accumulation of related goods like flatware and crystal over time. And this custom continues today. William J. Goode in his book *World Revolution and Family Patterns* (New York: The Free Press, 1963, p. 34) gives statistics that confirm Elsbeth's tradition: "In 1952, sixty-five percent of a sample of married German women said that they brought a dowry to their marriage." Earlier, when land would have been the primary source of wealth, land or cash would have been a major dowry component. In much of Germany education, occupation, and the more limited range of goods in a "hope chest" were what remained of the concept by the 1950s.

Today—in the late twentieth century—where it remains a viable tradition, dowry means the goods females bring to marriage: some traditional, some not. These goods, provided in varying proportions by the girl, her parents, or from friends (gifts over time or by "showers"), mark a rite of passage as well as a transfer of goods—from the future bride and her family to the groom and his family or the new family unit. The degree to which female dowry persists and in what precise format depends on individual and family preference and circumstance as well as the strength of the traditions of one's cultural community; being of a similar era is incidental as the contrast between my friend and me, or between a couple in New Delhi, India versus one in Port Allen, Louisiana, illustrates.

Today in Pennsylvania if one asks what dowry means for young women of urban, suburban, or small town surroundings, their answers might be, at best, as vague as mine was in adolescence past. Yet, if one inquires of our most tradition-bound group—the Amish and Old Order Mennonite—one sees a flourishing dowry or *aussteier* tradition for females and

DEFINITIONS

to a certain extent for males as well. For, in the late 1980s they are giving dowry portions that are sometimes nearly identical to those given by most Pennsylvania farm families of means over two hundred years ago.

The dictionary definition of dowry is "the money or property brought by a bride to her husband at marriage," (*The Second College Edition/The American Heritage Dictionary*, Boston: Houghton Mifflin Company, 1982); also "a present or gift given by a man to or for his bride" and "a 'gift' or talent with which anyone is endowed by nature or fortune, an endowment," (*The Compact Edition of The Oxford English Dictionary*, Oxford: Oxford University Press, 1982). In *Blacks Law Dictionary*, 3rd edition, (St. Paul, Minnesota: Henry Campbell Black, 1933), its origins are defined: "The property which a woman brings to her husband in marriage; now more commonly called a 'portion.' This word expresses the proper meaning of the 'dos' of the Roman, the 'dot' of the French, the 'dote' of the Spanish law, but is a very different thing from 'dower', with which it has sometimes been confounded."

"HOUSEHOLD TALK"

The "dower chest" as a gift for the newly betrothed maid is growing in favor and antiques shops in the country are searched for the old carved chests of Virginia and Massachusetts pioneers. Some persons with money to spare are sending agents to Europe to find real antiques such as figured in historical pictures. The dower chest of carved oak with massive handles of brass would be loved by every prospective bride. Some chests are of generous proportions, and if they are filled with rare and embroidered silks, cashmeres, and fine linens, as was the custom; their value will be enhanced very materially in the bride's eyes.

The Reading Daily Times
Thursday December 21, 1905

Blacks Law Dictionary defines dower, which indeed has often been thought to be synonymous with dowry, as "the provision which the law makes for a widow out of the lands or tenements of her husband, for her support and the nurture of her children. Dower is an estate for the life of the widow in a certain portion of the following real estate of her husband, to which she has not relinquished her right during marriage: 1. of all lands of which the husband was seised in fee during the marriage; 2. of all lands to which another was seised in fee to his use; 3. of all lands to which at the time of his death, he had a perfect equity, having paid all the purchase money therefor . . . the term, both technically and in popular acception, has reference to real estate exclusively."

In Marcus Bachman Lambert's *Pennsylvania-German Dictionary*, (1924), The Pennsylvania-German words that relate to dowry are *ausschteier* or *hausschteier* "to fit for housekeeping," "clothes and furniture which a bride brings to her husband, outfit." They are the phonetic spellings for *aussteier* or *haussteier* (which in the past were used interchangeably). Today *haussteier*, as practiced by Lancaster Amish, are those smaller household goods and tools given to newlyweds by people other than parents while *aussteier* are the larger items given to children by parents often over time. *Aussteier* is a term not used by the Amish in Mifflin County but rather the phrase "gifts from home."

A related Pennsylvania-German word, *ausbehalt* means "the reservation for life of houseroom, firewood, food, etc. (usually) made by parent (or by parents) in deeding property to another (Lambert)." *Ausbehalt* is often used in wills to signify the widow's rights or share; in other words, what is reserved out of the estate for her use. It can include but usually complements her dower. Historically both "dower" and *ausbehalt* were similar in that they were part of a widow's "life estate" (to be used by her while living but not hers to control) in contrast to goods given absolutely or forever as in a bequest.

In determining what has been the dowry tradition in Pennsylvania and how it evolved, we have restricted ourselves to the two largest, early cultural groups—those of Germanic or English extraction. The family records of these two groups (the former being far more plentiful as well as detailed) were of farmers primarily, so our study group has been further defined as "rural."

Young men and women, both single and married, who lived in nineteenth-century cities like Philadelphia had life styles vastly different from their rural counterparts. Their needs, as seen in their diaries and letters, reflect their urban environment. Both our research and that of Ellen K. Rothman for *Hands and Hearts/A History of Courtship in Early America* (New York: Basic Books, 1984, p. 77), showed a tendency for working young women in metropolitan areas, even like West Chester, to go out and buy the necessary household goods just before their wedding rather than be outfitted by parents along traditional family models.

Dowry and dower traditions long practiced in England and Germany were modified here. It is interesting to note which aspects prevailed and in what form. Also, of importance is how in reality the dowry and the dower actually worked among Pennsylvania's farming families and how they affected women, their husbands, their children and their descendants. These traditional family models always were a combination of law and local custom. "The old way" or orally transmitted rules tended to amplify the written rules (or law) in both the past and present. The result is usually a body of practical group knowledge and thinking. This has permitted modification from one region to another, from one set of circumstances to another just as seen in the Amish culture's application of their eighteenth-century *Ordnung* (written doctrine) to their contemporary living.

In discussing English dowry traditions or "portioning," Lawrence Stone in *Family, Sex and Marriage in England 1500-1800* (London: Weidenfeld and Nicolson, 1977) relates how it was an exchange of cash by the father of the bride for property from the father of the groom and that most united families were usually of similar means and from a close geographic area. The extent to which this exchange became a preoccupation for families was proportionate to the amount of money or status at stake. Primogeniture or the favorable setting of the first-born son was however of paramount concern in the English system. The concerns and life fortunes of the oldest son's siblings were of secondary or little importance. Also, the decisions were made by the parents, poetry or theatrical pieces to the contrary. But as Stone points out, the less economic leverage the parents had or could exercise, the more young people would decide for themselves. Nonetheless "the personal attractiveness of the spouse [still] mattered less than her dowry, health and practical competence." (Stone, p. 192)

Under English law, the woman, once married, had no rights over her dowry during her husband's lifetime although in practice she might have exerted fairly responsible controls over her own or their pooled resources. Stone also felt that, even among the aristocratic English families where children had more to sacrifice by not marrying according to parental dictates, by the end of the eighteenth century marriages increasingly were based on solid emotional attachment (p. 31). Such a shift would even then have been indicative of a less pivotal role for the dowry in the decision-making process.

Janet Senderowitz Loengard depicted even earlier English traditions in her article "Of the Gift of Her Husband: English Dower and Its Consequences in the Year 1200," (*Women of the Medieval World,* New York: Basil Blackwell, Inc., 1985). "Dos" or dower, she says, was the gift from a husband to his wife at marriage. It usually comprised one third of the land that the husband held free and clear at the time of marriage although it could include rents, services or goods. While he lived the husband was solely responsible for and managed the use of his wife's "dos" or dower as well as her "dowry" or patrimony (inheritance). If the marriage had not dissolved, the wife received both dower and dowry at her spouse's death for "use" during her lifetime under certain restrictions but the dower was to be passed on to his heirs upon her death as per *his* instructions. His prudent management of these portions was of concern to all parties—spouse, children, or second spouse.

Diane Owen Hughes pictures a similarly complex "web of gifts" among Germanic marriages during the Middle Ages: "brideprice, a payment made by the groom to his wife's kinsmen in return for their releasing their control of her *mundium,* a legal guardianship or protection exercised in Germanic society over women and other incompetents before the law; morning gift [*morgengabe*], a groom's payment to his bride the morning after the consummation of their marriage as the price or a reward for her virginity; and finally the father's gift [*maritagium*] or dowry that daughters might receive when they left their natal home to marry." (*The Marriage Bargain/Women and Dowries in European History,* the Haworth Press, 1985, p. 18. The book in which her essay appears, is an important collection which delineates the dowry in very different cultural communities. It should be referred to by those wanting to know more about other groups' traditions.) David Sabean in his essay "Aspects of Kinship Behavior and Property in Rural Western Europe Before 1800" (in *Family and Inheritance, Rural Society in Western Europe, 1200-1800,* Cambridge, 1976) illustrates a more recent Germanic peasant society where brides and grooms brought equally matched goods to their marriages. This appears to be a closer model to the Pennsylvania Germans' *aussteier.*

In Pennsylvania, as in most of the colonies, English common law became the practice. It was based on custom and long usage and was by its very nature conservative. As in England, women had no rights to control their dowry or their dower directly until their spouses died and the law offered little protection against mismanagement by the spouse.

Those husbands who died testate, or with a will, could and often did give their wives and children more than provided by law. Goods, cash or land given through bequest also meant direct control versus a dower portion which gave support but not independence. However, prior to 1850, if a man died intestate, or without a will, his estate had to be clear of debt before it would be divided with the widow getting her dower or one-third of the existing or "in process" real estate (not personal or moveable goods) for her life use. Pennsylvania law was weaker than that of the other colonies (later states) in that the widow's share was not protected from the liens of her husband's creditors. Pennsylvania law, in effect, was more concerned with their rights than with the estate of the widow. A widow had the option of taking her share of the estate according to the will's provisions or accepting the law's dower portion. Generally she had six to twelve months in which to make that choice.

Keep, keep the maiden's dowry.
   And give me but my bride,
Not for her wealth, I won her.
   Not for her station's pride;
For she is a treasure in herself—
   Worth all the world besides.

Is not her mind a palace,
   Wherein are riches rare,
Bright thoughts that flash like jewels,
   And golden fancies fair,
And glowing dreams of joy and hope,
   That make sweet pictures there.

Keep, keep my lady's dowry,
   Her hand, her heart I claim,
That little hand is more to me
   Than power, rank or fame;
That heart's pure love is wealth my lord,
   No more your coffers name.

Mrs. Frances B. Osgood
Godeys Ladys Book, January 1840, p. 9

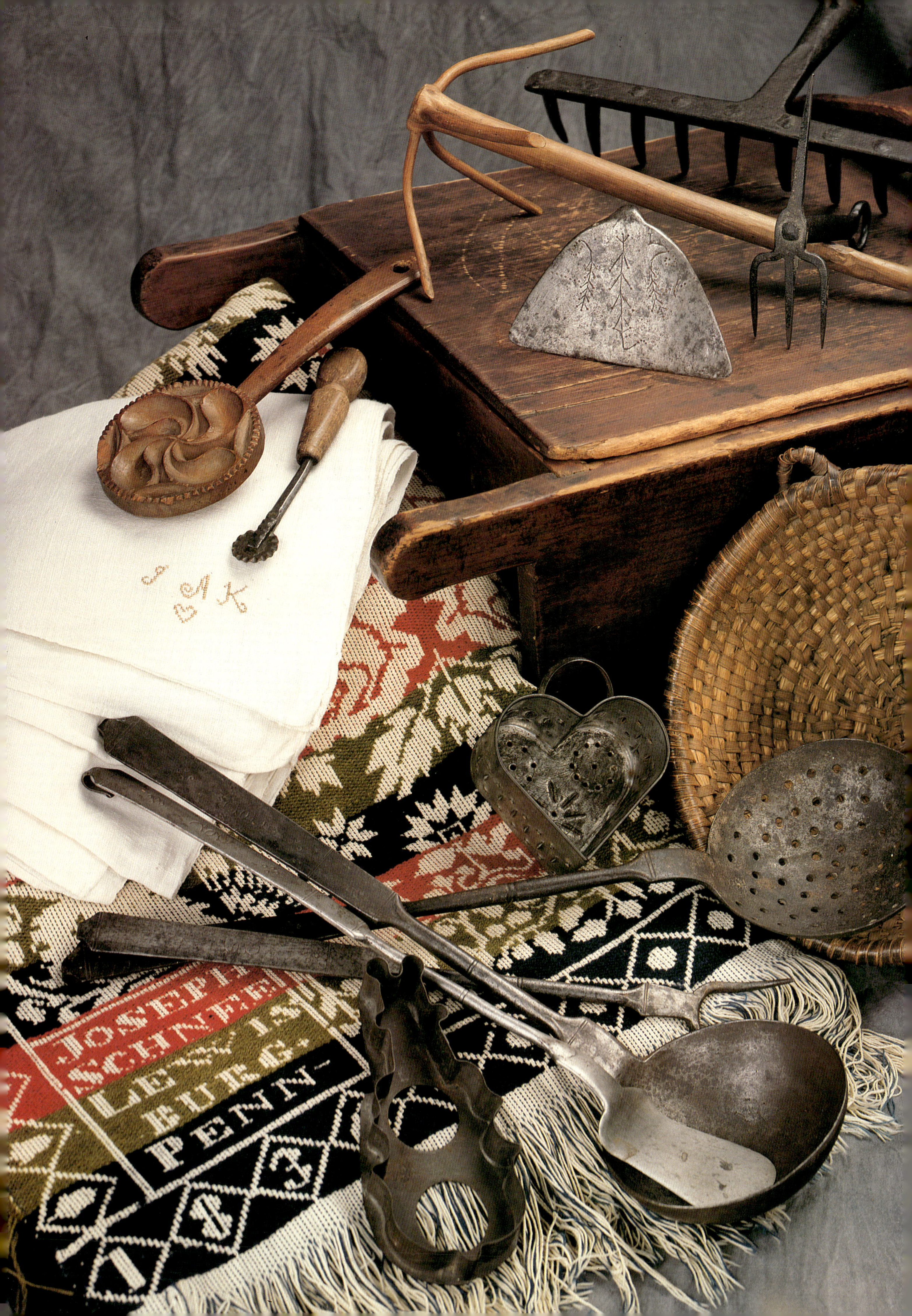
JOSEPH
SCHNEE
LEW IN
BURG.
PENN-

The remaining estate was then divided among the children with the eldest son getting a double share or "first birthright." After the Revolution, republican ideology made unequal division of the estate amongst siblings unacceptable and these last vestiges of primogeniture were removed. All children were then treated equally.

The Cumberland County estate of Francis Cunningham was £60,10 shillings and 7½ pence in total and its division illustrates Pennsylvania's common law practices of the time (1760). The widow's share or "dower" was £20,3 shillings and 7 pence (one third if there were children, one half if there were none) while five of the six children, both male and female, received £5,15 shillings and 3½ pence. A sixth child John Cunningham, presumably the oldest, got £11,10 shillings and 7 pence. Another sheet in Cunningham's estate papers lists "the account of goods given as a dowry" to one of his daughters—and includes a bed and bedclothes, personal clothing like quilted petticoats, a mantle, bonnet, caps, shoes and stockings—as well as a mare, saddle, bridle, a chest, pewter dishes and plates, a cow and books including a pocket Bible.

It was not until the Married Women's Property Acts in 1848 that Pennsylvania allowed women to handle their own estates. The main principle at work in Pennsylvania law prior to that time was that "by marriage, the husband and wife are one person in law; that is, the very being or legal existence of the woman is suspended during the marriage, or at least incorporated and consolidated into that of the husband; under whose wing, protection, and cover, she performs everything." (Sir William Blackstone's *Commentaries on the Laws of England, Vol. I,* Oxford: Clarendon Press, 1765-1769, p. 442) Only trusteeships set up by a girl's father or marriage contracts made with husbands prior to marriage could keep intact those legal rights she had had previously when she was a feme sole.

As Marylynn Salmon points out in her article "Equality or Submersion? Feme Covert Status in Early Pennsylvania," (*Women of America/A History,* ed. Carol Ruth Barkin and Mary Beth Norton, Boston: Houghton Mifflin Company, 1979): "Prior to marriage men and women held virtually equal positions before the law. As femes soles, women owned property, entered into contracts, bequeathed their possessions or served as legal guardians or administrators of estates. Once women married, however, their legal standing changed. They acquired femes coverts status." (p. 94) As a feme covert a woman gave up her rights when she became as one with the husband. What she gained, so to speak, was his assumption of any of her debts (as "guardian") and he was required to provide her with dower. The law as well as local customs assumed that a husband's control of his wife's property was in her (and their children's) best interests. As *The Spectator* observed at the time, "Separate purses between man and wife are as unnatural as separate beds." The first safeguards for women were added in 1770 when the Commonwealth required that a *separate* oral examination of the female spouse was required in the sale of a couple's property.

Marylynn Salmon presents a picture of actual practice that is far more fluid than provided by the common law. Women's property could be—and was—protected through parental bequests or devises and trusts that limited the otherwise absolute control exercised by husbands. Pre- or postnuptial marriage contracts were less frequently used but when administered and interpreted by a court of equity, women could and did exert considerable influence over their own property after marriage. Clear and indisputable wording of intentions was of paramount concern however in both the interpretation and enforcement of such documents.

Although women's legal status regarding the control of their "dowry" or parental inheritance and of their "dower" or widow's life estate was one of limited rights and of dependence—whether on a father, a spouse, an eldest son, or the court—local circumstances did, at times, liberalize their actual position. When uncontested, women could and did exercise more control over real property than given to them by law. The article, "A 'Man of Business'; The Widow of Means in Southeastern Pennsylvania 1750-1850" by Lisa Wilson Waciega, documents this through the analysis of nearly 900 wills which reflected changing attitudes among Chester County and Philadelphia Quakers (*The William and Mary Quarterly,* Vol. XLIV, No. 1, January 1987, pp. 40-55).

Starting in the late eighteenth century laws regarding women's property rights became more liberal and legal interpretations, based in part on local custom and precedent, became more flexible. This was symptomatic of changes in the public's attitude.

During the same time attitudes were changing regarding the importance of dowry also. J. Hector St. John Crèvecoeur

The female's dowry had the greatest range of objects and included a doughtrough—plain or on legs (*baketroft* or *backmuld*)—until the last quarter of the nineteenth century. One, shown here is painted softwood, courtesy of the Packwood House Museum, Lewisburg. Other items of the early nineteenth century might include an iron dough scraper, a wooden stirrer, a wooden side-handled butter paddle, a pie wheel made with copper coin, a sheet initialed "JAK/♥", a coverlet made by Joseph Schnee, (a professional weaver in Lewisburg, Union County in 1838), an early tin cake (cookie) cutter, a set of forged iron utensils made by a blacksmith or spoonsmith, a pierced *schmierkäse* or soft cheese mold, a rye coil bread raising basket (often given in sets of six), and forged iron garden tools. The butter mold, sheet and cheese mold are courtesy of Jim and Carol Bohn; coverlet, courtesy of the Union County Historical Society; all else courtesy of William and Jeannette Lasansky.

wrote in his *Letters from an American Farmer* in 1782: "As I observed before every man takes a wife as soon as he chooses, and that is generally very early; no portion is required, none is expected; no marriage articles are drawn up among us by skilful lawyers to puzzle and lead posterity to the bar or to satisfy the pride of the parties. We give nothing with our daughters; their education, their health, and the customary outset are all that the fathers of numerous families can afford. As the wife's fortune consists principally in her future economy, modesty, and skillful management, so the husband's is founded on his abilities to labor, on his health, and the knowledge of some trade or business. Their mutual endeavors after a few years of constant application, seldom fail of success." He was not alone in his observation of the breakdown of European models; ". . . [it is not] rare for a girl to refuse a man whose face and fortune are his only recommendations" (1788); "Young woman of the middling class. . . . seldom gives much of her thoughts toward the accumulation of a little dowry; for the question of what a wife will bring to the common stock is agitated much less frequently here than in countries more sophisticated" (1828); "It is quite common among parents to give their daughters only their parental blessing for dowry, and to make them wait till after death for the inheritance. . . . Fortune hunters are despised here, and men take a wife with the same carelessness as they would take a glass of brandy, especially when 'bound westwards.'" *Stars and Stripes* (n.d.) (from Arthur W. Calhoun's, *A Social History of the American Family Vol. II*, Cleveland: Arthur H. Clark Co., 1918, pp. 28-29)

> A woman's true dowry, in my opinion, is virtue, modesty and desires restrained; not that which is usually so called.
>
> Lewis Miller, carpenter and chronicler in York, Pennsylvania c. 1850

"Parents would not permit hasty marriages and few marriages take place without the parental consent of both parties. They must court long enough to know each other. Then too, her parents must know that Hans is *fleisich* (industrious) and not *betrünken*; and his parents must know that Theresa is a good housekeeper—whether she can cook, sew, milk the cows, and whether she is cleanly about her work and loves to work and that she is not 'highminded,'" wrote David C. Hennings, an observer of pre-Revolutionary War Pennsylvania Germans in Schuylkill County (from Stevenson Fletcher's *Pennsylvania Agriculture and Country 1640-1840*, Harrisburg, PA: Pennsylvania Historical and Museum Commission, 1971, p. 445). As families became less tied to the land, as others acquired cosmopolitan tastes, as certain areas became more industrialized, traditional agrarian life styles increasingly became a thing of the past. Standards for judging the suitability of mates and for "gifts from home" were changing as was the definition of dowry as the nineteenth century progressed.

The periodicals of the period: *Petersons, Godeys, The Designer*; later, *The Ladies Home Journal* and even *The American Farmer* began to illustrate a family divided into *separate* but equal spheres—the women's role as the one to impart family values became dominant. Starting in the 1840s there were countless articles giving motherly advice to young women on what qualities to look for in a mate as well as how to act in male company. Others debated the definition of "the meaningful person." Stories often showed men marrying frivolous women "for adornment"; women who might push others to live beyond their means.

In the June 1843 issue of *Petersons,* Mary Davenart's article, "The Two Weddings," captured one's worst fears about materialism when she wrote: "Dora was a sweet attractive hostess, and the house was beautiful, though a fitter residence for a millionaire than for one whose fortune was still embarked in commerce." (p. 184) Her language describing Dora Saunton Huntley's home furnishings was typically laden with negative connotation like "most grotesque." *Petersons* articles continued in this vein with "Advertising for a Wife" by Harry Sunderland in December 1848, who advised that physical appearances are *not* as important as they sometimes first seem, followed by "A Few Words on Marriage" by Dr. E. J. Tilt in July 1853, and "The Idol of a Man's Heart" by A. C. Mellett in November 1860: happy, intelligent, of warm heart, gentle, kind, of tender hand and voice were the virtuous graces advised for good mates, "whose love will shield him from avarice's power/In time of property's fleeting reign." (p. 389)

In an era where endless manuals advised young women on the how-tos of domesticity and of manners, dowry was generally absent from these discussions. Late in the century *Petersons* presented "Kathie's Wedding Dowry" (October 1877), the moral of her story being that a girl with good values and a willingness to work needs no dowry or, in the words of Kathie's grandpa, "You are a treasure in yourself." Was dowry becoming increasingly less significant in the non-rural environment of cities and small towns? Probably.

However, the close of the century saw it debated in a lengthy series of essays titled "Shall Our Daughters Have Dowries?" in *The North American Review Vol. 151*, 1890 (pp. 746-769). Dowry was defined by both its advocates and detractors such as Mrs. Henry Ward Beecher, Mary A. Livermore, Alice Wellington Rollins, Amelia E. Barr, Harriet Prescott Spofford and Mr. C. S. Messinger as marriage settlements for daughters although Harriet Spofford did raise the question of providing sons with business capital.

When mentioned, the dowry was associated with young women albeit infrequently in the contemporary prose and poetry of the nineteenth century. Its link to a single piece of furniture—the blanket chest and its textile contents became prevalent from the 1890s on. The chest and its contents, often incorrectly labeled "dower chest," became sex-linked to females exclusively where it had been *the* furniture piece given

DEFINITIONS

> GIRLS who are contemplating matrimony should have a dower chest.
>
> An old German fashion, but one that is being extensively revived. It is not possible for one person to present a prospective bride with a full chest; therefore, the custom of giving linen "showers" has become quite the thing among the young woman's friends.
>
> A member of her family or an intimate friend presents her with the chest, cedar lined, with the bride's initials carved or stamped in the center of the lid. Every member of the family, as well as relatives and friends, then proceed to contribute to the filling of the chest by making all sorts of useful articles.
>
> "For the Prospective Bride," *The North American*, Philadelphia, November 5, 1911

to both young men and women in the eighteenth century (before being replaced by the bureau and desk). This "dower chest," along with tedious chores like spinning and weaving became romanticized and elevated in status during the colonial revival as in Helen Blair's article "Dower Chest Treasures," *House Beautiful*, February 1904.

In the American mainstream culture of the early twentieth century, dowry, dower, and bridal became associated with the low, lid-hinged chest, sometimes cedar, and increasingly called a "hope chest." The definition of dowry had shrunk in scope and meaning for most. It remained a viable and complex tradition for only a few.

A blanket chest as well as a bed were the furniture forms often given to both males and females prior to their marriage, sometimes much earlier so that accumulated textile goods could be stored in them. Over time the blanket chest evolved into different dowry furniture forms: a slant top desk for males and a bureau or chest of drawers for females. An example of an early male's blanket chest is this one. It was made in Centre County for George Edinger who was born in Haines Township on August 28, 1816. His blanket chest, 28³/₈" h. x 22⁵/₈" d. x 5³/₈" w., is dated "1817" and survives with a descendant. George never married but rather lived with family. Courtesy of a private collection.

A Complex Inheritance System

INDENTURES, FAMILY BOOKS, WILLS

Indenture of Sarah Wade to Davis Wallace of Earl Township, Lancaster County, Pennsylvania on September 26, 1826. Courtesy of the Winterthur Library: Joseph Downs Collections of Manuscripts and Printed Ephemera. Manuscript number 76498.117.

*A*ussteier, as recorded in family account books or preserved in an oral tradition, was the Pennsylvania Germans' way of getting their children "off to a good start," and was the equivalent of their English neighbors' dowry. Appropriately translated "outfitting," "outsetting," or "advancement," it represented the first transfer of property to male and female heirs and more specifically at the time of their setting up a new household or family unit. Different in tone from European and Asian models, the Pennsylvania Germans never appeared to exchange goods for a spouse but rather to pool from each side resources which were delineated by sex-linked chores and spheres of influence or domain—the house and garden (female) and the barn and fields (male).

This transfer of purchased or family property at or near a wedding meant that *aussteier* or dowry was the marriage portion of a child's inheritance, given while parents were living. This portion might have begun to be accumulated slowly but in earnest in adolescence as the Amish do today or given all at once. The ability or inability to provide such a "good start" might affect the age and the order of marrying within the family as well as the type and place of first residence. The records show that it was the goal of many parents to rear not only healthy children but also to teach them a trade and to provide them with sufficient, if modest, goods to start off their adult lives.

When Pennsylvania-German parents were not able to provide this they not infrequently put out their children under a work indenture. In the examples which follow we see that in these instances the holders of the indenture acted much like substitute parents. At the successful completion of the indenture they usually gave the child several sets of clothes, bed(s) and bedding, chests and tools much as in the simplest parental *aussteiers* or dowries.

Phyllis Vibbard Parsons and William T. Parsons have done the most work on Pennsylvania-German indentures, some of which can be found in the Schwenkfelder Library, the Bucks County Historical Society, and the Lehigh County Historical Society. Phyllis Parsons in her article, "Indentured Servants in Montgomery County" (Norristown: *Bulletin of Historical Society of Montgomery County*, Vol. XXV, No. 1, 1985, pp. 43-45), dispels some popular notions about indentures and sets the record straight:

Such arrangements were made by parents, guardians or overseers of the poor who had responsibility for minors. Robert C. Bushong of Reading, PA, reminds us that the work indenture referred to a status rather than a simple contract relationship. Although even in 1800, apprenticeship sometimes carried a negative connotation, it was in fact a way up the ladder of work status. Stevenson Fletcher elaborates further, "Apprenticeship was not merely a system of labor, it was a method of education, especially of the poor. Although abused at times, it trained good workmen." Boys were normally apprenticed at twelve years of age and served to age twenty-one. Females went into service at twelve or earlier and served to age eighteen. Only minor persons could legally be bound out; certainly the community regarded it as a positive means to teach and to protect. More formally, masters owed instruction, protection, room and board to the servants under their care. That applied not only to the servants who worked out their passage money in eighteenth-century America, but to the sons, daughters and orphans who were put to service in the nineteenth century. They promised the worker to see to his welfare and to furnish the work tools of his trade. In many ways, the indentured apprentice became a part of the master's family.

Such indentures, or work apprenticeships, were made by the guardians for Lutheran and Reformed, Mennonites and Schwenkfelder children among others. As William Parsons points out: "Many German independent farmers and landowners made their beginning in Pennsylvania as indentured persons. In turn, they offered the same sort of opportunity to fellow Germans who came over later. North and South Carolina were similar, especially where German settlers were concerned. . . . While it is true that not every work contract was productive, the majority were. The relationship and camaraderie contributed to the continuing strength of the ethnic community. . . . They not only learned their trade from the master who was a surrogate parent, but they absorbed values and character traits as well." ("Schwenkfelder Indentures 1754-1846," *Schwenkfelders in America*, 1987, p. 44)

Of the eighteen indentures in the Schwenkfelder Library collection, several include *aussteier*-like listings of items given upon the successful completion of the apprenticeship. Such "outfittings" reinforce the parental nature of the holder of the apprentice papers. For instance, Catharina Hystand,

This Indenture witnesseth,

THAT John Wade of the Township of Earl in the County of Lancaster & State of Pennsylvania, Weaver, hath put his daughter Sarah Wade ———

—————, and by these presents doth, voluntarily, and of his own free will and accord, put her ——— Apprentice to Davis Wallace of the said Township of Earl in the County aforesaid, merchant, and to his wife Mary Ann & their heirs & assigns to learn the ——— art, trade, and mystery of an Apprentice, to serve from & after the seventh day of April A.D. 1827 ——— for and during and to the full end and term of Ten years then ——— next ensuing.

During all which term, the said Apprentice her said master & mistress faithfully shall serve; their ——— lawful commands every where readily obey. She shall do no damage to her said master or mistress, nor see it to be done by others, without leting, or giving notice thereof to her said master or mistress. She shall not waste her said master's goods, nor lend them unlawfully to any. She shall not commit fornication, nor contract matrimony, within the said term. She shall not play at cards, dice, or any other unlawful game, whereby her said masters may have damage. With her own goods, nor the goods of others, without licence from her said master or mistress shall neither buy nor sell. She shall not absent her self, day nor night, from her said master's service, without leave; nor haunt alehouses, taverns, or playhouses; but in all things behave her self as a faithful Apprentice ought to do, during the said term.

And the said master & mistress shall use the utmost of their endeavors to teach, or cause to be taught or instructed, the said Apprentice, in the trade or mystery of Housewifery in its various branches and procure and provide for her sufficient meat, drink, Apparel ——— lodging, and washing, fitting for an Apprentice, during the said term. And shall also send her the said Sarah to school during nine months within said Term — And at the expiration of said Term said master shall give unto said apprentice one Bed & Bedstead, one Bureau, one Cow, one spinning wheel & Reel, the whole of which shall not exceed sixty dollars in value — The said Sarah shall further have & receive at the end of the Term aforesaid one good & complete suit of Apparel in addition to her ordinary clothing, as & for her freedom Dues ———

AND, for the true performance of all and singular the covenants and agreements aforesaid, the said Parties bind themselves, each unto the others, firmly by these presents.

IN WITNESS whereof, the said Parties have, interchangeably, set their hands and seals hereunto. Dated the twenty sixth day of September in the year of our Lord, one thousand eight hundred and twenty six — 1826

Davis Wallace

Sealed and delivered in the presence of the Subscriber one of the Justices of the Peace in & for Lancaster daughter of Jacob Hystand of Hereford Township was bound over in June 1799 to Jacob Stauffer of Upper Milford Township, Northampton County, with the understanding that after ten years, four months and fourteen days, she was to receive: "a Customary New Suit of Cloathing. Also One Cow, One Bed and Bedstead with Curtains, One Spinning Wheel, and One Chest, either Poplar and painted, or one of Walnut boards." In March 1833 Abraham Oswald of Rockland Township, Berks County, bound out his daughter to Esther Long of Longswamp Township, Berks County. In return the girl was to get two suits of clothing, Bible lessons, a bed and bedding, a purse, and a spinning wheel. In June 1846 Jacob Huber of Douglas Township, Montgomery County, put his ward John Hoffman under the control of Absalom Huber of Upper Hanover Township, Montgomery County, who was to "... teach, instruct or cause to be taught and instructed ... the art, trade and mystery of a carpenter or cabinetmaker, and ... one fore plane, one Jack plane and one smoothing plane, one handsaw, one hatchet and square all to be new and of good quality and shall pay unto the said Apprentice, the sum of Twelve Dollars lawful money . . . ."

Other indentures show "outfittings," some of which were very spare—two suits of clothes—one old, one new, sometimes tools of the trade or cash, a cow and calf, a ewe and lamb as well as a pair of new sheets, or a cow or cash. Pennsylvania's Acts of Assembly, as early as 1683 and then in 1700, made it mandatory for two complete suits of clothes (one new), a new axe, a grubbing hoe, and weeding hoe to be provided as an "outfit" at the successful conclusion of an indenture.

Only one indenture indicated a very full "outfitting" similar to those *aussteiers* given to children of prosperous families. It was made between Eva Hootzin, a widow living in Heidelberg Township, Lehigh County in April 1818, and an Adam Michael for her daughter Magdalena (the original is in the Lehigh County Historical Society): "The agreement between Eva Hootzin, Widow and Adam Michael is as follows: For the first does Eva Hootzin provide her daughter, Magdalena Hootzin, to Adam Michael for four years; Adam Michael must give Magdalena Hootzin: a new cotton bed with 16 pounds feathers, a _____ cover for the whole bed; a flaxen linen cloth and a woven linen sheet of new cloth. Two new pillows, a big one and two little ones; a new blanket with three colors; a new low bedstead; in all a complete new bed, a new chest with 5 drawers; a cow or £9 money instead of the cow; a new spinning wheel; a new iron pot of the medium kind; and the same kind new pan; further he has to keep Magdalena complete in clothes for the whole time for Sundays and workdays and has to send her to school for 3 months and to the minister until she is confirmed and has to give her a free dress as she would like it, except not of silk."

Samuel Pennock was of West Marlborough Township, Chester County. His family account book covered the years 1810 to 1830. Courtesy of the Library of the Chester County Historical Society, West Chester, PA. Manuscript number 10723.

The transfer of property to grown children, done either by one's own family, or when family was unable, through indenture agreements, coincided with maturation and a child's reaching marriageable age. Along with the instillation of certain values and skills, these goods—sparse or fairly abundant—reflected the "good start" which each family felt compelled to provide. It reflected what was commonly thought as necessary—a basic set of goods for one starting out—to be complemented by a similar "outfitting" of one's spouse. What was considered basic by even the poorest was a bed, bedding, cow, chest, and some clothes. The *aussteier* reflected the higher socio-economic status of the family when cash and goods could be provided above and beyond this basic set.

One might start with a small "outfit" as did one Pennsylvania German who recalled how at the age of twelve he was bound over to a farmer for nine years. Upon reaching majority he was given only two suits of homespun clothes, four pair of socks, four linen shirts and two pair of shoes but how "at twenty-two he married and rented a farm of forty acres. Ten years later he bought a farm of sixty acres. Now he began to make money and gradually acquired more land. When his oldest daughter married he gave her one hundred acres of land and some of his best flax so that she could spin cloth herself. . . . When his second daughter married his wife *bought* kitchen utensils for her. His third daughter wore silk dresses." (*The Pennsylvania German Society,* 1922, p. 122)

One need not have been a wealthy father to be concerned about children's marriage portions. The records of George Erion, a ragdealer and farmer living in York County attest to this. In the 1790s he recorded both his promises to and, at times, his frustrations with his children. In 1798 he "promised" his daughter Barbary a cow, two sheep, bed and bedstead, chest, spinning wheel, a good set of clothes, a hat and cash if she was a "good girl," and to his son Philip £20 plus earnings "But He Tornd to a Bade Boy he Would Not do What I Want to have Done of him he Want and made Barkins [bargains] behind his Father Now he Shall Not have Enny of that Promise if he Dont Mind I will Bind him to a Shumakers Trade." (*Quarterly of the Pennsylvania German Society, Vol. 10, No. 1,* April 1976, p. 6) Erion gave his son George some cash, his daughter Molly a cow, and daughter Betsy a cow, bedclothes, feathers, and a brass ladle. But in spite of his provisions for Barbary to whom he gave the most, she became a whore: "March 18, 1802 I have payd my Daughter Barbary in Stor goods 3 Dollars and a halfe Ramaing [remaining] to her yat 4 Dollers and halfe. In the year 1802 I have paid all to my Daughter Barbary For she tornd out to a Hor." (p. 7)

While this is the only account book with portions explicitly linked to control, or the denial of "promised" goods if the children erred, one might assume that by its very nature *aussteier* giving would have implied pressure to perform one's duties (which included work on the family farm) and to live and marry with parental approval even if it were never stated. Perhaps it is not surprising that a mere ragman and modest farmer, George Erion, felt the need to promise and then withhold because with less at his disposal to give he had inherently less control: "I gave to my son George Erion just a 15 Dollar Note from my Hand which Shall Bare Entres [interest] from the Time as it above Written If I cant pay him he is to [get] paid out of my Estate What I . . ." (p. 10) Those families with more to give had more control. Rather than blatantly exercising control in *aussteier* records, the Pennsylvania Germans more frequently did that in their wills.

Wills were publicly-recorded documents which occasionally referred to "family accounts" or "books"—privately held. As Russell Gilbert pointed out in his text on Pennsylvania-German wills (Allentown: *The Pennsylvania German Folklore Society*, Vol. XV, 1950): "Both the atmosphere and wording [of the wills] portray the methodical, thrifty mind of the Pennsylvania German, who kept an accurate and detailed record of financial obligation. The desire to be fair and to treat all alike induced him to enter in a special book an amount of money or goods given beforehand to those relatives and friends he loved. References to the account books are rather prominent. Now and then the recipient of an advance gift had to return it, but more frequently he could keep it. The will served too as an official reminder of past rewards and of efforts at family equality." (p. 79) Seven wills from six of the seventeen counties in which they were studied used the phrase "Charged in my Family Book."

It was sometimes left up to the courts to interpret whether the accounts kept in these private documents were records of advancement—of inheritance at or about age of marriage—or whether the accounts were records of debt. The cultural communities which kept such records traditionally maintained they were "advancements." One case which went to court in Berks County ruled to the contrary as did its appeal before the state Supreme Court in 1887.

Jacob Leiby of Perry Township, Berks County, began to keep a book for his ten children starting in 1855 and continuing to his death in 1884. In the beginning of his book he wrote: "The contents of this book what each one has received for outfit who have worked til they obtained majority. John who was away three years before his majority shall be charged one hundred dollars for the three years [the amount at which his lost time on the farm was valued]. For what is charged in the book no interest shall be reckoned excepting what is more than 900 dollars. There they shall be reckoned." His will later stated: "I bequeath and direct that all my personal and real property shall, as soon as convenient, be sold at public vendue to the highest bidder by my executors herein after named, and also collect all outstanding money and divide the same among my children and legal heirs in such portions so that if all the notes I hold against them or any of them, my said children and heirs, and all money advanced to them or any of them, my said children and heirs, that their shares or dividends of such amounts the same share and share alike."

The initial court interpretation of Leiby's will was that his book concerned indebtedness, not advancement, and that therefore it did not affect the division of his estate; after expenses the estate should be divided equally. Eight of his sixteen heirs appealed this interpretation and insisted that the others had already received some or all of their inheritance while Jacob Leiby lived (inter vivos). The attorney for the appellants argued: "How the learned Judge who himself is so well acquainted with this particular and characteristic dialect (Pennsylvania-German), and is himself descended directly from an old and distinguished family of the same people could make such a grievous error we cannot understand. It is true, the book has the appearance of accounts. So has every family book that contains advancements. Advancements must be in the nature of accounts. The mark identifying them as advancements is evidenced by the significant and characteristic word, *Aussteier,* or outfit, uniformly entered in every instance against the ten children of the decedent from the oldest to the youngest. . . . An *aussteier* is an outfit, a portion, virtually to start out in life. The testator gives to each as they start out in life and who have worked for him until they have attained their majority, household goods, and as they received them, under the contents of this book charges them up as advancements." (John Seidel, "Dowry and Inheritance in Rural Pennsylvania German Society," unpublished paper for Don Yoder's seminar on Pennsylvania-German ethnography, University of Pennsylvania, 1980-1981, p. 20.)

The appellants further argued (unsuccessfully) that the money lent to his son Isaac for purchasing family property was likewise written up as a debt which was then removed when it was charged as part of his advancement. They also argued that only amounts of goods or cash over $900 were considered debt since interest was to be paid on sums over $900 only (Seidel, pp. 17-22).

This case hinged on a narrow interpretation of the will's mention of "all money advanced to them" including goods or cash itemized in the family book. The fact that "the family book" was not specifically mentioned was used by the judge in ruling against the appellants, the introduction of fourteen precedent cases and the testimony of a friend and neighbor, Charles Adams notwithstanding: "He [meaning Leiby] said to me more than once that he kept such a book in which he wrote everything from the smallest to the largest. He told me that in the shop where he was working. He told me a year before his death at my house on Ascension Day that he kept such a book, so that they could see what each one got when he was not here any more." (p. 23)

Lack of specificity regarding a "book" and how it was to be used after a father's death, was not always a problem in wills. Jonathan Kolb, of E. Vincent Township, Chester County, explicitly wrote: "I will and order that all the moneys arising from the sale of my real estate and on the sale of my other effects, together with the remainder and residue of my estate, be equally divided amongst and between my six children, or their legal representatives, equal shares alike and I do hereby give and bequeath the same to them in equal shares alike, except that my oldest daughter, namely, Elizabeth, wife of Benjamin B. Hendricks; Anna wife of Jacob H. Funk; Jonathan Kolb; Lydia wife of Davis Kimes; Mary wife of Isaac Slichter, and Sarah Kolb, and I do further order and direct that so much as each or either of my aforesaid children shall have been advanced by me in my lifetime, as will appear by a family book kept by me for that purpose, or the real estate

A set of chairs was a standard component of the female dowry. In the mid-eighteenth century Pennsylvania-German girls were receiving only a couple of chairs probably since they were still using built-in benches as their primary seating form. Slowly, two, four and then six chairs were given; later several sets in more affluent families. The earliest dowry reference to a set of chairs was in 1798 in the book kept by Abraham Wismer of Bucks County. The Clemens account books registers "chair with back" in 1799 (perhaps a reference to the English tradition). Once given, they became a standard part of the outfit which later included a rocker (as first recorded in 1832 by Johann Bomberger, Warwick Twp. Lancaster County).

This set of six chairs complete with rocker was made by David Ginter of Lewisburg; and they are stamped on the bottoms of their seats "GINTER/LEWISBURG" (David Ginter, chairmaker, was active from c.1831 to 1873). Courtesy of Roger and Arletta Zimmerman.

Isaac Pennocks's purchase of furniture from Mathias Foy of East Bradford, Chester County, was most likely for his daughter, Rebecca Pennock Lykens who married in 1818. Courtesy of the Library of the Chester County Historical Society, West Chester, PA. Manuscript number 77050.

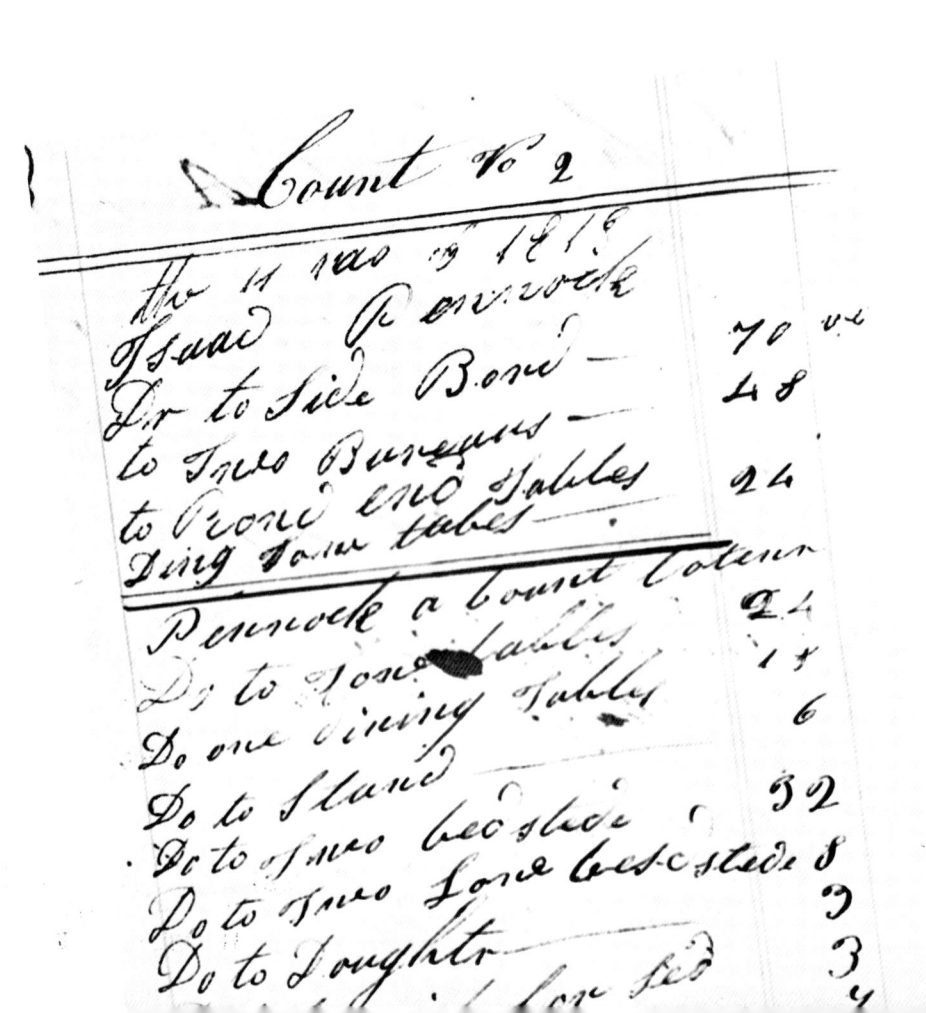

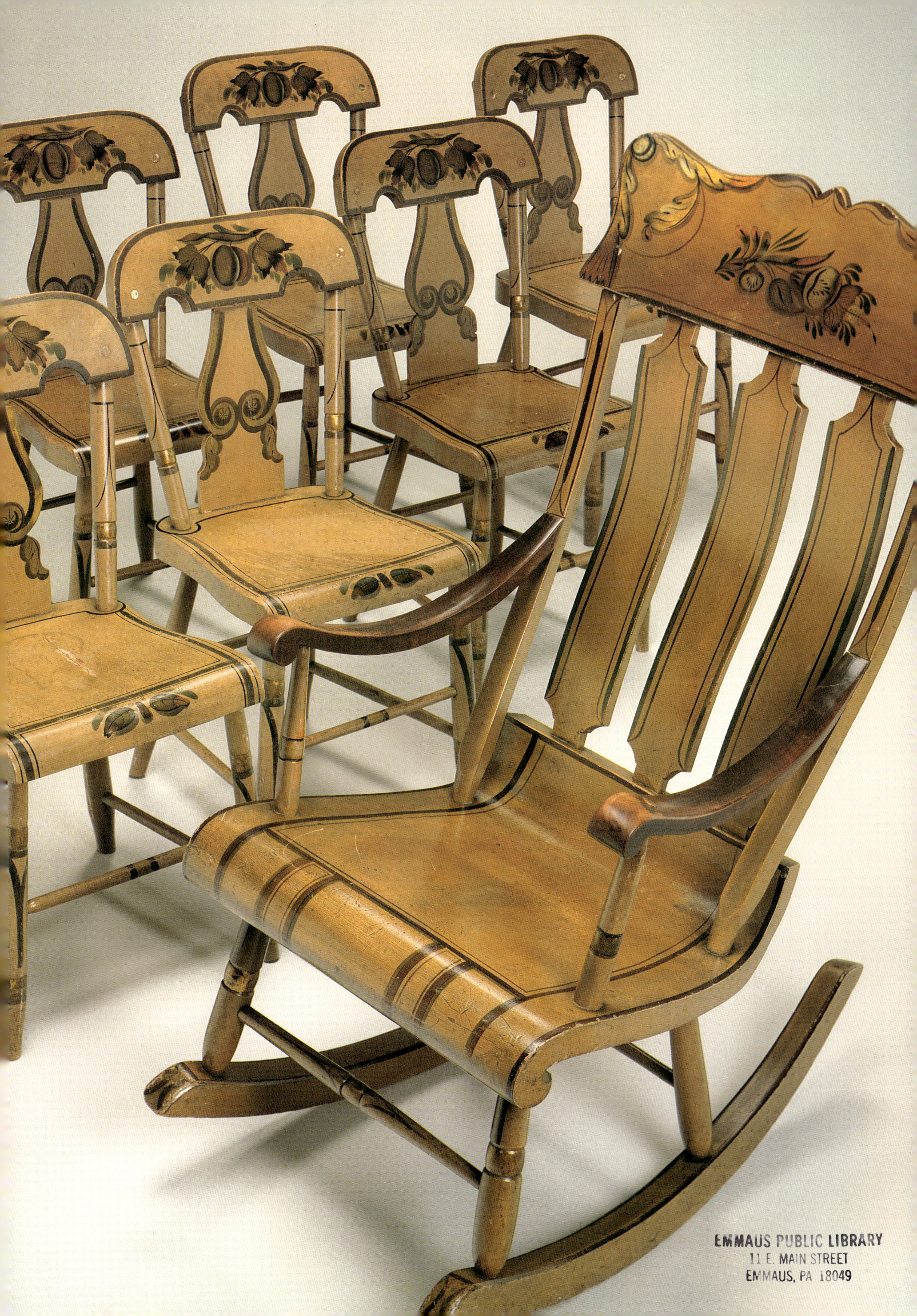

A COMPLEX INHERITANCE SYSTEM

before mentioned containing six acres and 102 perches before mentioned valued at $1000, to my oldest daughter Elizabeth Hendricks; they and each of them so advanced shall suffer a deduction out of his or their shares at the final settlement of my estate so as to make them all equal shares and share alike." (pp. 17-18, Kolb Family Record and Account Book, Mennonite Historical Society.)

Obviously, as the Leiby court case showed, a family could not assume that a judge of the same cultural community (Pennsylvania-German in this case) would rule in favor of the use in final estate settlements of privately-held documents along traditional lines *unless* so specified in the public instrument or will.

While *aussteier* or dowry records transferred particular goods at a child's marriageable age—or partial inheritance while parents lived, wills could also transfer particular items and the remaining property—or final inheritance, at time of death. Wills illustrate *aussteier* or dowry portions in several ways. First, by separating what the surviving spouse brought to marriage as "hers"—or dowry. Second, by specifying what children who had not reached majority were yet to receive, i.e. dowry portions to be provided for if indeed they had not been given by the time of the parent's death. Sons and daughters, as well as grandchildren, were often so provided for. The sex-linked objects in wills are again like those in *aussteier* accounts. Third, the will could provide for a "revolving fund" or flow of cash that was created by assigned responsibilities. Such funds allowed for continuity of traditional family practices by getting "each off to a good start" in their proper turn and by creating a realistic timetable for doing this. Fourth, wills could show or allude to what had already transpired.

Wills, more than any other kind of document, illustrated how parents could and did exert control through inheritance and provide for continuity of family traditions. In looking at great numbers of wills, "patterns" of broader cultural behavior and traditions emerge.

The Pennsylvania-German wills that Russell Gilbert surveyed in seventeen central and eastern Pennsylvania counties as well as the wills and will abstracts that we read for Lehigh, Berks, and Chester counties, all clearly show that, as indicated by Pennsylvania's written laws, the widow retained her one-third of the husband's estate, sometimes called *ausbehalt* or "dower" as well as any goods she brought as *her* marriage portion sometimes called *aussteier* or dowry. Typical is Christopher Bittenbender's specification that a son Jacob have the plantation "that I possess, with all the buildings, cattle and all the moveables belonging thereto, except the widow's share [dower or one-third] which shall be held inviolate. . . . to be withheld [from entire estate] is her [the widow's dowry] household goods that she brought with her, this she shall have in advance." (Lehigh County Will Book 7, p. 332) As Heinrich Romich, of Upper Milford Township, Lehigh County, stated in his will in 1830: "My beloved wife, Susanna shall keep all of her possessions that she had when she became my wife, and she can do with them what she pleases." Such phrases are used when husbands are not specific as to the wife's marriage portion or outfitting which might have included chests, pewterware, beds, bedsteads and bedding, clothing, bureaus, chairs and once "the Pear Tree which she planted." (Lancaster will of 1780)

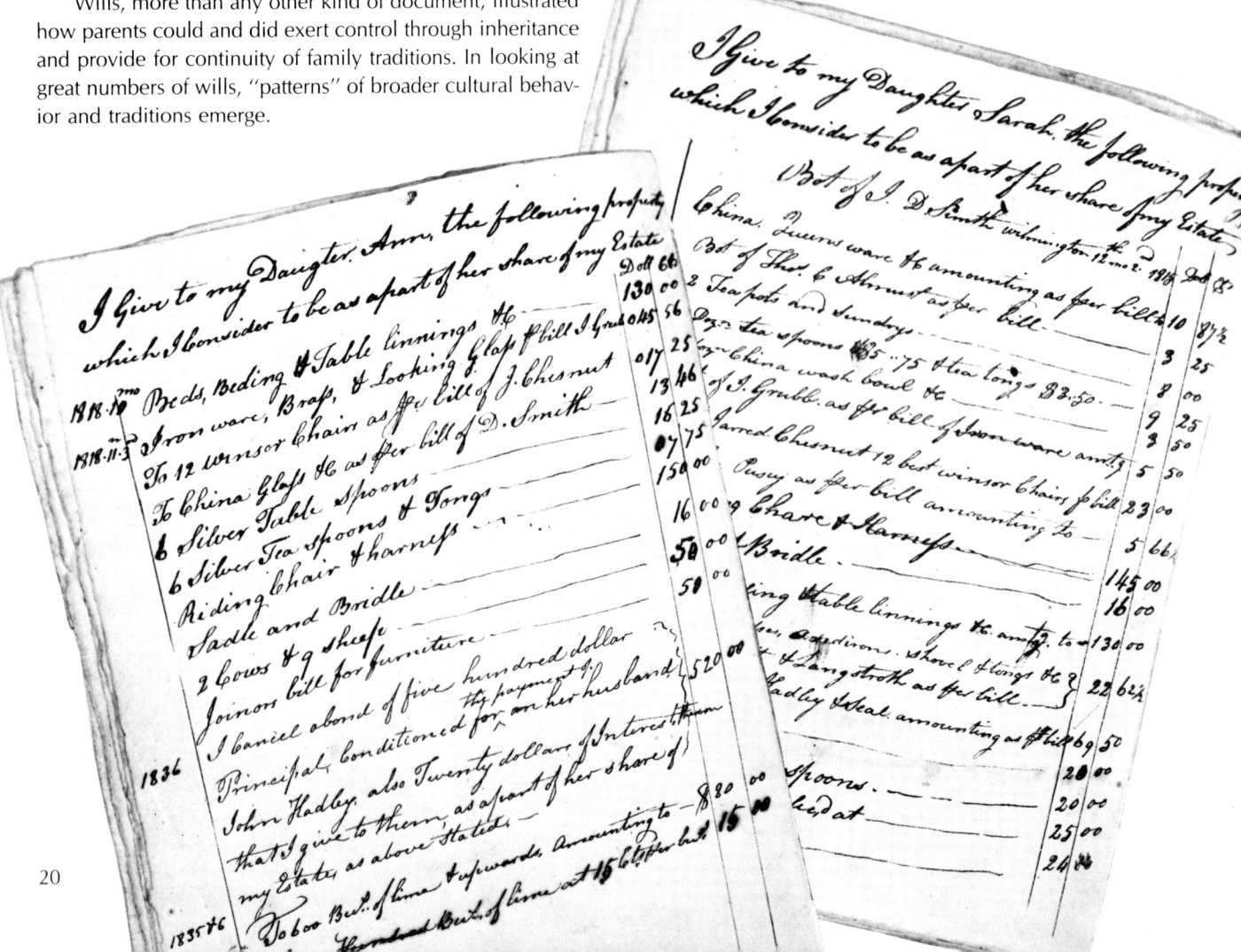

A COMPLEX INHERITANCE SYSTEM

The dower or third of the husband's final estate was given to spouses for their sustenance as long as they lived. Often the spouse said where the dower was to go when the widow died or remarried. When husbands enumerated the range of goods that they considered necessary for their wives the listing was not unlike what was given in family accounts to children as their start: beds, bedding, chests, tables, chairs, a doughtrough, dresser, corner cupboard, and looking glass as well as clothing, provisions like pork, beef, eggs, condiments, and spices in addition to milk cows, a riding horse, kitchen tools and a stove.

A husband often specified his will in great detail or drew up a separate support agreement that would provide for the care of his wife and widow. Martin Donat's last will and testament (1837) is about as detailed as any and includes not only such provisions for his wife but also a dowry or marriage portion for their servant:

I give and bequeath unto my dear wife, Maria, as follows: The use, occupation, and privilege of the front west room of my dwelling house where I now live, and also privilege in the kitchen, cellar and upstairs, springhouse, and garden, as she will have necessary for her use during her natural life; also, firewood to be delivered in her room, cut for her stove and kitchen, as much as is necessary for her use. My dear wife is to have one cow, the choice of my cows, and every three years she shall have a right of exchanging her cow for her choice of the cows that may be in the possession of the occupant of my farm or plantation whereon I now live, to be kept and fed with his cows as well as his own.

Further, I give and bequeath unto my dear wife, Maria, yearly and every year during her natural life, five bushels of wheat; fifteen bushels of rye; ten bushels of buckwheat; ten bushels of corn; twenty bushels of potatoes, delivered according to her directions. One bushel ground and one bushel fine salt; six pounds of coffee; six pounds of sugar; two barrels of cider, and as many apples as she wants for her use. One hundred and fifty pounds of good fattened pork and the offal of one hog; thirty pounds of good beef; ten pounds of tallow; ten pounds of hackled flax; ten pounds of fine and ten pounds of coarse tow; five pounds of wool; eight dollars in cash to be every year paid in advance or the beginning of the year. Three rows of early potatoes alongside of the occupants of the aforesaid farm or plantation, planted and worked as the occupant does his own. Attendance in sickness or infirmity, medical as well as all other that may be necessary. She is to have the privilege of raising a hog on the place aforesaid every year.

Further, it is my will and do hereby order and direct that five bushels of rye; two bushels of wheat; two bushels of corn; and three bushels of buckwheat of the aforementioned and described articles of dower and *ausbehalt* shall be given and delivered by the occupant and possessor of the farm or plantation which I have bought of Jacob Bear; containing about eighty-eight acres, and adjoining lands of Frederick Sechler, deceased; John Zehner; Michael Klingaman, and others, and shall be a lien on the same during the lifetime of my dear wife, Maria. All the remainder and other articles, monies, performances, attendances, mentioned and described hereinbefore is to be given, done and performed by the possessor and occupant of the first above mentioned farm or plantation, which containing about two hundred acres of land; adjoining lands of Jacob Sechler, Christian Henry, John Stine, and others, and shall be a lien on the same during the lifetime of my dear wife, Maria. Further, I give and bequeath unto my dear wife, Maria, two beds and bedsteads, the choice of all of my beds; one stove for her use to be kept in her room; and as much kitchen furniture as she

The cover and the first dowry entry of Samuel Pennock's family book appear on p. 16.

shall choose to keep. Also, one table; one bureau; three chairs, the house clock, which shall be in full her share of what she would be entitled to by the common laws of Pennsylvania.

Item. It is further my will and do order and direct that in case Fayethe Verner, who lives with me, shall continue and remain in the service of my wife or in the service of any of my children that may hold the farm whereon I now live, until she arrives at the age of eighteen years, she shall have eighteen dollars in cash and every Winter one or two months schooling and have her prepared to receive the Lords Supper, and to have good clothes, and if she shall continue in said service to her age of twenty-one years, she shall have a good farmers bed and bedstead, one cow, one spinning wheel, and a chest, besides the eighteen dollars, out of my estate." (Lehigh County Wills Book 2, p. 225)

Another will read:

My said two sons, Philip Kistler and Samuel Kistler or their children shall yearly give to my said wife, for the entire time that she remains a widow, one half of the rooms, closets, and kitchen, and a right in the cellar and on the second floor where she may keep her things, and to live in the house. Twelve bushels of rye; four bushels of buckwheat; six bushels of buckwheat; each cleaned and good grain to be taken to the mill and the product to be returned to her residence; a fattened swine with the lard of one hundred weight when cleaned and gutted. She shall have the right to have a pig. Yearly in Springtime a freshened cow for her use, that shall stay at this place. They shall feed it good in Winter and put out to pasture as they do their own; one half of the old garden shall be dunged for her use, and yearly one half acre for potatoes and corn to be dunged and plowed at the right time, and a quarter acre to be plowed at the right time and sown with flax seed. She shall have the choice of a row of apple trees in the orchard for her use. The cider shall be made and if she has use, she shall have yearly four gallons of brandywine; two gallons of whale oil (illuminating); a half bushel of coarse salt and one half peck of fine salt; a quarter pound of pepper and an equal amount of allspice; a pair of good new shoes for herself; four pounds of good wool. She shall have the right to keep six chickens. They shall provide firewood for her, haul it to the house and split it into small pieces, as much as she can use." (Lehigh County Wills Book 2, p. 200)

Should wives remarry, most husbands stipulated that their *ausbehalt* or dower revert to their children and be divided up equally among them. The range of spousal attitude ran the gamut from Johannes Hall's (of Hanover Township) who said: "In the case that she [his beloved wife Jutti] remarries, the lot and all thereon shall be sold and one third of the money derived therefrom shall be payed to her," (Lehigh County Will Book 2, p. 86), to Jacob Hartman's more typical frame of mind: ". . . my widow shall receive what she is promised by law and nothing more." (Lehigh County Will Book 1, p. 255)

Just as the wills frequently show what a man's spouse had brought to their marriage by calling it "hers," so they reflect parts of male marriage portions as "his." These items often included a clock and case, a room stove, farm animals. However, since the bulk of a couple's jointly held property was considered "his," differentiating what were his *aussteier* goods is often less than clear.

Sometimes *aussteier* is reflected in items set aside in wills for sons (though land and cash predominate). Wilhelm Peter is an exception. He gave land, the old brown horse and young mare with harness, as well as the new wagon with body, a plow, a cow, a chest and a room pipe with stove to one son Jacob; land, the young brown horse with harness, a cow, two beef cattle and a chest "such as has been received by the other," to a son Joseph; and land, the little filly, a cow and two head of cattle to another son Han George (just three of his thirteen children living in Heidelberg Township, Lehigh County in 1813) (Lehigh County Will Book 1, p. 17). Sometimes sons got tools of a trade like Abraham Butz from his father John in 1819: "He shall receive all of the smithing tools, namely, the bellows, vice, the tongs, the horn and what belongs thereto, the smithing iron onto which a smith threads, and a hoof knife." (Lehigh County Wills, Book 2, p. 28) Bibles were also mentioned.

Goods willed to females rarely included land but sometimes included cash and often included typical *aussteier* furnishings as in John George Peter's will of June 10, 1843: "In addition I bequeath to my daughter, Magdelena, one bed and bedstead, a cow, a chest of drawers, two coverlets, a spinning wheel as her outright possession." (Peter Family Records, Lehigh County Historical Society)

Equality was almost always stressed among siblings amongst the Pennsylvania Germans; when not equal, usually there were reasons given. Special considerations were made for the unborn, underaged, unmarried, infirm, or mistreated. One such instance was for Elizabeth Saeger who was given two-thirds of the rent from family property "as much as is necessary for her support because she is lame and can't help herself. If anything out of the rent money is left over, then it shall be divided among the other said children in equal shares." (Lehigh County Will Book 2, p. 106) Another father's concern extended to married children as when Johan Killian Leiby of Weisenberg Township wrote "Gertrand shall give of her inheritance to her son David, in advance, the sum of twenty-five pounds, and they shall be included in the distribution of what remains, because of his [David's] father's roughness. Andreas Knerr, Gertrand's husband, shall have no right to any of the inheritance because of his bad treatment against her." (Lehigh County Will Book 1, p. 206)

Most of the time, the special consideration, went to the eldest son but with the consideration came obligations to his mother and/or to younger, not-yet-established siblings. In other words, the eldest son was set up to become a surrogate father. When the main family property went to the eldest son it usually meant the father was old enough to retire, and though the gift or the sale of the homestead might have been at bargain sale or below market value, it usually entailed a series of payments to others—in effect it created a "revolving fund" that was to help mother or siblings. The will of Christophel Merkel, drawn up in 1806, typifies such an arrangement:

Further, I bequeath to my son Jacob Merkel, my plantation of two hundred acres, more or less, lying in Macungie Township, Northampton County; Therefore Jacob Merkel's four sisters must receive their hereditary share. My son, Jacob Merkel must pay the sum of eighteen hundred pounds current lawful money of Pennsylvania. One year after my death Jacob Merkel shall pay to his sister Magdelena fifty pounds in good money to her husband Peter Bär. The second year after my death to Catharina fifty pounds in good money to her husband [John] Peter Bär. The third year to Maria fifty pounds in good money to her husband, Michael Peter. The fourth year to Salome fifty pounds in good money. As she is yet of single circumstance, when she gets married my son, Jacob Merkel must give her a house dower equal to that received by the others, namely, a bed and new bedstead and all that belongs thereto with new curtains of the kind that she likes. Further, two cows, two sheep, two hogs, pewter and wooden utensils, iron utensils, like that of which the others have equally received. Should she, however, receive this from her father, then Jacob Merkel is released from giving her, her house dower.

Further, my son, Jacob Merkel, after the passing of four years shall pay each another four hundred pounds of good money in the following manner: As with the above fifty pounds, beginning the year with one hundred pounds and so yearly to give one hundred pounds and every year, in order to the youngest. Then beginning again with the eldest until each has received four hundred fifty pounds as their hereditary share from their father, Christophel Merkel.

That all of the above said points concerning the yearly dower for my said wife shall be held in truth and unbreakable for her lifetime according to the true intent and meaning thereof. Should she become sick then Jacob Merkel, or who after my death lives on my plantation, must in her sickness provide care and attendance in all cases as she needs it, or must see that this waiting is done. If God takes her away, namely her soul, so must my son, Jacob Merkel, see to the burial in a Christian manner of the deceased body and the funeral expenses he must pay himself.

If my wife, Christina, after my death, should remarry then my son, Jacob Merkel, shall let that of her household goods follow her. She is to receive five pounds in money yearly for the rest of her life, and no longer. The dower shall cease.

Further, it is my will that should any one of my children condescend against my said will, to alter it or disturb with dispute over what they, from it, are to receive shall, themselves, be excluded from any share or part of it or of my said estate and shall, themselves, be disinherited. (Lehigh County Will Book 1, p. 25)

Please note that the term "dower" is sometimes used incorrectly as in the will cited above. "Dower" is also used incorrectly (in place of "dowry") in another will which similarly assigns responsibilities to sons: "It is my will that both of my sons, in common, namely, Daniel and Jesaias Ledwig, the above said, shall further give to my daughter, Maria, her house dower [dowry] as the other daughters have received, namely, two good beds and bedsteads, the one a high one with curtains, a glass cupboard, a baking trough; a winged table with six feet; a drawer; a half dozen chairs; three cows; three sheep; two iron pots; two irons; a wash tub; a butter churn; also five dollars in kitchen or house utensils." (Lehigh County Will Book 1, p. 273)

This method of installment payments, as seen in so many of the wills reviewed, allowed for equal and adequate shares to be given to all children but not all at once. It allowed for giving a good start to other siblings by the eldest and for it to be done in a manner that was reasonable to the eldest child. When grown children were perceived by their parents as unable or unwilling to handle their financial affairs—or if they were women with irresponsible spouses—different arrangements were made to safeguard them or their heirs.

While quite frequently the father would hold notes on land that he purchased for his older son(s), who would then repay their father or siblings over time, it was usually the youngest, not the oldest son, who got the family farm. This was because the father might not be inclined nor able to give it up sooner. Sometimes the parents continued to live on the farm though in smaller quarters while the youngest took control of it economically. Such was the case in the Burkholder family of Muddy Creek, Lancaster County: "Daniel built his retirement house in 1901 attached on the Eastern side of the main farm house. In 1902 Daniel, Jr. (b. 1879, d. 1964) the youngest in the family, gradually began to take over responsibilities of the home farm, and he married in November of 1903 and soon occupied the farm house. Eventually Daniel W. Burkholder, Jr. bought the farm and had its purchase recorded on August 11, 1908: 'Excepting and reserving out of the hereby granted premises for the use of said Daniel S. Burkholder, during his lifetime, as follows, to wit: The use and occupancy of the new dwelling house, attached on the east side of the old dwelling house, and the southeast room on the first floor of said old House, part of the yard and garden belonging thereto. Room for one cow, one horse and all visitors' horses in the barn, together with sufficient long feed and bedding for the same, room in carriage house for one carriage. The one-half of all fruit grown on the hereby granted premises, right to pump and well of water, to use and carry away water for all kinds of uses. Right to work in blacksmith and general workshop, whenever he so desires, twenty-five bushels of good potatoes to be delivered in his cellar, by the grantee of the hereby granted premises, his heirs and assigns, during the time aforesaid. Also, reserving the right for said Daniel S. Burkholder to pass and repass, in, over and through the hereby granted premises at all times and seasons during the time aforesaid, with the right for him to send any other person or persons to do any work for him, which may become necessary by reason of all the above reservations.'" (*The Burkholder Family History*, pp. 25-26) (This same Burkholder family is the one whose account book is summarized on pp. 63, 71.)

Other than wills, which can yield detailed information over a long period of time for all cultural communities, inventories are a public record which held some, though not as much, information on family relationships. The inventories Scott Swank studied from Berks and Lancaster counties from 1730 to 1830 illustrate sparsely furnished homes—in the earliest period perhaps because of more built-in units and less furniture in general. He noted that the Pennsylvania Germans also kept a large proportion of their assets in the form of financial notes. He says they "had a proclivity for interest-bearing bonds and notes. A sampling of the inventories from Berks (Lutheran and Reformed) and Lancaster counties (Plain sects) makes this generalization possible. First, the majority of Pennsylvania-German farmers extended credit to someone, and the preponderance of their creditors appear to have been family members." (*The Arts of the Pennsylvania Germans*: W. W. Norton, N. Y. p. 47) Land was used to create "revolving funds" and mutual dependence. So would these interest-bearing bonds and notes.

Another observation about the inventories we looked at from Lancaster County is that often they show part of "the widow's share" which tends to read again like an *aussteier* listing: bed, bedding, small bedstead, two sets window curtains, a homemade carpet, a chest of drawers, a small tenplate stove, a looking glass with mahogany frame, a dining table, six Windsor chairs, another tenplate stove, a mahogany knife case and a tub and two buckets (for Rachel Bailey in 1798); a colander and pan, a small pewter basin, a milk strainer, six patty pans and other tinware, a frying pan and potrack, spoons, knives and forks, shovel and tongs, earthen pots, coffeemill, coffeepot, three candlesticks, six pewter teaspoons, a bake oven, tea kettle, pot, churn, doughtrough, tin buckets, the family Bible, two smoothing irons, a reel, a spinning wheel, stand, two coverlets, chest, keg, decanter, tumbler and gills, a gallon jug and black bottle (Mary Hoar, 1802); bedsteads and bedding, stove and pipe, looking glass, chests, doughtrough, barrel and tow, pair of hatchels and bench, barrel of soap, a wool wheel, flax bench and flax, wool, baskets, watering can, kitchen dresser, linen, tow, tubs, churn, washing machines, iron kettle, copper kettle, pair of choppers, buckets, wooden dishes, dining table, corner cupboard, looking glass, eleven chairs, an armchair, a case of drawers, a table, kitchen table, wash bench, set of ladles, iron pots and fire apparatus, and dripping pan (Widow of Jacob Eby, Leacock Township, 1834).

Certain furniture forms or tools that the widows frequently retained for their continued use were pieces the husband would have brought with him or which the couple would have gotten once married, but which would not likely have been in the wife's advancement: clocks with cases, room stoves, desks and bookcases, axes; also settees and looking glasses which were relatively rare *aussteier* items. Very occasionally a widow retained not only the goods one has come to expect but also very male items like augers, pincers, hammer and anvil, maul and wedges, fifth chain, log-chain, scythes, grain cradles, three shaking forks, dunghook, hayforks, jackscrews, etc. (Widow Landis, 1835).

All of these manuscript sources: indentures, family books, wills, and inventories present detailed descriptions and established patterns for the inheritance of goods and property among the Pennsylvania Germans of the eighteenth and nineteenth centuries. As reflected in their wills' references to family books, what was "hers" and "his," widow's shares, and the responsibilities to unestablished children, the interrelationships of these property transfers were generally well-thought-out, complex, as well as based on long-standing traditions. Families tried to provide for their own and close dependents from birth to death as had their parents. The *aussteier* or dowry was the central part of a complex inheritance system among the Pennsylvania Germans.

*J*ust as the *aussteier* was part of a complex inheritance system among our Pennsylvania-German communities, so the dowry portion appears to have been part of the English community's inheritance system.

In Pennsylvania's two dominant cultural groups, the wills in particular show that what was considered as basic "male" or "female" items was nearly identical. There are very few family account books in the English group so one cannot confirm that these "his" or "her" items in the wills were always the same goods given by parents to children before or at the time of marriage. Their marriage contracts do not have enough specificity to add clarity either.

We do know from the few extant family books and from several secondary references that English dowries did exist and consisted of objects like chests, Bible boxes, beds and bedding, horses and cows. The range of furniture forms and textile pieces which have survived with the initials or names of single women, or dates that predate, or are at the time of a couple's marriage, also indicate the dowry concept at work. Again, the goods are similar to those given to or made by Pennsylvania Germans of the period.

It appears however that the English communities had a stronger and more complex inheritance dowry system for daughters than sons. Their marriage portions also involved cash and land to a greater extent than those of the Pennsylvania Germans while equality among siblings seems not as important a concept for them.

Although the family account records surveyed were from Adams, Chester, Delaware and Chester counties, it was to Chester County that we turned our attention in looking for marriage contracts, indentures and wills. By limiting our search we could also draw upon the excellent published and unpublished work of Barry John Levy: "The Light in the Valley: The Chester and Welsh Tract Quaker Communities and the Delaware Valley 1681-1750," (University of Pennsylvania Ph. D. thesis 1976), and *Quakers and the American Family/British Settlement in the Delaware Valley* (New York: Oxford University Press, 1988) as well as Lee Ellen Griffith's doctoral thesis: "Line and Berry and Inlaid Furniture: A Regional Craft Tradition in Pennsylvania 1682-1790," (University of Pennsylvania, 1988) and her article in *Antiques* (May, 1989, pp. 1202-1211) based on the material gathered for the thesis.

Today a substantial number of the manuscript records and material goods of Chester County's dominant English communities are housed, maintained, and interpreted by the Chester County Historical Society in West Chester as well as by the Friends Library at Swarthmore and Haverford colleges. They include cabinetmakers' and family records, indentures, diaries, and wills.

Chester County was one of the three original counties drawn up by William Penn in 1682 under a charter signed by Charles II. At that time it included present day Berks, Delaware, and Lancaster counties as well. Although there were already English, Dutch, Finnish, and Swedish settlers when Penn got his charter, the greatest number of settlers later came from Great Britain: English, Welsh, and Irish Quakers, Anglicans and Scots-Irish Presbyterians. Another large number of settlers were Pennsylvania Germans. Each group settled in fairly distinct areas of the county. The English Quakers were dominant in the southeastern part, the Irish Quakers and their Scots-Irish Presbyterian counterparts in the southern and western parts and, quite separate from the others, were the Pennsylvania Germans to the north.

As Margaret B. Schiffer points out in her book *Chester County Inventories 1685-1850*, (Exton, PA: Schiffer Limited, 1974): "For over two hundred years the population of the county was primarily rural, conservative and middle class with a strong Quaker element . . . Most family names found in the eighteenth-century tax assessment lists are still found in the same township in 1850. Although the county was primarily agricultural it did not have a purely rural culture. The Quakers went to Philadelphia for Yearly Meetings and also to market and there they had the opportunity of seeing city styles which they would adapt to their own tastes." Indeed the 210 weavers, 118 blacksmiths, 104 carpenters, 23 joiners, 7 potters, 7 cabinetmakers, 5 clockmakers, and 5 spinning-wheel makers recorded in the 1796 direct tax list of Chester County could have supplied most of the basic household advancements of furniture, textiles and tools as these same groups of craftsmen had in similar rural and culturally conservative areas of the state (see Schiffer p. 5).

In the *Quakers' Rules of Discipline of the Religious Society of Friends* their young people were exhorted to obtain counsel and consent of parents, relations, and friends especially as it pertains to the choice of a "helpmate." In 1857 they explicitly stated: "And seeing that the real enjoyment of life is far more effectually secured by contentment with simple habits than by any appearance or mode of living which entails anxiety or risk, we would strongly advise parents, whilst they exercise a prudent care over the interests of their children not to be unduly anxious to secure worldly advantages for them on entering the marriage state. And we would affectionately encourage our younger members when looking towards this most important step, to be satisfied to set out in life in a manner befitting their circumstances, instead of seeking to imitate in their style of living the example of those who possess larger resources." (*Rules of Discipline,* London: Darton and Harvey, p. 103)

Dowry, which was the partial advancement of one's inheritance at time of marriage, was of importance. As Jerry Frost points out in his book, *The Quaker Family in Colonial America,* (New York, St. Martins Press, 1973), "Nearly all the instances of the link between money and matrimony occurred among wealthy Friends in England and America, and show that like rich Puritans and Anglicans, prosperous Quakers saw marriage as involving a financial arrangement. [However,] the very few dowries mentioned in correspondence and the absence of Quaker marriage contracts preclude generalization about the majority of members." (p. 158) He went on to note: "In England in 1797 a few members of the Society of Friends set up a 'Marriage Portion Fund' to provide virtuous young servant women with dowries so that they would not need to postpone marriage. [This is of major concern to Quakers as according to Barry Levy.] The need for some kind of financial settlement was considered far more important in England than in rural America where the high price of labor and the availability of land made the amount of work that a woman could do her most important asset." (p. 158) Nonetheless Frost points out, and indeed it is implied in their *Rules of Discipline,* that the American Friends did have an eye on each other's ability to provide a dowry and that most often the dowry included cash and/or land, sometimes exclusively.

The paucity of extant family records delineating the children's initial household *may* be a result of a dependence on a cash dowry in lieu of goods: "While marriage for money was universally condemned, Friends did not consider wealth unimportant . . . 'Like many other Englishmen Friends attempted to marry virtuous wealthy girls of good background.' " (Frost, p. 156) Frost points out that eighteenth-century French traveler Jacques Pierre Bussot de Warrille observed that most American women married without dowries in the conventional European sense—cash and land primarily. On the other hand he stated: "In rural areas a

Levis Pennock's accounting with daughter, Mary Pennock Passmore on May 5, 1777. Courtesy of the Library of the Chester County Historical Society, West Chester, PA. Manuscript number 10549.

father might contribute some livestock, however and his daughter might accumulate feathers on a bed, linens, some pewter, or a chair." (Frost, p. 158)

Wills show that when the dowry goods were delineated they resembled the male and female *aussteier* of their Pennsylvania-German neighbors. James Miles of Kennett Township, Chester County, in his will dated December 11, 1852, stated: "I give and bequeath to my wife Sarah C. Miles the use of twelve hundred dollars that is to say the interest during her natural life in lieu of Dower, agreeable to our Marriage Contract. I likewise give her all the house and Kitchen furniture that she brought to me." Abraham Marshall of West Bradford Township, Chester County, withheld from his wife and daughter the two articles most often associated with male dowry: the clock and desk, and instead gave her the rest or female-related items: "I give and bequeath to my beloved wife Sarah, the sum of one thousand dollars to be paid to her within one year after my decease by my said Executor. Also one good Cow, the first choise [sic] of my cows: together with all my Household and kitchen furnature [sic]: (Except the Clock and desk) all which said bequest to be held by her in her own right during her life and at her decease (or at my decease if it should last take place) to go to and desend [sic] to my daughter Rachel Marshall."

Even more detailed than these two references was the will of Quaker John Watson who was living in Middletown, Bucks County, when he drew up his will on September 16, 1832:

Secondly—I give to my Daughter Rachel Watson 2000 dollars to be paid as herein after directed, I also give her the bed my mother made for me with the bedsteads on which it has been used, also 20 sheets, 12 pillowcases, which were made for her and marked with her name, 4 blankets, 1 Bedquilt, 1 Bureau, all of her choice. My will is that if she remain with my Executors or either of them, that they provide a suitable way for her to go to Meeting, and see her friends, and my desire is that in all cases as becomes brothers and sister; and if that should be the case my wish is that she should sew for the one that she lives with, as she has done for me; I direct my Executors to pay her 50 dollars a year with them or either of them; which sum and privileges is to be in full of Interest on the 2000 dollars while she so remains with them, but if it be more agreeable to her to live elsewhere then my Executors is to pay her 100 dollars a year and every year which sum is to be in full consideration of the Interest on the 2000 dollars Legacy bequeathed to her, and it is my will that the 2000 Legacy remain lean [lien] on my real Estate until paid, and my desire is that it remain so unless she should marry, and in that case as much of it that she may be willing to let remain, that she may have a small income yearly which she will find convenient, and my will is that in all cases when the said Rachel Watson shall receive either Interest or Principle [sic] whether married or single that her receipt shall be a full discharge for said sums; and in no case shall any person have the power to call the money out of my Executors hands but herself during her life.

Thirdly—I give to my son William B. Watson the sum of 400 dollars to be paid by my Executors in 4 annual payments of 100 dollars each, without Interest. I give him the mare which he has had sometime in his possession and my good wishes for his prosperity, believing that what I have given him heretofore is his just share and it is my request that he should give medical attendance to my wife and daughters Mary and Rachel while they remain where they are, free of any charge for services they have rendered him, and still may render if he and they should remain single—

Fourthly—I give my son Isaiah P. Watson the sum of 2000 dollars to be paid by my Executors with 3 percent Interest from my decease until paid, but my desire is that he let the money remain in the Executors hands until it shall appear that there is good prospect of its being used to more advantage, and then to consult his best friends on the subject—

Fifthly—I give to my daughter Mary Watson the sum of $2000.00 to be paid as herein after directed—I also give her the second choice of my beds, bedsteads, 14 sheets, 12 pillowcases that was made for her and marked with her name, also 4 blankets, 1 bedquilt the second choice of my bureaus and my will is that she remain where I now live unless she should choose to marry, or my executors should both marry, in that case she must act as is agreeable to her—My will is if she remains with my Executors either of them, that they provide a suitable way for her to go to meeting and to see her friends, and my desire is that in all cases they act as becomes brothers and sister; and if that should be the case my wish is that she should sew for the one that she lives with as she has done for me—and I direct my executors to pay her 50 dollars a year while she remains with them or either of them, which sum and privileges is to be in full of interest on the 2000.00 dollars while she so remain, but if it should be more agreeable to her to live elsewhere, then my Executors is to pay her 100.00 dollars a year and every year which sum is to be in full consideration of the interest on 2000 dollars legacy bequeathed to her—and it is my will that the 2000 dollars legacy remain a lean [lien] on my real estate until paid, and my desire is that it may so remain unless she should marry, and in that case as much of it as she may be willing to let remain, that she may have a small income yearly, which she will find convenient, and my will is that in all cases when the said Mary Watson shall receive either interest or principal, whether married or single, that her receipt shall be a full discharge for said sums, and in no case shall any person have power to call the money out of my Executors hands, but herself during her life—

Sixthly—I give to my two sons John Watson and Joseph Watson all the remainder of my Estate which has not otherwise been disposed of by me in my will, after my just debts and funeral expenses are paid, both real and personal to them, their heirs and assigns forever, to be divided equal in value between them taking into consideration the difference in the value of the improvements and the value of the land, and if they cannot make a satisfactory division, that they choose three or 5 disinterested men to assist them, a majority of them shall be final—the goods left for the use of my Widow cannot be divided until the time specified in my Will arrives. (*A Quaker Saga* by Jane T. T. Brey, Philadelphia: Dorrance and Company, 1967).

Other wills list males specifically as getting: "one Large Bible, one Bedsteed Bed & furniture, one Large Chist, one Longsettle in the house & one Littel Cubert wherein I Lay Books; Six black Chares"; also, "one spring Clock; one Large walnut table; my Clock & Case wherein it hangs; one Large Case of Bottles"; "one littel table in the house; one table in the parler; one new Chist in the Loft; one Case of Bottles with pewter tops; one Bible with frame to set it on; also Barclay Apology; my Sadle & Boots My best Hatt & Case one steel Cross bow; one Little Cane with a fishing rod belonging it—together with all my Carpenter tools of what sort so ever; the bettur sett of Coat & Vest plate Buttons." (Thomas Watson's will of December 30, 1737)

Wills also list the females as receiving chest of drawers, beds, bedding, quilts, coverlets, clothing; also pewter dishes and salt, chafing dish, brass skimmer, pepper mill, and sidesaddle.

Lee Ellen Griffith's search for line-and-berry inlaid furniture, sometimes bearing initials and dates, often found furniture so marked as being reserved as the widow's—most often chests of drawers. Other forms with female dowry connections were Bible boxes. As Jane Brey recounts about a female's dowry" . . . [a woman to be married] must be supplied with linen quilts, blankets as well as a good supply of extra clothing 'to start her off properly'. . . . a bride's chest was the customary piece of furniture used to hold such collected goods. Numerous examples of these chests remain as family heirlooms, and sometimes they have been known to contain some pieces of homespun linen on which a long-ago ancestress had worked her initials in finest cross-stitch as a young bride. Once, I remember seeing a chest completely filled with linen sheets, pillowcases, blankets, quilts, towels and table linen—all handmade of homespun materials, each piece marked with miniature cross-stitch initials." (*A Quaker Saga*, p. 244) Rodney Cavernough wrote of his great-great-great-great-grandfather's will written in 1812 which reserved out from his estate for a great-granddaughter, Elizabeth Davis: "A new feather bed and bed cloathes, a cow, a spinning wheel, a new Bible, two new suits of Sunday clothes besides her common wearing apparel," and for his wife "pots, pans, bed, cow & etc. including her saddle and bridle"—all items associated with traditional female *aussteiers* among the Pennsylvania Germans of the past and of the Plain sects of today.

Sometimes fathers offered "protection," or exerted continued control, over their daughters' marriage portion by never formally giving over these items to their girls (hence to their sons-in-law). For example, Caleb Johnson enters "lent" when he recorded his three daughters' cupboards, chest of drawers, beds and bedding, china and glassware.

Marriage contracts also offered protection to a female when in some she retained control over those things she brought to the union—which under Pennsylvania law would otherwise have been under the sole control and ownership of her husband until his death. For instance, Charles McKeever in December 1831, agreed prior to his marriage with Catharine Neilor to the following restrictions: he permitted her "his intended wife, peaceably and quietly" to possess and dispose of all her "ready monies, bonds, notes and all other securities for money" and "all her household goods, chattels, real and personal estate" and suffered her to "buy, sell, bargain, pay and receive in her own name." He also allowed her to dispose of all her goods to any person or persons and by her choice of means. This was typical of other marriage contracts where the females or their fathers for whatever reason considered control of property for women essential.

As Barry Levy points out in his thesis: "It was a complex system of mutual obligations with property going generally from father and mother to sons and daughters, but also going backwards from son to father [dependent upon age and circumstance] and from sons to sisters. It served two uses: chiefly it helped assume that all children were adequately portioned and it involved all children financially in the family and by extension in the community." (*The Light in the Valley*, p. 189) An important difference between Pennsylvania-German records and those of their English neighbors is the word "adequately." It did not always mean "equality" as among the Pennsylvania Germans. Interdependence as shown in the Quaker wills was similar however to that which was already shown to be operating among Pennsylvania-German families of some means.

Levy gives several "typical" examples of this economic relationship as in the case of Thomas Massey of Marple, Chester County, who "married Phebe Taylor in 1692 and died in 1708, age forty-five, leaving six children: three girls and three boys . . . The eldest son, Mordecai, was to take over the father's role. Thomas Massey gave him the house and plantation in Marple which he was to enter at age twenty [and which the widow might continue to live in as long as she did not remarry] . . . Mordecai had to pay James and Thomas [his younger brothers] the sum of £100 [over time, and those two also divided the 470 acres at Willistown at maturity] . . . Each of the [three] daughters got twenty pounds to be put out at interest at the age of eight and received at twenty-one or when married. They also received unworked black walnut, some walnut chests and a quarter of the livestock [the other three quarters having been given to an equal number of males]." (*The Light in the Valley*, p. 188) These payments to children—in this case siblings—were staggered, as would the father's have been to his children if he had lived to see them establish their own households. In the end, the males were treated relatively equally (the first son got more but he had obligations which his younger male siblings did not have) and the females were treated to adequate but not equal portions when compared to those of their brothers. This trend was repeated when reading wills of other English farmers. It contrasts sharply to the pattern established by Pennsylvania Germans where equality across sex groupings was as essential as among the members of the same sex.

The eldest son often had to postpone his own marriage because of these obligations: "In such families, oldest sons married at an average age of 35.7, the mean for all sons being twenty-six. In a society that put great stress on portioning all the children, being the eldest son was no privilege; it often meant a disciplined life devoted to unfinished family business." (*The Light in the Valley*, p. 191)

Equality among sons, particularly as it pertained to land, was not a priority for all English cultural communities here in Pennsylvania. According to Levy, ". . . Anglican parents saw no need to bankroll every son's love story to ensure them all dignified and protected situations [as did Quakers] . . . Anglican farmers and artisans who easily could have afforded land for their children did not buy it [in the eighteenth century] . . . only slightly more than half the Anglican settlers [in the Delaware Valley] wrote wills . . . [and those] who did leave wills tended to invest in the family line rather than in individual children." (*Quakers and the American Family*, pp. 180-181)

Levy gives us an example of this type of thinking. Thomas Dawson, a cordwainer and farmer in West Caln Township, Chester County, in his will of July 11, 1748, gave his entire 551 acres and £219 in bonds to his eldest son's advancement or to his son's heirs leaving his other sons and three daughters with nothing; his second son to be a substitute heir in case of the first one's death. This Anglican tradition, as Levy perceives it at work in Chester County, appears to reflect the English tradition of primogeniture. It is quite different in concept and application to the equal advancements or traditional interdependence through "revolving funds" maintained by their Quaker and Pennsylvania-German counterparts. As Levy says, "Dawson's thinking was nevertheless common among Anglicans who left wills. Most Anglican Fathers, who held 259 acres on the average, favored one or two sons." (*Quakers and The American Family*, p. 181) There were exceptions but as he notes of all those fifty-two Anglican families who had more than one son: eight gave all to one son, six divided their land or cash sale of land among all the children in their wills while the remainder made no wills at all. According to Stevenson Fletcher in his book, *Pennsylvania Agriculture and Country Life, 1640-1840* (Harrisburg, PA: Pennsylvania Historical and Museum Commission, 1950, p. 17): "The Scotch Irish proceeded on the theory that all girls would marry and hence needed no estate; so in their wills, they generally devised about nine-tenths of the estate to their sons and divided the remaining tenth among their daughters."

In contrast, Quakers in the Delaware Valley, as shown in their wills and inventories, bought land to farm for themselves as well as to give to their children as their "good start." Barry Levy found that these fathers hoped to settle their sons and sometimes grandsons on farms and those with sons tended to accumulate more land for this purpose. "Sons received over 200 acres on an average and daughters received somewhat less than the equivalent in Pennsylvania currency . . . The average [Quaker farmer in Chester County in the first half of the eighteenth century] had a small herd of animals (6 cows, 4 steer, 6 horses, 14 sheep and 8 pigs) and was cultivating between 40 and 50 acres for wheat, barley, and corn. The rule of thumb in eighteenth-century farming was three acres for one cow, so the cows and steers would require at least 30 acres. The six horses would need about 6 acres and oats, and their 13 sheep about two acres a year. This gives a figure of at least 80 acres in use for the average farmer who had 700 acres. The additional 620 acres awaited children." (*The Light in the Valley*, p. 136)

Second-generation Quakers, Levy points out, began to give less land to their children but they gave more moveable goods. The land which was given often was cleared and with "improvements" however (*The Light in the Valley*, p. 237). This parallels conditions among the prosperous Pennsylvania-German farming families of the second generation. (This is well illustrated in the three generations of the Clemens family in Lower Salford Township, Montgomery County, see pp. 52, 53). Also the goods owned and perhaps considered essential to setting up a household, were increasing in number and reflected a more leisurely and refined way of life even in rural surroundings: before 1730 there were trunks, boxes and chests to store clothes. Eating was often from pewter without the benefit of knives and forks but with spoons and fingers. After 1730 the average moveable goods rose from £192 to £331 which often included chest of drawers, desks, clocks, looking glasses as well as teapots and tea sets, knives and forks, table linens, and books. Instead of an average of three chairs there were nearly ten (Frost, *Quakers in Colonial America*, p. 237).

Of the two major English groups in Pennsylvania there were major differences regarding dowry. Marriage portions or "advancements" were either given by Quakers while fathers were alive and prospering, or set aside in wills, were given directly or by an elaborate "revolving fund" maintained among siblings through mutual obligations. Anglicans, it appears, did much less of this, relying instead on the younger siblings to fend for themselves while investing in the oldest surviving male sometimes exclusively.

Inheritance for English families as well as for Pennsylvania Germans when it was provided was done so over a lifetime—in large part out of economic necessity both for parents as well as for children. The dowry or *aussteier* portions of their inheritance were received by children at a crucial juncture in their lives.

Red earthenware was the pottery of choice given girls for their dowry for well over one hundred years (1740s to 1860s). It was slowly replaced by china and queensware, later by stoneware, depending in part upon the form: the former replaced earthenware tableware while the latter replaced earthenware serving and storage vessels primarily. The earthenware listed in the dowry records was not specific by form as later china store-bought entries sometimes were, but might have included some of the examples seen in these pieces and made by potters Adam or John Maize and James Neiman who worked in Union County. Adam Maize worked in New Berlin or Union Township from 1804 to 1860 and John Maize from 1838 to 1849; the Maize ware includes the large covered crock and the small and large dishes. James Neiman worked in Mifflinburg or New Berlin from 1854 to 1887. His ware with its characteristic runny manganese glaze includes the covered beanpot, pitcher, and cake molds. Courtesy of Packwood House Museum, Lewisburg (two large plates in foreground and large covered crock—all by Maize); courtesy of Jim and Carol Bohn (plates in center, covered beanpot, bottommost large sponge cake mold and small one on left; courtesy of William and Jeannette Lasansky (large pitcher, large and small Neiman sponge cake molds on lower right—all by Neiman, and plain homespun wash towel). The pieces range in size from 5½" d. for small cake molds and from 6⅛" to 9⅞" d. for the plates.

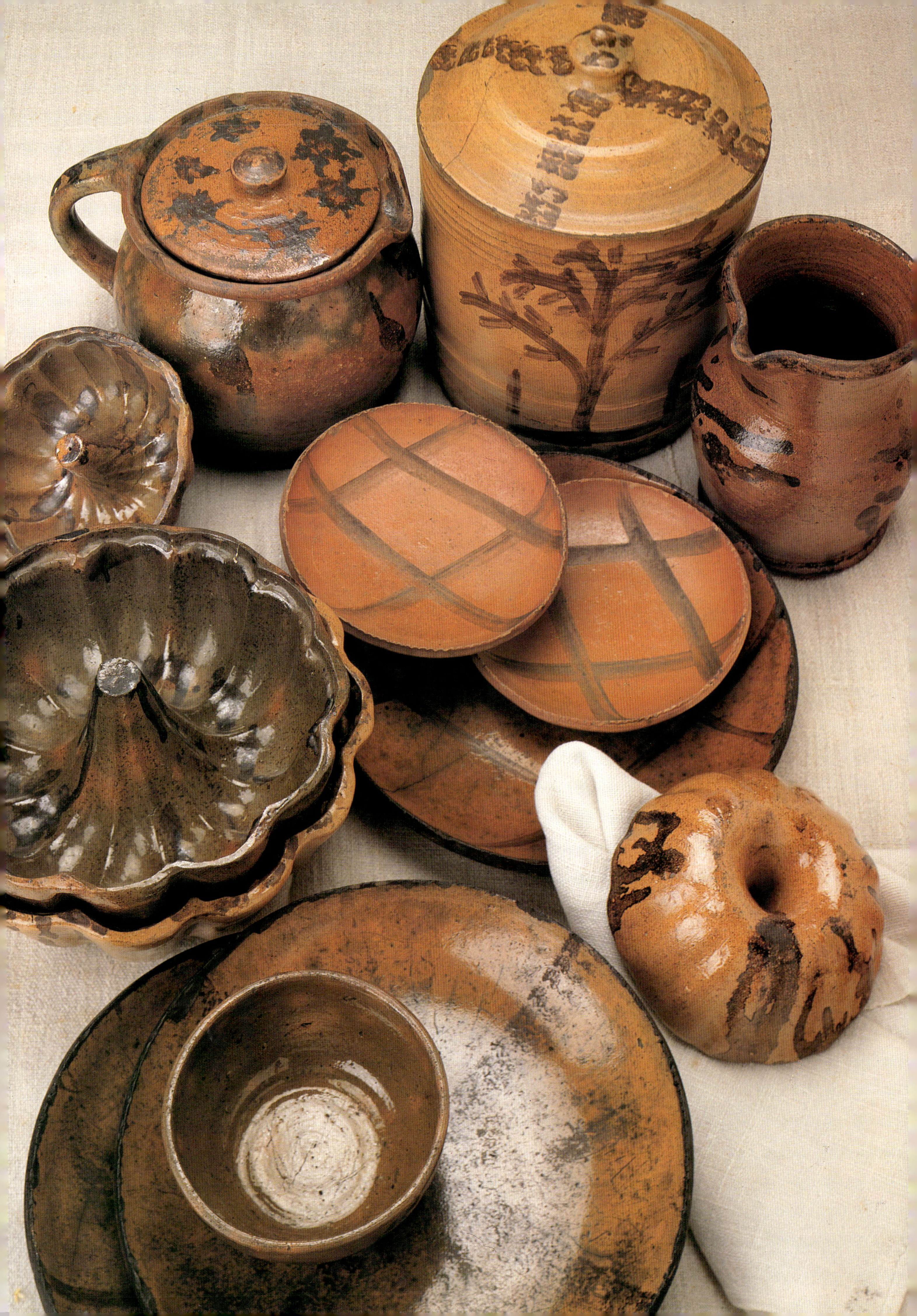

It's in the Accounts

Written and Oral

Based on the reading and analysis of twenty-seven Pennsylvania-German family accounts that were recorded for nearly two hundred years (1749 to 1945) and after talking with over two dozen Amish and Old Order Mennonite informants living in Centre, Clinton, Lancaster, Mifflin, and Union counties, observations can be made about the *aussteier* or dowry traditionally provided to young people here. When typical male and female *aussteier* of contemporary Plain people are compared with those of their earliest counterparts, it is interesting to note how many elements in the traditional dowry remain intact. These marriage portions were also recorded as "outfittings," "outsettings," or "advancements." Today, just as in the past, no one family's way of giving marriage portions or outfits to their young people can be said to be the rule. Nonetheless, patterns of giving do emerge in conversation with these very tradition-bound Pennsylvania farm families just as analysis of written dowry records kept for two hundred years illustrates patterns of retention, evolution, abandonment, and the introduction of new forms (see charts, pp. 46, 54, 55, 64-69). These patterns reflect group thinking or custom as well as personal circumstance and preference.

Sarah, or "Sadie," and her husband, Joseph Beiler, live alone in the "grandfather (*gross dawdi*)" part of the house on the Beiler farm in Lancaster County where he was born and which he, as the only son, bought from his parents. When we visited, it was Mr. Beiler's 66th birthday (May 12, 1989) and Sadie commented that he still would like

Next to tall case clocks, the kitchen cupboard or dresser (*schiessel schank*) was among the more expensive items which fathers bought for their children. Samuel Schultz of Hereford Township, Montgomery County, charged customers from $19 to $25 for them in 1815, while Jacob Bachman of Lancaster charged $14 to $16 for softwood cupboards and $24 for a walnut one in 1823. This black walnut example from c.1750-1800 measures 81¾" h. x 63" w. x 21³⁄₈" d. It is filled with pewter of the period. Courtesy of The Henry Francis du Pont Winterthur Museum. Accession number 65.2720.

to move elsewhere, but she described herself as "an old post" who would just as soon stay where she is.

When asked whether the family ever kept records of what they gave their children before or at the time of marriage, she responded, "No, we never did." Neither did she know of others who did. In fact, she stressed that she did not know what others did, but that they tried to do for their children what their parents had done for them. There were no rules but everybody was guided by tradition, so that she felt certain "patterns" evolved. They never worried what their neighbors gave their children because everybody had different financial means. It is just that everybody will "stretch" themselves (*na de deck schtrecker*) to do the best they can. But, she observed, young people often compare what each "gets from home." This among the Amish is called *aussteier*. Sadie, after being asked, could think of no other name for it.

Sadie and Joe Beiler have eight daughters. The oldest, Rachel, was married in 1968; the youngest, Liddy, in 1986. The Beilers tried to give equally to each, that is in items not in dollar amounts. The latter would be impossible because of inflation over the eighteen-year period—the cost of the food alone for the weddings had tripled between the first and the last wedding. Their daughters' *aussteier* included a bedroom suite plus two beds and a supply of bedding including two topmost coverings for each bed. Today, the tops are usually a quilt and a "spread" among the Lancaster Amish. When Sadie married, spreads were more popular because they could be washed, whereas they could not wash the quilts. She felt that today quilts are "in" partially because spreads are too expensive. Sadie is trying to make a quilt top for each of her forty-two grandchildren to be given to them on their eighteenth birthdays. She made all the quilts for her daughters.

While the girls were growing up, she and her husband bought various furnishings as they became available at bargain prices and stored them in their attic. Sadie's brother owned a used furniture store and "that helped a lot." Their daughters "never handled money much" (neither did the son), but when they got married the parents set them up with all necessary furnishings, household items, clothing, and food for the first year or until the newlyweds' first harvest was in. The interval between the couple's marriage in November and their setting up housekeeping in the spring was "grabbing time" as Sadie called it—"they grabbed what they

IT'S IN THE ACCOUNTS

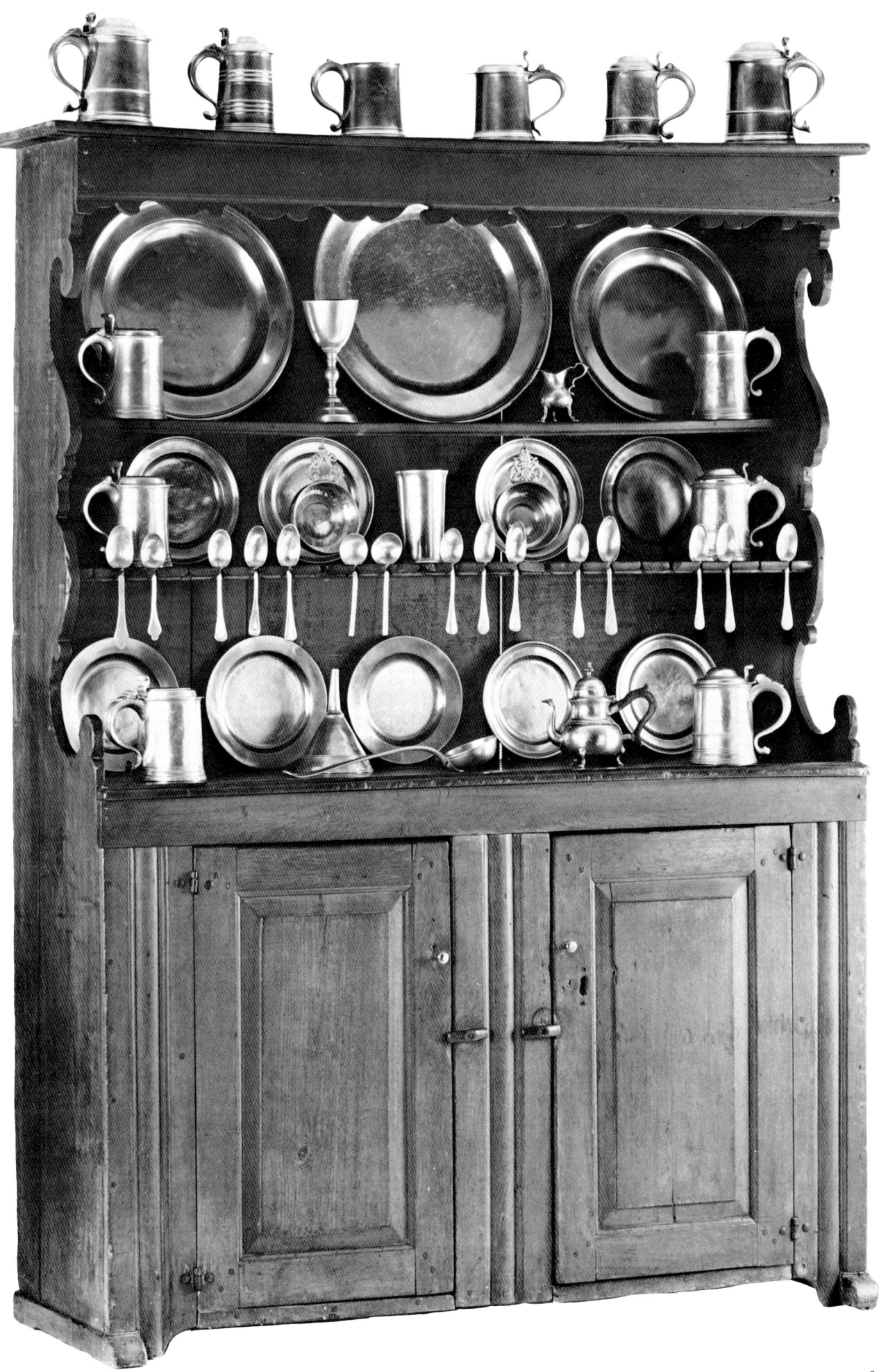

could." But the children always had to be satisfied with what their parents provided, "They were raised that way." Nowadays everything has to match for some young people, Mrs. Beiler feels.

When questioned about what the Amish do for their sons at marriage, Sadie stressed that they, the Beilers, might not be typical as they have only one son, Chris. However, they tried to do what their parents did for them, carrying on tradition. Chris got two beds and the necessary bedding including four tops. His wife, Anna, brought the furniture to the new household. (Chris married three years after starting to purchase the cows and then the family farm from his father. He married younger, at age 21, than is usual for Amish males.) Sadie noted that Chris like other young men received "a team" (meaning a horse and a buggy) from his parents when he was sixteen. Sometimes, she said, the first horse is not right and a substitution has to be made later.

Sadie was the tenth of sixteen children. One died in childhood, three were stillborn, one girl was handicapped, and one girl was mentally retarded. All the healthy girls married and all the boys went into farming. Her father provided financial backing for all her brothers to purchase a farm but did not give them one. The boys paid for their land as well as the equipment "over time." As far as Sadie could remember the boys in her family were not actually given farm equipment, seed grain, or farm stock at their marriage, but "just the usual" (meaning bedding, a desk, some food, etc.).

When Sadie married it was war time. Consequently, her kitchen equipment consisted of various odds and ends, "I remember, Mother gave me five aluminum tablespoons. I was thrilled. But you can imagine what the food tasted like with those." She also got a second-hand bedroom suite. She remembers her oldest sister getting "new things." But they all got "a dozen pillowslips, a dozen sheets, tablecloths, towels, tea towels and so on." Some of these items had been given to the girls at various times by different people as presents and stored away until their marriage. Sadie also got her grandmother's rocker (her grandmother died when Sadie was just four weeks old and her mother bought the rocker at the sale and saved it for Sadie until she married). Sadie and all her sisters were also given a corner cupboard, a dropleaf table and a sideboard for the parlor; a stove, a kitchen table, and a "combine" or hutch for the good dishes. On looking at her combine, Mrs. Beiler remarked, "It was exactly like my mother's, except hers had the wooden sink and mine had drawers from the start. That was a new 'pattern' then." Sadie kept her "dry goods" in the combine's bottom half while in the sideboard she kept her bonnets and good things that were not used too often. Her combine was new and made especially for her by a neighbor. He used green wood and she remembers how for years the drawers and doors would stick. It still has a place of honor in her kitchen. It is now a "catch-all," she remarked. For instance, it now holds two footed pink glass bowls—one bought for her by her father and one inherited from her sister. All her girls used them to hold fruit at their weddings and she has often lent them to others for the same purpose.

Sadie observed that each piece of furniture that she received or that she in turn gave to her girls, had a definite function and place in the home. Sometimes they were made by a father if he was handy with tools. For example, her daughter-in-law, Anna, had her father make her "combine." Other pieces might be passed down as was Sadie's rocker, or some might be bought at sale or from another source, as Sadie had done over the years for all her girls. Buying the *aussteier* all at once was nearly an impossible thing to do although some did. Accumulating the goods over time was an economic necessity for the Beilers.

Susie and Amelia Bender of Mifflin County observed that while there are some Amish families who can afford to give all new furniture to their children, many others give old furniture or a mix of old and new. In their family their four brothers got desks while all the girls got corner cupboards. These two maiden ladies have the standard set of female house furnishings.

Sylvia King, who lives in Mifflin County, tells an interesting story about her first major dowry item—a corner cupboard. Just before her parents moved from Mifflin County out west to Iowa with most of their family, they provided a stove, bed, table and chairs, later a chest of drawers, as well as a corner cupboard to their oldest daughter Lizzie who was about to marry Sam Detweiler. Lizzie, however, preferred a corner cupboard that was to come up at sale, so Sylvia at age twelve or fourteen was the recipient of her sister's "reject" which had been made and grain-decorated by a local craftsman. Lizzie has since given her cupboard to her only girl while Sylvia King still has the original piece standing in a place of importance in her living room.

Reflecting upon more recent practice, Mrs. King noted how she and her husband provided a car for each of their five children. Today, she felt that people still try to give equally to their children as they leave the family and go on to establish homes of their own, but that *aussteier* is not done to the same extent in part because of finances. Also, she observes that needs are changing because so many of her people are not working on farms (this was confirmed by Sadie Beiler who said only a third of her district worked a farm).

The "outfitting" of children remains important as an economic tool to get a new family unit off to a good start—particularly among farming families with prescribed traditional needs. It is therefore not surprising that the *aussteier* is intact today among Pennsylvania's Amish and Old Order Mennonite communities. As they struggle to retain the farm as the family/work unit integral to their faith, *aussteier* will continue to have a valid and central role to play. In families where males are no longer farmers, but rather craftsmen or factory workers, certain aspects of their *aussteier* traditions have lapsed or will in future. In part, because of scarcity of land, some Amish are instead employed at sawmills, pallet plants, machine shops, etc.

Mrs. King's sister, Lizzie, feels that *perhaps* the Lancaster Amish have more elaborate and complete outfittings. "Of course, each child gets several quilts made by their mother, the girls receive about three and the boys, one or two," she noted. Lizzie felt that much is accumulated between a fall wedding and the spring setting out on one's own.

Kate Emerson, a friend of Sadie Lapp who lives in Lancaster County, remembered not only Sadie's wedding to Stevie King in December of 1986 but also the goods Sadie had assembled: three beds complete with several sets of bedding, one being part of a bedroom suite of bureau and night stand, a corner cupboard, a dining-room table and chairs, a couch and parlor chair, two hooked rugs made by the grandmother, five needlepoint chair cushions made by Sadie, a second kitchen area rug, a "combine," a refrigerator but not a stove (since that was included in the house that would be rented), a complete set of dishes and twenty-five balls of rolled rag strips—one and one half pounds each. Stevie King as the male was expected to add twenty balls, which when combined with Sadie's would be brought to a local rug weaver to be made into carpeting. When woven each ball will make about a yard of carpet thirty inches wide. Stevie also brought to the marriage his "team" complete with harness, bridle and horse blankets (roughly the cost of an automobile), a desk, tools of carpentry which was his trade, and a bentwood rocker which was "his" chair.

When asked whether the itemization of the *aussteier* was written down, as we know was done by some in the past, most of these informants were unaware of such a record. However, Anna and Barbara Fisher, who are older maiden ladies recently moved from Lancaster County to Sugar Valley in Clinton County, do remember such a record.

Levina Huyard, who lives in Lancaster County, distinctly remembered the "paper from a tablet" on which her grandmother on her father's side (a Fisher) had itemized the *aussteier*. Levina's father also kept such a record, perhaps she felt because he had two sets of children—from first and second marriages—and that, as a consequence, he was still giving to young people when he was at an advanced age. He therefore might have needed to "write it all down." Levina now has "none of those writings" nor is a written family account kept by her or her husband Amos—deliberately so. She said her husband's family tradition was not to write the *aussteier* down; Levina and Amos adhere to his family's way reinforced in part because of severe price fluctuation over time that makes it seem fruitless to do so. Instead, they keep "in their minds" what has been and needs to be given to their nine children.

Such price changes were illustrated by the examples Levina cited: the chairs she received at the time of her marriage in 1947 cost eight dollars a piece. Recently she had them stripped and repainted for one of her children and the cost was twenty dollars each. "Still a bargain," she said when it probably would now cost as much as fifty dollars to purchase each one new (as well as the fact that the older chairs would last from one generation to the next in contrast to newer ones). In recent years prices have changed even more dramatically: a daughter-in-law was provided with three sets of six chairs: one with cane seats and two all wooden like the old plank-bottom ones. All "new," these three sets alone cost the girl's father about one thousand dollars. Having three sets and all "new" was not typical, Levina thought.

Nowhere has price affected what the Amish can do for their children more than the price of land today. Traditionally fathers have helped their sons get started with a farm and sometimes, if there were no boys or fewer boys than farms owned by the father, land went to girls as well. Land purchased for children was often passed on by bargain sale that was based on the land's original purchase price plus costs of improvements.

When asked about how land was provided, Levina responded, "That's something else" and that now it "must be done so many different ways." In talking about her immediate situation she said, "I don't know how it's ever going to end up." As in the Huyard family, sometimes not all of the sons are in farming and therefore they may not be interested in the family's land holdings. In other instances, the young males marry a girl whose father provides the land or the means of getting land. Few parents are able to give land outright to the son or sons who want and need it. Most are involved, even in a bargain sale which is well below assessed or actual market value, with holding notes that the sons are expected to pay off. Few parents can afford to "write off" a land transaction even if they were so inclined and the siblings all agreeable.

The size of an economically viable farm is changing but has its limits. While local tradition in the late eighteenth/early nineteenth century held that a 120- to 150-acre farm was small enough, today the Amish in Lancaster stop subdividing their land for their farming sons at around sixty to forty acres. Intensive farming methods and different crops have allowed them to put off the inevitable search for more land or diversification of occupations to some extent. Their need to extend the boundaries of their settlement areas, particularly in Lancaster County, as well as to move outside the county, is dictated almost exclusively by their need for additional farmland for new family units.

All the ways of dealing with land transactions as well as other aspects of *aussteier* are dependent on a family's economic conditions at the time and that is dependent on the number of children, status of daughters' husbands, consideration of handicapped or single children, and location of land holdings, among other things. As Levina reflected on the future of their family farm and the fact that it will go to the one son at less than market value, "If he gets a break, all [his brothers and sisters] will understand because he helped out [worked for parents]." In fact wages are often withheld and used later to purchase articles in the *aussteier*.

One important aspect of both male and female *aussteier* is that it represents, at least in part, the earnings of children. Whether they work on the family farm or are hired out, children's earnings are often kept by the parents (actually the father) to be saved or reinvested in the family business—the farm. The return to the children is in the form of their *aussteier* or dowry. Historically, when a child left before the accepted age—about twenty-one for males and eighteen or so for females—the parents might "charge" the missing wages, real or applied, against their inheritance (Jacob Leiby did this with his eldest son, see p. 17). These centuries-old patterns of wage saving and giving are valid today among Old Order Mennonite and Amish farm families.

Farm equipment for the Lancaster Amish boys seems no longer to be a part of the male *aussteier*. Like others interviewed, Levina Huyard noted that the men tend to buy what they want at farm sales. There seemed to be no pattern among Amish families as in the past: some males might use their own wages, saved by parents, for purchasing new equipment; some might inherit what still was in use on the farm; some might assume financial notes held by parents for family farm equipment. She feels that aside from the male's horse and buggy, desk, clothes, beds and bedding, it is the "girls [who] are much more set in what they get and they get more objects, but the basic value of what the boys get is the same [equal value meaning the items' importance and their necessity—not necessarily the financial consideration though that too may be the same]." "This system works as long as we stick together," is the conclusion.

Levina Huyard noted that "things haven't changed much." Some traditional items such as woven rag rugs had been made out of necessity and adherence to frugality in the past. Continuing to give rolled rags for a woven floor covering is no longer an act of economy, Levina maintains. Buying linoleum floor covering is now less expensive than having such rugs woven. But, some of her people adhere to having the latter done simply out of tradition or their sense of "fashion." More families may now use linoleum but she is sure that there will always be some who want rolls of rags for a woven rug. Similarly, the fashion had been for spreads more than quilts at one time, particularly in the 1940s and 1950s, but this was no longer so: "It's not so much a case of economy but of what you want."

The role of tradition was reinforced in our conversation with Elam Beiler of Centre County. Now living in Brush Valley, after moving from Lancaster County fifteen years ago, Elam noted that "tradition can go against the faith." He cited the saving and showing off of "precious" things in the woman's corner cupboard as an example of this. Their religion teaches them not to put value in objects or material goods, and yet, the accumulation of what his wife called "precious things" or "treasures"— articles given or owned by your "namesake" and others close to you—shows that such "added value" exists. These articles are prominently displayed in the corner cupboard as others might be on the girls' bureaus or the family's sideboard. The Beilers shared with us a family register of Mary's aunt and an early decorated pillowslip made by another aunt, which they had purchased at public sale the day before our visit. Family-related articles such as these are obviously very special. The corner cupboard's role is to display, in particular, those glass and china objects that might have such association—given by a "namesake" or as a "keepsake"—or that are in some other way designated as "precious."

Mary Beiler confirmed their tradition of having a rag rug woven in rolled lengths for the parlor. These rolled rugs are cut and bound for a specific room often just before the couple moves in. She and her husband also felt the traditional male's *aussteier* is not as complex now—grains and farm tools are no longer part of it. The desk is, however, and Elam noted that the desk he had been given as a young man was not a particularly good one. Later on, he made himself a desk/bookcase which is now in their main living area, while the one he was given earlier is in one of his boys' bedrooms. There it is used for general storage. Often he said the desk would be placed in the couple's bedroom and in it would be kept the family's records.

Elam's family did not keep an *aussteier* record so far as he could recall, but Mary's mother kept "a paper" of what Mary and her three brothers and sisters received as advancements. Among the larger items she received was her bedroom suite which included a bed, dresser, and chest of drawers (sometimes also a stand). The dresser was low and had an attached mirror, while the chest was higher. Such a suite was usually purchased from non-Amish sources until about ten years ago. Nowadays, along with the female's other furniture, the suite is most likely made by a local Amish craftsman.

The suite, as well as the other beds, the sideboard, drop-leaf table, parlor chairs, kitchen or "combine," table and chairs, and stove are usually purchased by a girl's parents at the time of her impending wedding (added to the bureau and hope chest she had previously been given). When such furnishings are not family pieces or already set aside but rather purchased new, a local Amish cabinetmaker is given the order in the fall, executes and then delivers it in the spring to the couple's new home—or, if they are not settled in yet, to the bride's family home. Antique furniture pieces, even if a couple prefers them, are becoming harder to give because of their increased cost.

Hannah Stoltzfoos, the third youngest of twelve children and the mother of three, lives on a Lancaster County farm with her husband Amos, a son and daughter-in-law and their young family. The two women share the formal parlor because what might serve as Hannah's is used as a small shop for locally made quilts and small handsewn items. Our visit there began with her showing her own *aussteier* quilts and one of her father's. Hannah's mother made one light and one dark quilt for each of her surviving seven children. The light one is white with colored embroidery and is smaller, intended to be used with "fancy pillows." They had been put in Hannah's hope chest.

This "hope" or blanket chest was the second piece of furniture she had received and in it she accumulated, as do other females, the larger and heavier pieces of bedding of the *aussteier*. (The male's heavy bedding, like quilts, just "gets put somewhere.") Her first piece of furniture had been given several years earlier—a chest of drawers. In it, Hannah accumulated the smaller pieces of bedding: pillowcases and sheets plus towels, tablecloths, and handkerchiefs. Small area rugs—braided or sewn—might be placed there also. Sometimes these pieces of furniture are made by a "handy" father but she laughed saying "if that had been the case with me, my hope chest would have more resembled a wood box." The order of receiving these two "female" furniture items, at either Christmas or birthdays from about age fifteen to nineteen, is a fairly uniform "pattern," as is the kind of items stored in them.

Hannah's dark quilt was made for her in 1936 and is in the "Sunshine and Shadow" pattern. It is made of small crepe blocks (the same material as used in her wedding dress) and was made by Hannah's mother when Hannah was seventeen or eighteen. (Hannah did some quilting work on it but it was her mother who conceived and organized the project, hence she says that her mother made it.) She also had one of her father's *aussteier* quilts in the "Diamond in the Square" pattern. One of Hannah's sons who is particularly interested in family history will get this.

She feels that males traditionally get two quilts or spreads and females get three, numbers that were mentioned by others. These would correspond to the numbers of beds brought to the new household by each of the young people, male and female. Hannah said most parents try to give the boy two beds—one of which will be used by a hired hand, one for a guest—while the girl gets the same plus the bed of the suite.

Textiles are given to both young men and women throughout their lives and those not to be used immediately are stored in the girl's bureau or chest of drawers and later hope chest, and in the young male's desk drawers. When shopping a mother is often asked: "is it for the drawers?" The textiles include not only several sets of changes for each bed, but also towels, tablecloths, and small articles of clothing. Depending on the group's rules, some can be purchased like socks, underwear, and new shirts but not pants or dresses—they must be handmade. Males might have as many as a dozen changes and girls might have a dress in each color. Hannah made one dress each of purple, blue, green, magenta, aqua, gray, brown and black (for funerals) fabric for her girls when they were full grown (about age sixteen). But, she said, these were fairly worn by the time of marriage so they were generally replaced about then.

Hannah Stoltzfoos mentioned that women were often given a yard of cloth from each friend or relative at the time of a child's birth. For a while that amount would suffice for the child's clothes but later the amount would be insufficient. At that time, a woman might save the material or "pile it up" for the child's *aussteier* quilt—often a "Sunshine and Shadow"

"Precious" items in *aussteier*, then and now, were often highly decorated such as these Pennsylvania-German sgraffito red earthenware plates. The top one was made in 1804 by Jacob Funck in Haycock Township, Bucks County. The German inscription around its rim is translated to "In the dish stands a house. He who would pilfer — keep out. East, west, my wife is the best. 1804", 2 1/8" h. x 11" d. Courtesy of the Philadelphia Museum of Art, purchased by the John T. Morris Fund. Accession number 21-46-66. The bottom plate was made in 1816 by Henry Roudebush and John Kichline in Upper Hanover Township, Montgomery County, for Sally Steiner, 2 1/8" h. x 11 7/8" d. Courtesy of the Philadelphia Museum of Art, gift of John T. Morris. Accession number '01-5.

Pennsylvania-German sgraffito decorated red earthenware plate made by John Neis, Upper Salford Township, Montgomery County. The German inscription around the rim is translated to "As I have gathered I will soon be coming to your wedding", 1 1/2" h. x 9 7/8" d. Courtesy of the Philadelphia Museum of Art, purchased by the Baugh-Barker Fund. Accession number '38-15-9.

pattern which would well utilize yardage as well as scraps. She confirmed Amish young peoples' current requests for quilts rather than store-bought spreads, though the latter were sometimes used on beds where the topmost covering would get a lot of wear and need much laundering. Hence the *aussteier* quilts were often used in the guest room. Nowadays, she said, of course they can be washed where previously airing was more common and sometimes the exclusive way of cleaning. "Air cleans them and saves the colors," and like her mother, Hannah feels it is best done on a "windy raw damp day to freeze the germs and bugs out."

Traditional needlework includes the *aussteier* pincushions (*schpella kisse*) which will eventually be hung in pairs from a couple's parlor and/or kitchen clock mantels and in the corner cupboard. Needlework also ornaments some bedding as well as tablecloths. Hannah Stoltzfoos's family has pattern boxes with designs that have been handed down through generations. Numerous needlepoint chair pillows in several patterns and techniques are also executed by the Amish and set aside.

Farm tools are generally no longer given by parents to sons nor is kitchenware to girls as in the past. Rather, small tools such as hatchets, hammers, axes, hacksaws, pitchforks, and tablespoons, cups and saucers, or a roaster are given by relatives as wedding gifts and are called *haussteier*. The *haussteier* articles complement those articles accumulated since early adolescence or given by the parents. Together, *aussteier* and *haussteier* make for a total "outfitting" as done in the eighteenth and nineteenth centuries by parents alone. Aunts and uncles provide the larger of these items and generally agree as to who is giving what while married cousins give the smallest articles like a screwdriver or bucket which might be duplicated. "Yes, that's so," Levina Huyard smiled as she recalled getting three agate buckets! Hannah says that she always gives the tablespoons to her nieces and nephews and that is understood.

When responding to making a distinction between dowry and wedding gifts, Elam Beiler also said *aussteier* is for them what other people call "dowry," a term not used by any of the Amish, but when Levina Huyard read of it in Longfellow's poem "Evangeline," she recognized it as being their *aussteier*. To give this to children is important because parents feel children are "entitled to get a good start when first married." For this reason, a basic food supply that feeds the couple until their first canning and butchering season is part of the *aussteier*—"fifty quarts or more of canned stuffs: peaches, applesauce, pears, cherries, red beets, pickles, corn, peas, lima beans, and string beans as well as a whole pig or half a beef. Enough is given to last through the first summer so they needn't go to the store and buy. It's a helpful system."

The beginning of an adolescent girl or boy's *aussteier* can be seen when visiting with Amish families as with the family of Fanny Kauffman of Clinton County. Her two oldest girls had their chest of drawers (with large drawers below and two small ones on top) in the guest room. On their top surfaces were displayed the china and glassware given by family and friends—"keepsakes"—things which will eventually be put in their future homes' corner cupboards (*kleidershrank*) or on the sideboard. Glassware patterns that are popular now are clear pressed glass sometimes called "Wexford," in sherbet, creamer, butter and "fancy" dish (with "little" feet) varieties.

According to Reuben Beiler who has a store in Lancaster County, the "Moon and Star" pattern in green, blue, and amber is also popular as are punch bowls, but the latter is no longer made. Fanny Kauffman maintains that she and her husband will later give the major furniture gifts to their girls and that they will write down or account for such gifts as she does when selling her and others' quilts. She also proudly displayed the quilts that both she and her husband brought with them at the time of their marriage in 1967—"Sunshine and Shadow" patterns.

Our final interviews were conducted among the most conservative of the Amish—the Nebraska called "white tops" because of their white canvas buggy tops—and the most conservative of the Mennonites—the Wengerenites or "team" Mennonites. It was interesting to contrast their accounts of "gifts from home" to those of the Lancaster Amish we had talked with in Lancaster County or in Centre and Clinton counties where some of them moved fifteen to twenty years ago.

Aussteier and *haussteier* had become familiar terms to us but we found they were not for any of those Plain people living in Mifflin County. "Oh, that's probably what they call it in Lancaster," was the reply. "It's what they [grown children] get from home."

A Nebraska Amish man, Sam Yoder, made the analogy: "You got to lift a child onto a horse to give him a good start." "We each got a plough; the rest we had to get ourselves: harrow, disc, hayloader," he said when recalling how it was when he "started up forty-four years ago" in January 1945. Sam was one of seven Nebraska Amish boys who grew up together with his lone sister on the farm on which he now lives with his wife, Katie. Sam was the oldest surviving child and he remembers being given provisions: a hog, a quarter of beef and canned vegetables for example—to see them through the first year; also a cow and calf, a horse, fifty bushels of feed corn and twenty-five chickens which complemented the twelve Katie "brought with her."

Sam Yoder's desk, which came from his grandmother, has since been replaced by a new one he made after he and Katie moved into a smaller attached house on the family farm in 1968. The new part or *gross dawdi* also required a smaller corner cupboard which he made. Sam pointed out tables with nicely turned legs and a wood box that he had made as well—often of oak—unpainted and bright with a clear varnish. The desk was made from a cherry tree which he cut down in the pasture and then dried for four years.

When asked if he had been given clothing as "gifts from home," Sam said "yes" but could not remember how many changes. Katie, his wife, was specific—"it would have been about a dozen shirts, but not near so many pants." Sam also got several beds as well as bedding changes. What he did not get, which some Lancaster still do, were rolled rags for rugmaking. No rugs were in sight on the Yoders' scrubbed, untreated wooden floors—not braided, sewn, hooked or woven: "We do not use them."

Twenty years ago, when Sam's only son Chris was

twenty-one he took over the farm. An agreement, not unlike many seen from the eighteenth and nineteenth centuries (see pp. 22, 23) was drawn up between father and son and filed in the local court house. It delineated mutual rights and obligations: "right to a garden, a patch of corn to feed a horse, and more." As Sam notes such a formal agreement "should be done. One never knows what can happen—accidents do happen." Indeed, some are not so fortunate as to get anything from home. The parents of the husband of his only married granddaughter were not living when the young man set out. There was no outfitting.

Most young men and women, however, do have quilts made by their mothers. Some children get as many as seven among the Nebraska Amish, some as few as one, but most about three along with some comforts or "haps." Pieced quilts, and many of them, seem to be the preferred bedding among the "white tops"—there are no spreads or embroidered work in these homes. Instead of the Lancaster Amish needlework chair pads, often worked in almost iridescent shades of wool, the Nebraska Amish have pieced (but not quilted) chair seats and back pads in their clothing fabrics—blues, purples and browns being dominant. The "Nine Patch" and its variations are favorite patterns. Window covers or loose hanging panels are also made up in these fabrics in contrast to the others' store-bought rolled shades.

Katie Yoder and Franey Hostetler, who lives nearby, both confirm that a long list of goods is "what the girls get from home": a dry sink and kitchen dresser (separate items in their homes as distinct from the Lancaster County "combine,") kitchen table and chairs, rocking chair, cook stove, pots and pans, rolling pin, skillet, coffeepot, tea kettles. Katie was one of thirteen children "that grew up" in her family and five were girls. She knows that her oldest granddaughters (and she has ten grandchildren now) have begun to get some small pieces like shelf clocks bought at "sale" by their father.

As Franey Hostetler sat and surveyed her kitchen, listing the items she would give her girls, she noted how her husband has recently made some new pieces to replace what they had when "setting up housekeeping" twenty years ago. The new oak kitchen dresser's blind front doors, when opened, exposed a tidy display of dishes and glassware accumulated over the years. Some were the "pretty dishes" given her before she married by the family on whose farm she worked for three summers. Others like the pitcher and glasses, a "berry set," a fruit bowl, were sometimes given by one's namesake. "It seems to work that way." At first, she like other Amish girls would have kept them on top of her bureau. Eventually they were placed in her kitchen dresser.

All of Franey's furniture had been made locally, which seems to be a tradition held in common by all the Plain sects. Her nephew, who works in a sawmill, makes furniture "in between." She felt that only a short time ago there seemed to be fewer—not enough—of their own making furniture; now there are more, and most of the young people "like the new pieces." Older furniture of theirs, if sold at a public sale, goes "to antique dealers at outrageous prices." It is for that reason, sales are sometimes held solely for their own community or goods are merely divided up. Franey's husband is now contemplating doing a dropleaf table to replace their first and current kitchen table. They often do fine work based on traditional forms.

"Patterns of giving" play the dominant role in these Nebraska Amish families also. As Franey noted, some people give the boys a desk, but "my husband had to make his own, so our [two] boys have to make theirs." A desk is an essential piece for them to have to keep their records in and books on top. Similarly with the "female's" corner cupboard she said, "I had to get my own so my [three] girls have to get their own." Tradition is paramount in her mind.

Their boys will probably get what their father did—horse, cows, pig, chickens, beds and bedding, half a dozen chairs, clothing, some canned goods, some farm tools, and perhaps a wagon. Usually the boys are buying farm equipment themselves today from money they accumulate from "working out," outside of the community. (Wages given within their community, though greater than in the past, are considerably lower than "outside" wages; two hours might be one day's pay for example).

Franey like Mary Beiler, Barbara and Anna Fisher, mentions mother as having kept a record of all these things—a book, a tablet, or "a paper." Franey's mother had seven girls and with all that was required for "setting up a household" for the girls, she remembers her mother recording what the first girl got and trying to do the same for the others—to give equal value; "boys are simple [i.e. fewer items]."

Before our leaving, Franey's young daughter, Leah, brought out her recent attempts at counted cross-stitch and chain-stitch needlework. Embroidery is done to a much lesser extent by the Nebraska Amish than others but her new sewing skills will be used as she simply initials and maybe dates her bedding textiles. Leah, like her mother, will in time learn to make quilts. If she becomes a mother she will make perhaps three or four for each of her children as well as knot several comforts or haps for each.

Amos Hoover, an Old Order Mennonite, moved to Mifflinburg, Union County, from Farmersville, Lancaster County, the year four of his children were to marry. His move allowed him to help provide farms or "a good start" for these children, something that would have been difficult or impossible to do where he had grown up near Ephrata (for farm prices in Lancaster County in 1968 were roughly four times what they were in the Union County area). He made the move at age 48 along with thirteen other "team" Mennonite families. They had no meeting house, school or ministers at first but they brought shared values and mutual support with them.

Among their traditions was the giving of "things from home," a tradition which is much like that practiced by their Amish neighbors. *Aussteier* was not a word he used, however, but rather the phrase "things from home." He was the only one we interviewed to have kept a record of such items though others knew of such papers.

Amos shared several of his account books with us. One had a detailed accounting of the items he bought as a young man with his accumulated wages. It began in 1939. Half of what he had earned had always been given to his father, who in turn helped Amos acquire a farm.

The other half was mostly saved by Amos so that money was available when he, the youngest son, was to take over the family farm. This was just before his marriage in 1942. With his saved two thousand dollars plus what he got from home, he bought such items as a buggy for $150, a two-horse wagon for $36.66, a plow for $22.00, a cultivator for $18.33,

Salt boxes were occasionally listed in dowry "outfittings" in Pennsylvania as were other small wooden kitchen furnishings such as wash tubs, butter churns, and buckets. John Bomberger gave salt boxes to two of his daughters and Jacob Leiby gave one to both a daughter and son. This painted white pine salt box, 11" h. x 7¼" w. x 8½" d., was made for Anne Leterman and inscribed "ANNE LETERman/Anno Domini 1797/John Drissell/his hand May/ 2nd 1797". The maker lived in Milford Township, Bucks County and several of his small painted wooden salt boxes and tape looms survive him. Courtesy The Henry Francis du Pont Winterthur Museum. Accession number 58.17.1.

two hundred chickens for $75.40, and five sheep for $66.60. Much of his first equipment was used and refurbished as were many of his wife's household furnishings which she brought to the marriage. She too brought some cash from "earnings off the farm" but, because she married soon after beginning "to run around (socialize with other young people)," her cash was not substantial. They married in the fall of 1942, and like so many farming couples, were prepared to take over the Hoover family farm the following spring.

April 1st is the single date most often recorded in such accounts—as it was then and is now the beginning of a new season. Provisions like a cow, half a pig, a barrel of vinegar and many canned goods were given to these young people by both sets of parents—as Mrs. Hoover said, "enough to keep us 'til we had a garden." These same kinds of provisions were recorded by Amos as he outfitted his oldest daughter, Ada (in 1967), and his fifteen other children: eighteen quarts of meat, six pounds of bacon, twelve pounds of flour, nineteen pounds of ham, twenty-one pounds of bologna and ten pounds of sugar. Her most expensive item was a new sewing machine for $208.00 followed by a refrigerator, sofabed, and couch.

Amos, like Hannah Stoltzfoos and Sadie Beiler, linked the amount of goods "from home" to wages turned in or work done on the farm to a certain extent, but Amos was more emphatic than Sadie or Hannah. He said if the children do not save and turn over some of their wages they will have less. All of his children—young men and women—have started off with some land. Not all families can do this but he notes, "they went the same way we did." Again the traditions of his Old Order Mennonite parents were and are maintained, when at all possible. Moving to Union County allowed tradition to be maintained for his family.

Abe Yoder, Jr., who has organized the Mennonite Historical Center in Belleville, remembers a small account record for his parents' family of thirteen children. He mentions that he would not have known particularly what his siblings got, especially those much older or younger than he. However, he did remember that the sister nearest in age to him got the family doughtray and desk nearly fifty years ago. Luckily, he said, his was not a family that was picky about being treated exactly the same. As Sadie Beiler had stressed, "Our children are raised to accept what they are given without complaint." Others echoed that sentiment.

Obviously the keeping of such *aussteier* accounts was not always done. It may not always be necessary nowadays as noted by Mennonite Amos B. Hoover of Denver, Lancaster County who, like Mrs. Daniel King of Mifflin County, saw to it that each of his children simply had a car. Mennonite Miriam Hershey of the Goschenhoppen area said her family considered equal education opportunities in the same way—as an "outfitting for life." These examples clearly reflect a drastic evolution in the form of the *aussteier* for some but not the concept which is to give the children "a good start,"—"to lift a child onto a horse."

Mr. Hoover, who is an historian as well as a farmer, notes that many of the known historical records appear to be coming out of the Franconia Meeting Mennonites, perhaps because they are from a Dutch tradition that included exceptional record keeping. Whatever the reasons—whether because of particular family patterns or larger group dynamics—*aussteier* records then and now are hard to find. It would not be surprising that some families would have thrown out such records especially when they were in German (which they could no longer read). John Hostetler, author of *Amish Society*, (Baltimore: Johns Hopkins University Press—first printed in 1963 and revised as recently as 1980), when asked said that aside from seeing dowry portions in Amish wills, he was not aware of it being a tradition that was written down.

Stephen Scott in his *Amish Weddings*, (Intercourse, PA: Good Books, 1988) notes that the parents of the bride and groom do provide a "dowry" of furniture, livestock, etc. He points out that in 1987 these furnishings might come to between two and four thousand dollars depending on whether they were new or old. Hannah Stoltzfoos said that a friend of hers calculated that it takes about ten thousand dollars for parents to provide a typical *aussteier* and wedding dinner for each daughter. Initially, preparing boys for marriage costs less, but as Hannah cautions that when a farm needs to be bought, costs are much higher and sometimes are prohibitive. Equitable distribution which seems central in all our conversations among the Plain people and in analyzing past written records of the Pennsylvania Germans, may not always be "entirely fair"—or even possible today.

When comparing these contemporary male and female *aussteier* or dowry practices with what the old records reveal, one sees many similarities throughout the entire time span (1749 to the present): outfittings could be broken down into five main groupings—furniture, tools, livestock, grains, and food, as well as miscellany. Some items were always given to males and females alike such as beds and bedding, blanket chests, Bibles, livestock, and foodstuffs. Either sex might get a clock, saltbox, baskets, garden tools, cow chains, buckets, or later, something like an umbrella. However, most objects were (and are) sex-linked—often by task in the house or on the farm. The garden was usually in the female domain as was the kitchen although occasionally one sees a male getting earthenware, porcelain, eating knives and spoons, carpeting, or a broom. Most often dowry articles are sex-linked by repeated entries over hundreds of years (see charts, pp. 46, 54, 55, 64-69), but there is that isolated object like a flax hatchel which was given too rarely to establish a pattern. Equality in giving (i.e. total value) among daughters or sons and between them appeared to be as now of paramount concern.

An advertisement in the *Pennsylvania Packet* delineated the womens' sphere in 1780: "Wanted . . . A single Woman of unsullied Reputation . . . perfectly qualified to direct and manage the female concerns of country business [a farm], as raising small stock, dairying, marketing, combing, carding, spinning, knitting, sewing, pickling, preserving, etc . . ." Both in work around the house—helping one's mother—as well as in the preparation of some of her dowry textiles, the future work world for a young woman was prescribed and reinforced traditional roles. In contrast, the male's dowry was not comprised of goods he prepared but rather of "life" skills he acquired and then gifts of occupational tools from his parents—carpenter's, mason's, or blacksmith's sometimes but most often farmer's seeds, animals, implements, and vehicles as well as land.

The male's "outfitting" language as a whole has changed less over time and it has always involved fewer but sometimes more expensive items. It is thought of less as a concept today, though among the Nebraska Amish, the most conservative group, it remains most intact. A young man's household goods traditionally were limited to one or several beds and their necessary bedding. The male blanket chest evolved into a desk though more slowly than its female counterpart. In the records reviewed for this study, a desk was mentioned in 1818, 1832 and 1835 but it was not until 1880 that it took over as the most important personal piece of a male's furniture (sometimes as a secretary/desk).

The only piece of male machinery that appears to have been in some homes was a loom and they were all early entries (1765 to 1818) and were most likely for weavers. Only two other times were specific tools of a trade mentioned in a male *aussteier* and that was for blacksmithing and masonry. Most of the tools which males received were of general use like an axe or for use on the farm: ploughs, harrows, hay knives, strawbench cutters, work forks, grubbing hoes, wheelbarrows, grain cradles, cow chains and later patented cultivators, corn machines and grain drills. The most expensive items for a male—then and now—were vehicles

Pennsylvania-German black walnut table (*diesch*) c.1750-1800, base: 30″ h. x 32″ w. x 23¹¹⁄₁₆″ d., top: 47⅛″ w. x 33⅝″ d. Courtesy of The Henry Francis du Pont Winterthur Museum. Accession number 65.2749.

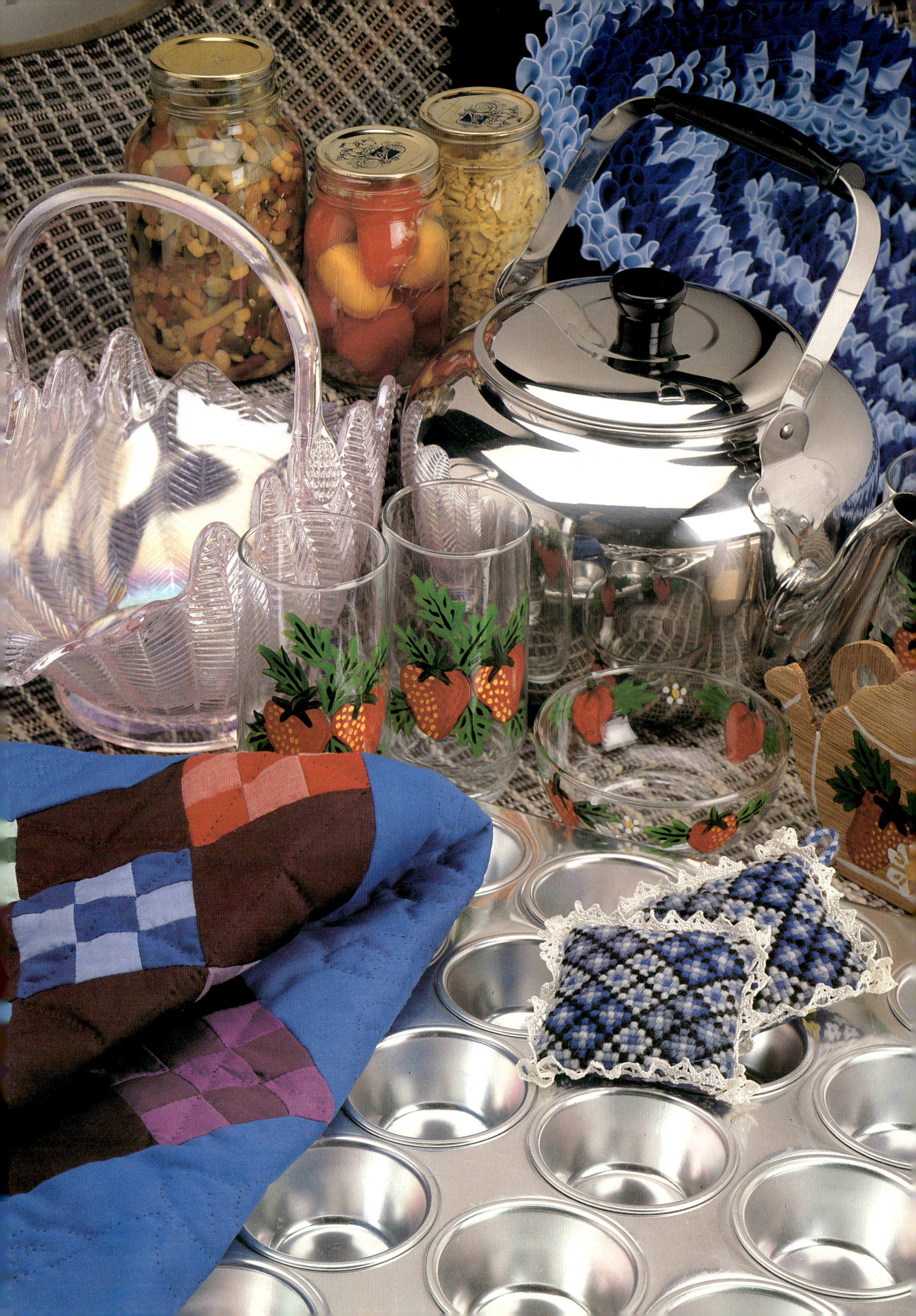

like a wagon, a sleigh, or a buggy, as well as the horse with its saddle, bridle and harness.

Foodstuffs, whether in the form of grains: wheat, oats, rye, or corn; or later potato, pork and beef entries, continue to be part of the *aussteier*—male and sometimes female. Sets of six, twelve and twenty-four grainbags were listed through to the 1860s but then were dropped as an entry as were Bibles which occasionally a female might get also. Horses, cows, pigs, and earlier, sheep, were given to both sexes though today it is the horse which is a standard gift for young Amish males as is the saddle, bridle, harness and blankets; sometimes cows. In some families, like Levina Huyard's and Hannah Stoltzfoos's a cow is still "an option" for the girls while chickens and pigs are no longer given among most Lancaster and Mifflin County Amish but are among the "white tops."

Cash played—and still plays—a more important role in the male "outfitting" than for females—in a different sense where it was used to equalize the gift giving. Cash today, as it sometimes was in the past, is given to help a male purchase a farm, often with expectations of full or partial repayment to the parents or siblings.

Today, it appears that far less, if any, farm equipment is purchased ahead of time for Amish males by parents. This is in part because fewer are able to become landowning farmers but mainly, as Elam Beiler and others note, because that tradition has lapsed. Again, the most conservative Amish group, the Nebraska, still give ploughs and sometimes other tools like discs. In general, the contemporary marriage outfitting or *aussteier* is considered less of a male tradition although it has always existed in a role complementary to that of the female. The female's "outfitting" on the other hand is intact much as it has been. Also it is more detailed in its items although it is generally equal in its total cost to that provided young males.

Contemporary Amish female dowry items include small and large items gathered since adolescence and also things accumulated from the time of their fall wedding to the establishment of their own household the following spring. Small items in their *aussteier* and *haussteier* might include glass and chinaware, rugs, quilts, pin cushions and kitchen utensils as shown here. The painted glassware is by the Abraham Z. Peachey family of Belleville, Mifflin County; the rug is by Mrs. Daniel N. King of Barreville, Mifflin County; the quilt is courtesy of Mary Koons; the pin cushions are courtesy of Hannah Stoltzfoos, Smoketown, Lancaster County; the muffin tin and ten litre stainless teapot were purchased at Peight's Store and the glass basket from Peachey's Store, both in "Big Valley," Belleville, Mifflin County.

Because of the greater variety of articles within the females' *aussteier*, evolution of materials as well as forms and function can be seen in both furnishings and household tools. There is a greater number of abandoned as well as newly-introduced articles as well. In contrast, more items in the male "outfittings" have remained unchanged or little changed just because of what they are: livestock, horse and buggies, Bibles, food grains and stuffs, saddles, bridles, harnesses, and cash settlements. While patented and mass-produced cultivators, threshers, corn machines, and grain drills were introduced and added to the male's "outfitting" in the second half of the nineteenth century, Amish farmers' basic farm tools and machinery today are not that different from those earlier implements such as the plough and harrow—which evolved slowly over a long time period. Few male entries were dropped (looms c.1818, sheep c.1840, axes c.1850, and grainbags c.1860) as compared to female entries (spinning wheels, yarn winders, doughtrays, rye coil bread baskets, cedarware, pewterware and more).

The female's "outfitting," in contrast, reflected major changes as her implements evolved. The evolution in the home was more like a series of revolutions which dealt with change in material and form as well as function—often dictated by changes in technology.

Pewter tableware gave way to locally-produced red earthenware examples which in turn were replaced gradually by manufactured white earthenware dishes, porcelain, and queensware; later, by stoneware and glassware. China and glass are now complemented by plastic containers in Amish gift giving while stainless steel and aluminum have replaced many, though not all, tin or cast iron containers. An article like the kettle survived though in new materials: from iron to copper to tin, then to aluminum or stainless steel. So did the basic kitchen utensil set of skimmer, ladle, flesh fork, taster and spatula evolve from handforged to die-stamped.

Forms of all metal cookware changed radically however as the hearth was abandoned as the cooking center. Stoves introduced new cooking methods and transformed equipment needs and consequently the cook's workday and week, as did refrigeration for food's preservation. Other forms became obsolete like hearth "kitchens" and bird roasters, rotating iron griddles, and hearth toasters (except for camping). Dramatic changes were made in a tool like the toaster while other items like rye coil bread baskets and oven peels for outdoor bake ovens disappeared; in their place were tin bread raisers and steel bread pans designed for the stove's oven.

*E*volution of forms represented not only sometimes rapid technical changes in the nineteenth and twentieth centuries on the home front but also ethnic acculturation and assimilation. As Pennsylvania Germans worked and prospered beside their English neighbors, eating with just a few table utensils evolved to the use of numerous spoons followed by knives and forks. Tea drinking emerged in the early nineteenth century as a custom not only pursued by the English settlers. Germanic bedding of feather ticks, blankets, and coverlets was augmented starting in the

IT'S IN THE ACCOUNTS

Beds and bedsteads were sometimes listed as high or low posted in some family account books. Textile entries indicated high post beds were given because of their occasional listings for bed curtains or bedhangings. This Pennsylvania-German painted poplar high post bed (*hockstolliche bethlad*) from c.1790-1810 measures 85" h. x 74¾" l. x 49½" w. Courtesy of the Philadelphia Museum of Art, Titus C. Geesey Collection. Accession number '58-110-3.

1830s with the "English" quilt. Many Pennsylvania-German families would then maintain and provide dual bedding traditions well into the twentieth century.

As families of both major cultural groups became more comfortable and affluent and were able to give more, furniture forms also proliferated: chairs were not noted just as single or in pairs as in the mid-eighteenth century but in sets of six and later nine and twelve—in rush, Windsor and later cane styles—sometimes with matching rockers. Tables, first noted only as kitchen tables, were joined by dropleaf examples (1830s) and stands of various types (1860s). Sideboards were added later in the nineteenth century (1870s) as were flour chests and dry sinks. When the sewing machine became part of the "advancement," it is not surprising to see it mentioned along with sewing tables (in the 1860s).

Not all evolution took a steady course. Much depended on how tradition-bound a family might be. For example, although a bed quilt and its accessories (perhaps a pieced or appliquéd bolster cover and pillow covers) were mentioned as early as 1831 in the *aussteier* weaver Michael Albrecht gave his daughters, other families embraced the Anglo quilt tradition less enthusiastically and not totally. As late as 1883 feathers for ticks and pillows were still being entered by some more conservative Pennsylvania-German families. On the other hand, the doughtray or trough or table, was an English furniture form quickly embraced by Germanic neighbors and mentioned until the 1870s. Home spinning and weaving (as reflected in the account entries in their yarn winders and spinning wheels) seems to have encountered a sudden death by the late 1830s.

These are the *aussteier* or dowry traditions as reflected in the following Pennsylvania-German family account books or in the ledgers of craftsmen making goods for these clients. The study of the retention and evolution of certain forms as well as the abandonment and introduction of others in Pennsylvania-German family *aussteier* is made more complete in that it can be brought up-to-date by looking at contemporary Amish and Old Order Mennonite patterns of giving. But as a reminder, Sadie Beiler's admonition is important in that "these are patterns, not rules."

Unfortunately, less can be said about the English dowry traditions here in Pennsylvania because far fewer records were found and they form a picture of gift giving over a far shorter time span (1782 to 1828). Contemporary tradition is almost non-existent. Even the Lane Furniture Company's chest which sold to a broad audience here in Pennsylvania starting in 1912, is no longer even called a "hope chest" but rather a "cedar chest." References to any accumulation of textiles, table- or kitchenware and their placement in such a chest appears to be a tradition of the past.

In looking at the four account books that were charted and analyzed as well as a few others which were summarized, several points emerge. Dowry goods in the English communities are almost entirely restricted to females. Only two fathers mention outfitting males and their range of items is very limited: a horse with saddle and bridle, a cow, beds and bedding, cash, a bucket and table linens. The females did get items not unlike the Pennsylvania-German young women of the same late eighteenth/early nineteenth-century period: horse with saddle and bridle, cows, sheep, pigs, beds and bedding, a chest of drawers, chairs in sets of two, twelve or as many as eighteen, dough troughs, tables, table linens, tea kettles, and china or pottery.

Some of the forms appear to have been introduced in this cultural group earlier than in Pennsylvania-German homes: knives and forks as well as glass plates and bowls (1782 to 1787); looking glasses, rocking chairs, carpeting, (all 1809 to 1828); andirons, shovels and tongs (1810 to 1828) for example.

Equality seems to be of less concern in this group however. Fathers do not "even up" their giving totals with cash settlements as seen in many of the Pennsylvania-German family records. Sometimes, in fact, the differences between siblings of even the same sex are substantial as in the case of Elizabeth Yeates Conyham who got £2720 worth as compared with her sister, Mary Yeates Smith with £1138. The few males mentioned generally received more than their sisters.

Little can be said until the sampling is larger, however, as four families' gift giving patterns are not sufficient to draw conclusions.

Small tables or stands were introduced into the dowry in the mid-nineteenth century and remain popular today in Amish families as part of a bedroom suite in the *aussteier*. This grain-decorated stand, 31" h. x 21⅝" w. x 21⅞" d., is inscribed on the underside of its top "Made by Levis John/1853/For daughter Sarah/Cocalico Twp [Lancaster County]". It may well have been part of her dowry. When a father was able, there is a tradition of his making furniture rather than going to a carpenter or cabinetmaker. Collection of Dr. and Mrs. Donald M. Herr.

IT'S IN THE ACCOUNTS

The following fifteen family account books or cabinetmaker records yielded data on dowry items in Anglo-Saxon or "English" communities in Pennsylvania. They are arranged in chronological order from the earliest dowry reference in 1777 to the last in 1877. All but one of the family account books were those of farmers (when the occupation was known). The geographic area for these families was Adams, Chester, Delaware, and Lancaster counties. These manuscripts can be found at the Chester County Historical Society in West Chester, the Friends Historical Library at Swarthmore College, the Lancaster County Historical Society, and Spruance Library at the Mercer Museum in Doylestown.

When they proved useful, the account books were summarized. Primarily they are dowry references hidden in family accounts. As with the Pennsylvania Germans, English descendants might have kept strictly family or dowry account books but the only one we found was Samuel Pennock's. His slim book lists in detail the goods given to his five girls. Most of the dowry entries we found for the Anglo community were found instead in cabinetmaker records. This source makes it more difficult to make comparisons by sex. Consequently, the following chart is restricted to those few entries in family accounts. Since fewer families gave very detailed listings as the Pennsylvania Germans did, this chart is brief by comparison. Generic dowry references and more cash line items made this body of information far less interesting.

With fewer and far less detailed family account books available to us than from the Pennsylvania-German community of the eighteenth and nineteenth centuries, it was necessary to look elsewhere. A large body of primary source material—in the form of diaries and letters—is held by some historical societies. We went through over seventy diaries, primarily of Quakers, at the Chester County Historical Society in West Chester, Pennsylvania. Those listed in the bibliography yielded *some* pertinent information for us either in their recording of dowry preparation and attitudes toward marriage or, in the absence of the same, as contrasted to very detailed accounts of other household and family chores.

LEVIS PENNOCK'S ACCOUNT BOOK

On the 7th day of May 1777, Levis Pennock of West Marlborough Township, Chester County, wrote "an inventory of what goods I gave to Dater Mary att and after marage." A year earlier, on April 24, 1776, Mary Pennock had married George Passmore. Her father's gift of goods totaled £78, 8 shillings and 3 pence for a mare, saddle and bridle (£26), two beds and furniture (£20), two tables and a case of drawers (£11), cattle (£10), two pots and pewter (£5, 13 shillings, 3 pence), and smithwork, thirteen chairs, woodenware and sundries (£5, 15 pence).

Mary Pennock Passmore was deceased in 1822 when her mother Ruth wrote a will that divided her moveable goods into several dowry-like outfittings for grandchildren including Mary's: "I give and bequeath to the sons of my daughter Mary (deceased) late the wife of George Passmore the sum of twelve hundred dollars to be equally divided among them, and to the daughters of the said Mary the sum of eight Hundred dollars to be divided amongst them. Also, I will to my said daughter, Mary's daughter, Margaret my best feather Bed and bedsteads, the looking glass that was her Aunt Elizabeth's, six chairs, one pair of fireiron tongs and shovel used in the back-room downstairs, And to the said Mary's daughter, Rachel, one feather bed and bedsteads, one case of drawers and six chairs."

CALEB AND ROBERT JOHNSON'S ACCOUNT BOOK

The receipt book of the Johnson family was begun by Robert Johnson in 1766 and then taken over by his son Caleb after Robert's death in September 1769. In it are recorded the deaths of Caleb's mother, Catherine, in 1777 and his siblings: Hadley in 1780 and Simon in 1786. Also listed starting in 1782 are Caleb's dowry portions to his three girls: Margret Sharp, Deberah Burrey, and Mary Peirce.

The listings give his daughters' married names and "what goods _____ had when married in _____ ." In the case of Margret and Deberah, he later pens in the word "Lent" as contrasted to his daughter Mary where he wrote out "Lent" at the time of making the dowry listing. It appears Caleb Johnson maintained parental control over the goods in doing this; not giving them to the daughter nor to her husband who would normally have controlled the goods brought to the marriage.

The first two girls' marriage portions were roughly equal but the third, Mary Peirce, received much more: some major pieces of furniture like an armchair, a candlestand, a case of high drawers as well as walnut and mahogany cupboards being given at a "later date" than the marriage. She was also given finer housewares: a set of china, glasses, knives and forks, tablecloths and towels.

JACOB MINSHALL'S ACCOUNT BOOKS

After the death of his father, Thomas Minshall, in 1783, Jacob handled his mother's affairs for another thirty years or until her death in 1813 at nearly ninety-nine years of age. She lived in the eastern half of the family home and his accounting of her widow's share included the following: five beds and bedding, two cases of drawers, two looking glasses, sixteen chairs, two chests, two trunks, a spicebox and table, a desk, carpet, table linens, earthenware, glassware, queensware, pewter, brassware and kettles, tinware, ironware, cedarware, dough trough, flatirons and flesh fork, buckets and frying pan, cask of molasses, butter tub, knives and forks, lamp and lantern, mortars, churn, malt and powdering tub, three casks and dried apples, salt and casks, bedcord, as well as a horse and cow.

As Jacob noted: "The before Mentioned articles are goods taken by My Mother Agness Minshall to the amount of one Hundred and sixteen Pounds sixteen Shillings, one Hundred whereof being her Due agreeable to my father's will. The Remainder I Do Releas unto her free Disposal except the after Mentioned articles which is to be mine after her Decease [a desk, a chest, a lignamvita morter, a large iron pot and bake iron and hanger]."

Jacob Minshall was a fourth generation English Quaker who lived not on the original family tract of 625 acres, which had been divided over time, but on land that his father had acquired, built on, and enlarged in Middletown, Chester County.

WILLIAM AND JAMES GIBBONS'S ACCOUNT BOOK

William Gibbons, a farmer living in East Bradford Township, Chester County, had six children. The two youngest girls, Lydia and Mary, were listed in his account book by their married names (their husbands' names are inserted later): "son in law Richard Jacob & his wife" and "son in law William Gray." Although another daughter, Phebe Gibbons Smith was not listed she was mentioned in her father's will as having been advanced her amount as were Mary Gibbons Gray and Lydia Gibbons Jacob. His will refers to his book of "Private Accounts" and undoubtedly that is what is now held by the Chester County Historical Society (MS #76850). The private account book has fairly detailed accounts for Lydia and Mary.

Lydia's account was first started in 1789 and contains entries as late as 1805. The bulk of the household entries span from March 31 to April 15, 1789 and included: cash furnished to go to Philadelphia to buy necessaries for housekeeping, 33½ lbs. of feathers, nine yards of homemade bedticking, nine rushbottom chairs from Charles Hall, an armchair painted blue, a pair of green bedsteads made by William Sharpless and a sacking bottom, a teatable and a case of drawers from Benanuel Ogden, eight pewter plates not quite new, two part worn pewter dishes, a small part worn tea kettle, a coverlet part worn, ten pounds of flax bought at vendue, twelve yards of huckaback table linen, two pair of tow sheets part worn, a pair of new flaxen sheets, and a young bay horse of his own raising named "Durgan."

On the other hand, Mary's entries are substantively different because of her moving with her husband to Virginia. After the initial gifts of bed and bedding "when first married," the father is recorded as having "sent the following articles by _____ , who lives near my daughter in Virginia": mainly cash but also homemade linen for apparel, handkerchiefs, a rose blanket, worsted hose, and crepe material.

JASPER YEATES'S ACCOUNT BOOK

Jasper Yeates (b. 1745, d. 1817) was no ordinary man in eighteenth-century Lancaster County nor was his account book typical of others of either the English or Pennsylvania-German communities. He was not a farmer or craftsman, as were the other keepers-of-accounts, but rather an attorney and jurist though also a landholder.

His records (1771 to 1816) included "accounts of advancement to . . . " his two married daughters and his one son. His other daughters remained single and no advancements were listed for them. Jasper Yeates's records did not reflect the diversity of furnishings typically given females; making things equal among the siblings seems not to have been a concern either. The girls, who received substantially less than their brother, John, were not favored equally either.

Mary (b. 1770) was the first to marry in 1791 and her account began with wedding clothes valued at £72, 3 shillings and 7 pence. The remainder of her advancement was either in cash—$2,000 or £750—or goods which seem intended more for her attorney-husband Charles Smith: a ten-

Walnut gateleg table with drawer c. 1720-1740. Secondary woods are poplar and pine. It belonged to Humphrey Marshall of Marshallton, Chester County and measures 30" h. x 58¼" w. x 47½" d. Courtesy: Chester County Historical Society. Accession number 1982.15.61.

	JOHNSON 1782-1787	GIBBONS 1789-1796	CASSET 1809-C.1829	PENNOCK 1810-1828
Riding horse, horse(s)	F, F, F	F	F, F, M	F, F
Cow(s)	F, F, F	F, F, M	F, F	F, F, F, F
Chest of drawers, bureau	F, F	F	F, F	
Bed(s) and bedding	F, F, F	F, F	F, F, M	F, F, F, F, F
Sheep	F		F	F, F, F
Cash	F	F, F, M		F, F
Large pot	F		F, F	
Chairs (2, 12, 18)	F, F, F	F	F	F, F, F, F
Dough trough	F, F	F	F, F	
Reel	F, F			
Warming pan	F, F			
Pewter dishes	F	F		
Pig(s), sow(s), swine	F, F			F
Wheel (spinning)	F, F, F			
Table	F	F	F, F	
Tea kettle	F	F	F	F
Set of china, pottery	F		F	F, F, F, F
Glass plates and bowls	F			F
Towels	F			
Knives and forks	F		F	
Bucket	F		F, F, M	
Arm chair	F			
Candlestand	F			
High drawers	F			
Cupboard	F			
Saddle and bridle	F		F, M	F, F, F, F
Table clothes or linens	F		M	F, F, F, F, F
Feathers		F	F	F
Coverlet		F		
Flax		F		
Wheat		F		
Meat		F		
Lime		F		F
Hankerchiefs		F		
Blanket(s)		F	F	
Loom		M		
Salt		M		
Coffee boiler			F	
Teaspoons (silver)			F, F	F, F, F, F
Cedarware			F, F	
Quilting a quilt			F	
Carpet			F, F	F, F
Copper kettle			F	
Bread basket(s)			F	
Flat iron			F	
Rolling pin			F	
Grid iron			F, F	
Rocking chair			F	F
Bible			F, F	
Dye stuff			F	
Looking glass			F	F, F, F, F
Ironware				F, F, F, F
Queensware				F, F, F
Joiner's furniture bill				F, F, F, F, F
Kitchen furniture				F
Skillet				F
Lumber for house				F
Harness				F, F, F
Riding chair				F, F
Andirons				F
Shovel and tongs				F
Brassware				F, F
Tablespoons (silver)				F, F, F, F, F
Pewterware				F
Gig				F
Tea tongs (silver)				F, F, F, F

plate office stove with pipes, office window curtains and Venetian blinds, Hale's *History of the Common Law* and numerous other books for a total of £1,138.10. A camp bed, a field bedstead, curtain and counterpane, and four yards of calico for the camp bed were among the few "traditional" female items. Mary Yeates Smith's account was also unusual in that it shows a Gerhart Martin plastering her kitchen as well as expensive paper hangings for her two parlors.

Yeates's second daughter, Elizabeth (b. 1778) also married an attorney, Redmond Conyham, but she, or rather they, seem more favored than the Smiths with a larger cash gift of $5,000 or £1,875. Elizabeth, like Mary, received very little directly from her father in the way of furniture although she may have used her cash advance to purchase some herself. She did receive the wood for making a case of bureau drawers and someone was paid for constructing it. £1 and 2 shillings was paid for the fringe and binding of a quilt, in addition to handkerchiefs, cotton stockings, gloves, two frocks, a dress and gingham, dimity and muslin being purchased for a grand total of over £2,720.

In contrast, Jasper Yeates gave his son, John (b. 1772), over £10,808 according to the family records. Much was in cash for the young man who occupied the father's property called "Belmont Farm," but there were also numerous entries for newspaper subscriptions and law books. Also entries included cleaning a watch, making a coat, purchasing chocolate, cloves, wine, cherry brandy, coffee, tea, whisky, molasses, flour, raisins, meat, sugar, as well as linen, muslin, cambrick and indigo. Farm equipment like wagons, a plough, wheelbarrow, a pair of traces, horses and cows appeared along with some traditional dowry furniture forms like bedsteads, a flour chest and "yellow" chairs. The two large walnut dining tables for £3; a small tea table and a small walnut table with folding leaf for £1, 10 shillings; twelve walnut chairs with leather bottoms for £9 and a chess and backgammon table for £1, 17 shillings, 6 pence. Such items showed that John's household furnishings were not of the average sort however. Most of the time his father indicated the craftsmen or tradesmen who sold the goods: Francis Mekil made three beehives at three shillings nine pence each, Christopher Mayor mended his tinware and made tin funnels, cups and watering pot while Peter Getz did silverwork. Great detail was also recorded with the purchase of typically generic goods such as ironware. Jasper indicated for instance that in one transaction John received a twenty- and an eleven-gallon iron kettle; a six-, five-, four-, three-, two- and one-gallon iron pot; a large-, middle-, and small-sized iron skillet, an iron bake oven and a camp kettle.

For all the detail yielded in the son's accounts (which cover eighteen pages) Jasper Yeates's outfittings for his daughters are therefore particularly frustrating for their brevity and lack of detail. It appears that a much smaller cash transaction was their chief dowry gift. However, John's accounts may have been as lengthy as they are because he ran Belmont Farm for his father rather than because of his sex. Indication of the nature of their relationship is revealed in a note written toward the end of John's account on April 27, 1808 "[Memo—The Piano forte at Belmont is not given to my Son; I purchased the time of *Negro Peter* for £25 until he should become 28 years old, viz on the 13 March 1817. He has lived at Belmont since my son kept House but I have not given up my Title]." At that time Jasper added £4,019.60 to John's account for "the sum of buildings and improvements at Belmont Farm" bringing John's total to over £10,587.

ENOS THOMAS'S ACCOUNT BOOK

Living and working in East Goshen Township, Chester County (1747 to 1805), Enos Thomas was a farmer, sawyer, and cabinetmaker. Although his records from 1791 to 1804 show him doing more sawmill work and coffinmaking than furniture making, he made three dowry furniture ensembles that are very detailed and of particular interest.

In March and April 1792 he crafted for James Massey a bureau, a clawfoot dining table, a card table, a dough trough, a common walnut table and a pair of bedsteads painted blue. Later, in November, he sold him another pair of bedsteads (for ropes) and painted brown for a total sum of £12, 8 shillings, and 6 pence.

From March to May, 1793, Sarah Nox purchased two bureaus, a writing box, a double case of drawers seven feet high with column corners for £10, a dining table four by five feet for £2, 12 shillings, and 6 pence, and a cherry dining table with maple legs for £1, 17 shillings, and 6 pence. She also purchased a large poplar chest painted mahogany for £1, 2 shillings, and 6 pence, a pair of bedsteads with short posts,

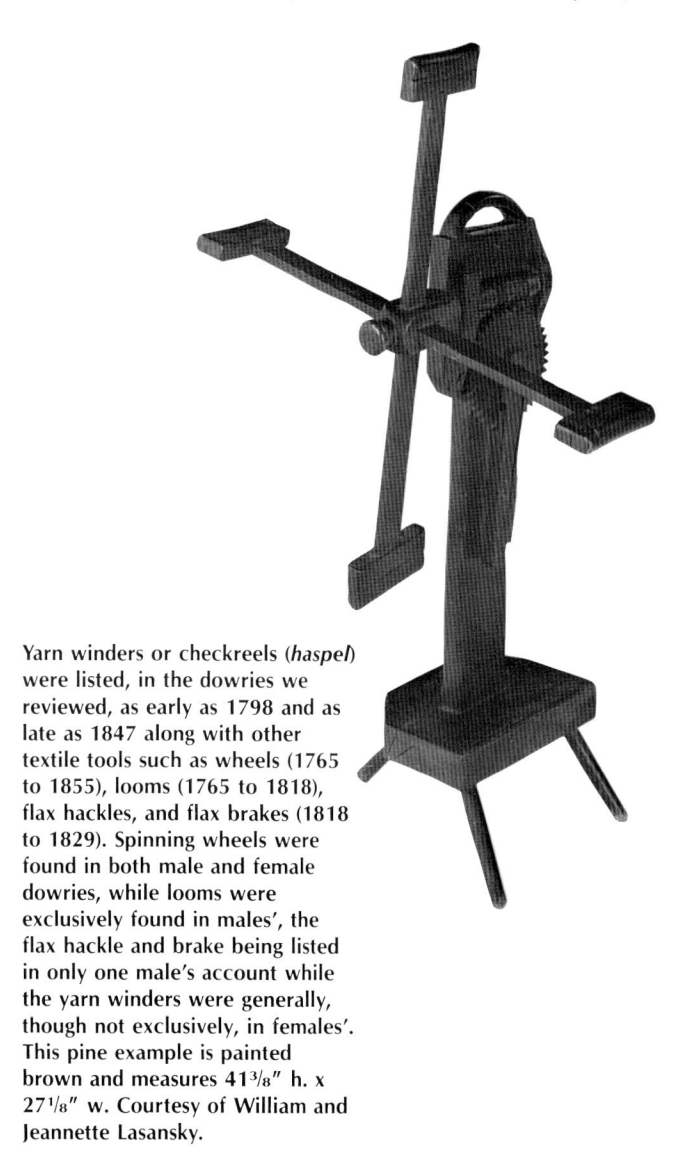

Yarn winders or checkreels (*haspel*) were listed, in the dowries we reviewed, as early as 1798 and as late as 1847 along with other textile tools such as wheels (1765 to 1855), looms (1765 to 1818), flax hackles, and flax brakes (1818 to 1829). Spinning wheels were found in both male and female dowries, while looms were exclusively found in males', the flax hackle and brake being listed in only one male's account while the yarn winders were generally, though not exclusively, in females'. This pine example is painted brown and measures 41³⁄₈" h. x 27¹⁄₈" w. Courtesy of William and Jeannette Lasansky.

a walnut candlestand made in tea table form for £1, 2 shillings, and 6 pence in addition to a common poplar table with a drawer painted brown for 15 shillings.

Lastly, Nathan Cooper was charged on November 3, 1800 for a walnut case of drawers (£7), two "cheretree beaurows" at £4 each, a walnut dining table for £2, 12 shillings, and 6 pence, a breakfast table for £2, 5 shillings, a doughtray for 18 shillings, 9 pence, and two pair of bedsteads: one high post pair painted mahogany and one low post pair.

Enos Thomas obviously was capable of making fine and varied furniture pieces. His accounts are exemplary (from an historian's point of view) in their detail, not only on woods used or surfaces painted, but in his notations on size (table 4 by 5 feet, 7 feet high case of drawers) and other details: clawfeet, columned corners, "tea-table-like."

AMOS DARLINGTON SR. AND JR'S ACCOUNT BOOKS

Both Amos and his son were cabinetmakers who made furniture for Chester Countians over a long period of time that spanned the eighteenth and nineteenth centuries, 1764 to 1852. Both had occasional listings that appeared to be the furniture groupings now associated with setting up a new household and indeed they may be group furniture purchases by fathers for their daughters' marriage portions.

For instance, the elder cabinetmaker entered five such groupings over nine years (1796 to 1805) that had very similar items in each. There was always a high post bed (£3), a dining table (£2 to £3), usually a bureau or chest of drawers (£7 to £9), and a doughtray (15 shillings to £1, 26 shillings). Sometimes a card table, a candlestand or a chest were added to the basic set of household furniture. Details were noted, to some extent, in the listings that differentiate between dining-, breakfast-, poplar-, or card tables. Beds were listed as high post or field, low post and with or without curtain frames. The price range, however, was the main indicator of a difference in time spent in making the piece. All the furniture was purchased by males.

In contrast, women purchased three of the fifteen dowry-related furniture groupings found in Amos Darlington Jr.'s two account books starting in 1792 and finishing in 1852. The range of furniture within each grouping was quite similar to those pieces made by the elder cabinetmaker with a few new additions: "Pembroak" tables ($8 to $12), washstands ($2 to $4), corner "bason" stands ($6 to $10), end tables $30, and knife boxes (50 to 75¢). The wood type was often cited—cherry or maple bedsteads; cherry, mahogany, or maple bureaus; small tables in poplar or pine; several cherry dining tables, a walnut breakfast table, and small poplar or maple stands. The dowry grouping cost as little as $40 for a bureau ($11), dining table ($9), cardtable ($7) and bedstead ($10) purchased by Isechar Hooper in May 1819 or as much as $137.25 in March 1828 when Amos Worthington bought a pair of bureaus ($60), a pair of end tables ($28), a breakfast table ($10), a high bed ($14), a field bed ($8), a corner basin stand ($6), a square stand (no charge), a candlestand ($4.50), a doughtray ($3.50), a knife box (50¢), a footstool (50¢), a sampler frame (62½¢), and glass (87½¢). The average furniture outfitting for his other thirteen customers was $90.72; three customers had $113.50 bills.

Over the entire time of these account books (1764 to 1852) no piece of furniture was eliminated as a necessary component of the dowry: dough troughs, beds, chest of drawers, or tables. Others were added over time but they appeared to reflect as much the circumstance and needs of a particular customer (as with cardtables or sideboards) as change in period furnishings (as with washstands or corner basin stands).

SAMUEL PENNOCK'S ACCOUNT BOOK

Samuel Pennock was one of three Pennocks (all Quakers living in Chester County) for whom we have found a dowry reference. He is, however, the only one to keep what he called a family account book. In the slim book are his written entries for his five daughters: Susanna, Sarah, Ann, Elizabeth, and Philena. Starting in 1810 and going through to 1828 he records what he gives to each, "the following property which I consider to be as a part of her share of my Estate." The entries for the girls were made either in one month's time as was the case for Elizabeth, or over quite a period of time, which extended to twenty-eight years for Ann. He did not total their entries nor did he give equally for all the girls received very different totals: anywhere from $541.15 to $1,111.27 in goods and cash.

Samuel Pennock sometimes recorded the store where he made his purchases or the craftsman he employed. For example, Jarred Chestnut made twelve of his best Windsor chairs for Sarah Pennock in 1815 for $23.00, another dozen (though not the "best") for Ann Pennock in 1818 for $17.25, eighteen bentback Windsors for Elizabeth Pennock in 1825 for $22.00, and an undetermined number and type for Philena in 1828 for $20.50. J. Hadley, a joiner, presented Samuel with bills of $38.50 and $83.00 for furniture, James A. Sparks sold him feathers for $27.00 and $6.33, and Joseph Grubb sold him ironware, brassware, and looking glasses. Rag carpeting cost $10.60 for twenty-four yards and a dozen rush bottom chairs and a rocking chair cost $14.50 when outfitting Elizabeth in 1825.

MATHIAS FOY'S ACCOUNT BOOK

Mathias Foy was a cabinetmaker in East Bradford Township, Chester County, and in the last of his account books he registered the amount owed him by Isaac Pennock for a group of household furnishings. These appear to be some of the goods

Tinware replaced some of the ironware and pewter items in the late eighteenth and the nineteenth century dowries. It was first mentioned as part of the *aussteier* in Abraham Wismer's book in 1798. Items such as these candlemolds, candle box, sifters, graters, cake or cookie cutters, cup, dipper, grease lamps and hearth bird roaster were but a few of the tinware items which might have been part of a female's kitchenware hoard. Courtesy of William and Jeannette Lasansky; small grater (top) and grater/sifter/cutter combination (center), courtesy of Robert and Shirley Kuster.

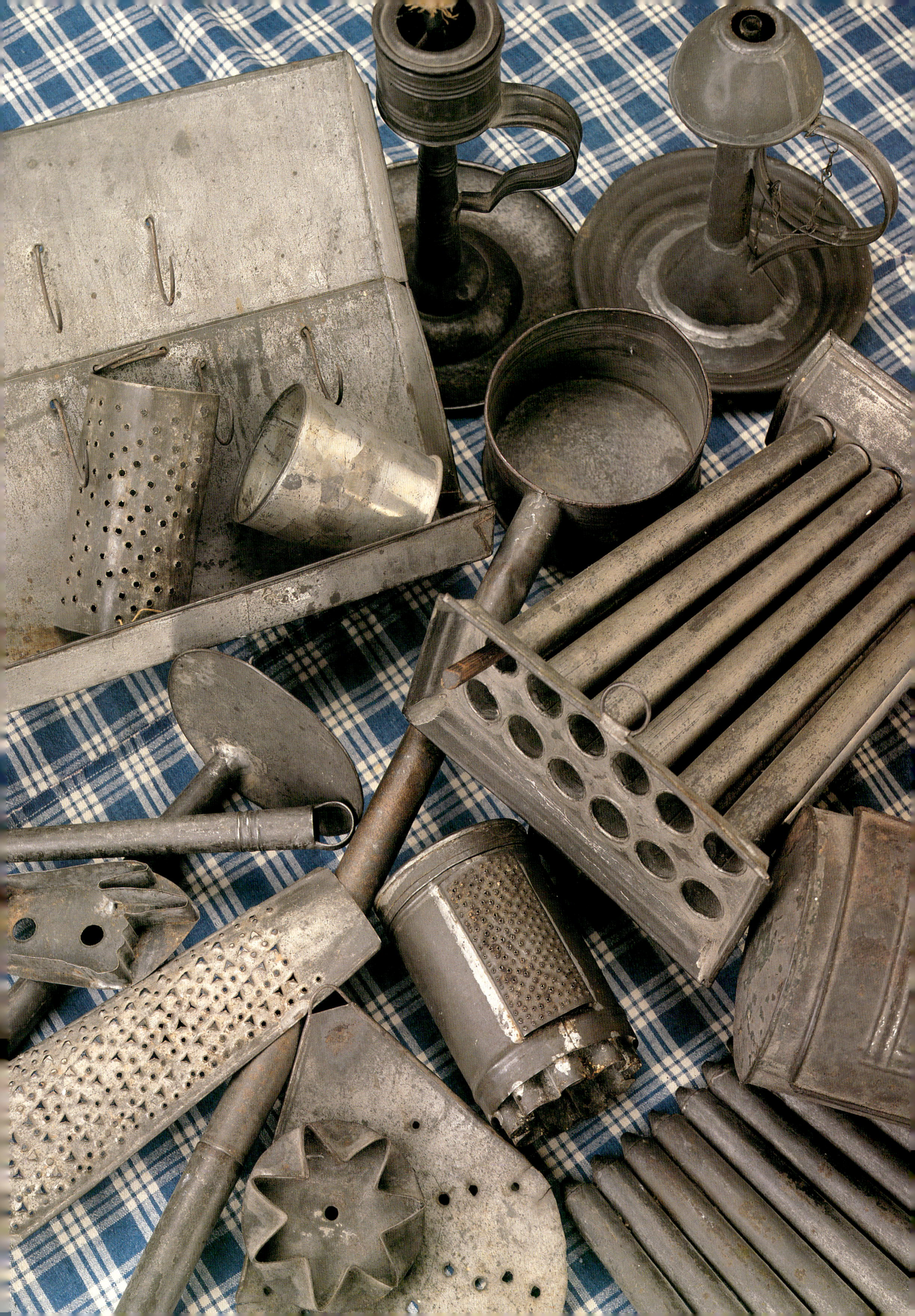

Isaac would have given to his daughter Rebecca Pennock Lykens at the time she was about to marry in 1818: various bureaus, tables, bedsteads, chairs, a doughtray, and a washstand for $260.00. One realizes how partial a dowry outfitting was when compared to what was in her father's home at the time his inventory was taken in West Marlboro Township just six years later.

In Isaac's first parlor were twenty-two fancy chairs, two tea tables, a sofa, two mirrors, andirons/shovel/tongs/bellows and hearth brush, and twenty-five yards of India matting for the floor. In the second parlor were a tea-, breakfast-, and two dining tables, ten fancy chairs, a sideboard, a looking glass, andirons, fireplace shovel and tongs as well as a large array of china, glass, japanned waiters, a bread basket, table brush and yards of floorcovering. In the Pennocks' hallway were a clock, a corner cupboard with lots of plates, two armchairs and seven Windsor chairs as well as twenty-nine yards of domestic carpet on the floor. There were eight bedrooms, usually each had two beds with their appropriate bedding, bureaus, window hangings, looking glasses and sometimes a bookcase, candlestand, rocking chair, breakfast table, spice box, washstand, pitcher and basin and chairs. A chest, trunk, cradle, clothes basket and sixteen pair of sheets, twenty-eight blankets and four comfortables were in the eighth bedchamber which served as a storage unit as did the garret with its extra carpeting, rugs, yardgoods, wool, spun yarn and cotton spinning wheel, an old chest of drawers, desk, trunk, stool, sausage knife and watering can. The kitchen and the cellar contents included a dough trough, table, chairs, pewter dishes, smoothing irons, knives, forks, kettles, pots, pans, boilers, skillets, jars and jugs, Dutch oven, gridirons, brass and iron candlesticks, tin kitchen coffeepots, canisters, candlebox, sausage stuffers, funnels, milk strainer, pepper box, iron bread toaster, ladles, tea kettle, shovel and tongs, potrack, andirons as well as pepper and coffee mills. His moveable goods or estate totaled $110,622.75.

Compare this with the goods, even when varied, that either he or his cousin Samuel, outfitted their daughters with and one sees that indeed the daughters' goods were just the *beginning* of life's accumulation of moveable goods or estate for the more affluent Pennsylvanians in the early nineteenth century.

The complete listing, including individually assessed values, for Isaac Pennock can be read on pp. 346-349 in Margaret B. Schiffer's book *Chester County Inventories 1684-1850* (Exton, PA.: Schiffer Publishing Ltd., 1974).

JACOB CASSET'S ACCOUNT BOOK

Four daughters and one son had their marriage outfittings mentioned in their father's account book, alongside entries for his work credits as a farmer, tanner and surveyor. Jacob Casset lived near Gettysburg in Adams County and his records reflect diverse activities over a seventy-eight year period. Unfortunately, some of the handwriting was impossible to decipher, so when he cites "November 1, 1829 articles purchased for my daughter Sarah at the time of her marriage," not all the entries are clear. Those that were legible we listed in the accompanying chart. Most of Hannah's were not however. In his dowry entries there is often specificity as to who made an item or from what store something was purchased.

THOMAS MONTAGUE'S ACCOUNT BOOK

Thomas Montague, a farmer living in Hartsville, Bucks County, briefly recorded the amounts given to each of his eight children. The amounts were equal only by sex—the five daughters each received $266.67 for an outfit while the three sons each received $400.00. For example, in 1822 he wrote "Eliza Watts Montague-DR. To Sundries outfit as before charged to my other daughters $266.67." In 1823 he mentioned "Henry W. Montague To Be charged against him in the settlement of my estate as part of his legacy he having received the same. To amt of his time in going to learn his Trade this was agreed to by him $266.67. To sundries of clothing when at Trade 11.33, To amt of spending money 5.00, To cash paid 30.00 To cash when he left home 17.00 To amt paid for him to . . . 47.04 To amt paid for him to . . . 22.96," or $400.00 total.

JONATHAN C. LARKIN'S ACCOUNT BOOK

Jonathan Larkin was a furniture and coffinmaker (as well as a gravedigger) in Chester County and his account book (1827 to 1841) has one furniture grouping that appears to be part of a typical female dowry outfitting: Robert Tearwood purchased a bureau for $12, bedsteads for $4 and $2.50 as well as a "dotray" for 62½¢ for the grand total for $19.12½ in 1833.

WILLIAM CANBY BIDDLE'S ACCOUNT BOOK

Quaker William Biddle's account book is like most of the others kept by non-Pennsylvania Germans. It shows that a dowry outfitting, outsetting, or furnishing for children was considered important but it lacks many specifics. The importance of equality in giving was usually a factor, if not for all, at least within a sex for the English families. In this case this is well illustrated in the entry of his second child and the oldest female.

Frances Canby was born August 10, 1842 and married Clement Acton Griscom. Her father enters on her page in his ledger: "In acct with Frances C. Griscom Cr" "1863 1st mo. 1st day By part of the amount paid for her outfit and furniture on her marriage; which is to be counted as part of her share of my estate without addition for interest 1,500,00." Three years later he enters "By cash paid to her to purchase additional furniture, which makes this a/c equal to HBT's [her sister Helen Biddle was given 2,000 as an outfit in 1866]." In January 1877 he made another notation on Frances's page, "To Cash paid her to equal Mary B. Woods [her other sister, Mary Biddle Woods, was outfitted as the first two had previously been but in 1869 it cost $2250!]."

William Biddle's account book, though spare in details of furnishings, does clearly illustrate a father's attempt to keep outfittings' costs up to date and equitable by bringing his first daughter to marry current to the amounts spent on the second and third outfittings. He also makes the account of the second to marry, Helen Biddle Thomas, equal to the third and last girl by adding $250 to Helen's total at one point. Their brother, Clement Miller Biddle, the firstborn, was noted as having received $1693.83 in cash only on December 31, 1865. More on him was not found in this book.

IT'S IN THE ACCOUNTS

Tall case clocks were sometimes given as *aussteier* though not with the frequency of other furniture forms. For instance, in the first generation of the Clemens family of Montgomery County only one girl of nine received one. They were expensive items costing from $31 to $36 in those accounts surveyed. Later clock entries for about $6 were most likely for shelf clocks. This Lebanon County Pennsylvania-German black walnut tall clock was made by Jacob Graf prior to 1760. It has a pewter face and measures 98" h. x 24 1/2" w. x 12 9/16" d. Courtesy of The Henry Francis du Pont Winterthur Museum. Accession number 65.2261.

The following account book records provided information on items traditionally set aside as marriage portions or *aussteier* in Pennsylvania-German communities. The books are arranged in chronological order by their earliest dowry reference rather than by the books' first entry. The earliest known reference was made in 1749 and the latest was one entered in 1902 from an account book started in 1858. While most of the family account books were those of farmers, when occupations were known, others were of weavers as well as one of a potter, of a schoolteacher, of a blacksmith and of a justice of the peace. These families happened to have lived in Berks, Bucks, Lancaster, Lebanon, Lehigh, Montgomery, and York counties and their manuscript records were found at the Lancaster County Historical Society, Lancaster Mennonite Historical Library, the Lebanon County Historical Society, the Lehigh County Historical Society, and the Mennonite Historical Society in Lansdale; also, the Muddy Creek Farm Library in Denver, the Spruance Library at the Mercer Museum in Doylestown, the Schwenkfelder Library in Pennsburg, the Joseph Downs Manuscript Collection at Winterthur, and the Historical Society of York County as well as in several private collections.

For comparing those *aussteier* or dowry references to twentieth-century practices as recorded by the Amish, we then included the account book of Moses A. Kaufman from Holmes County, Ohio. His book ends in 1945 and is in a private collection.

The books are all summarized and they include not only family account books but also furniture maker or store account records which, at times, yielded dowry information also. Sometimes family account books were kept exclusively for the purpose of recording birthdates and marriage outfittings as was Michael Albrecht's. More often though, *aussteier* references were hidden among other and very varied entries within general accounts. We looked through several hundred such books before finding the relatively few that had dowry references.

Following the book summaries are two charts which include some of these books. Only those manuscripts which yielded information that could best be analyzed in chart form were broken down this way. Books that yielded a small or very narrow body of information, even if important for corroboration, were not included in the chart but rather, just in the summaries.

The first chart illustrates the dowries given to the Clemens children in each of three successive generations starting in 1749 and ending in 1857. The Clemens book illustrates the longest run of dowry entries for one family. The goods given are broken down by generation and are listed in the order in which they are mentioned. The sex of each recipient is noted. Changes in the type of goods given over one hundred years, as well as terminology, can be traced in the listing which runs from top to bottom, earliest to latest citing.

The second chart illustrates the marriage portions given in fourteen other families. The account books are listed chronologically from the earliest dowry reference in 1765 to the most recent *circa* 1945. The dates below the account book's title are for the first and last dowry references in a particular account book—not necessarily the opening date of the account book as cited in the bibliography. The variety of goods is listed down the side of the chart and from top to bottom, from the earliest citing of a particular item.

Trends in outfitting children can be seen, as in the Clemens chart. But, in the second chart there are more problems in *how* goods are listed. In the beginning, terminology tended to be more generic like "house furniture" or "earthenware" rather than later when there was more specificity. This tendency to be more specific seemed to be a trend but the personality of the party making the entries was always a factor. When deemed appropriate, the author took the liberty to group some items together in one category such as "hog" and "sow" with "pig." The listing of meat, for instance, included any animal that was not livestock. These steps were done for efficiency and the author hopes that there were few distortions in doing this.

THE CLEMENS ACCOUNT BOOK

The Clemens family, prosperous Mennonite farmers living in Lower Salford Township, Montgomery County, kept a family account book from 1749 to 1857. It is the only book found to date that covers three generations. Its information on *aussteier* or dowry portions for all their living children is very complete, with as much or more detail than any other family record seen. Jacob Clemens started the book in 1749 with accounts of money lending. His accounts were followed by those of one of his sons, Gerhart, in 1820 and one of his grandsons, Heinrich, in 1857. Both Jacob and Gerhart Clemens mention the "family" book in their wills as a point of reference in making the children's share of the estate equal.

Jacob Clemens came to America with his parents, Gerhart and Anneli Reiff Clemens, in 1709. Eventually he purchased the family farm from his father and also ran a distillery there. He married Barbara Clemmer and they had nineteen children, twelve of whom survived to adulthood and ten of whom were mentioned in the accounts. Nine were girls. Two of the sons, John and Jacob, are not mentioned in the book. However, it is known that Jacob, Sr. did sell a farm he had purchased (probably for that purpose) to his second eldest son John in 1782 and sold another in Gwynned Township to his youngest son, Jacob, who is recorded to have made staggered payments to his siblings. So, to a certain extent, all Jacob's sons were helped in terms of their land needs. A single entry for his eldest son read: "In the year 1768, I Jacob Clemens, sold the farm on which I first lived to my [eldest] son Gerhart Clemens. It contains 136 acres and I sold it for 650 pounds. Of this amount I allowed him 200 pounds to be charged against his inheritance. For the balance he gave me notes which he is to repay."

The girls, on the other hand, all have numerous and detailed entries for moveable goods. They received similar although not identical items: bedding, bedsteads, spinning wheels; "English" dough troughs, blanket chests, and cupboards as major pieces of furniture. Several got a table as well as a wardrobe. It was not until the portion of the eighth daughter, Magreda, was recorded that a chair "with back" was mentioned (c.1774). The last daughter, Susanna, was the first to get a coverlet (1781). These two items illustrate a transition that was being made in the Clemens family from Germanic forms like benches to English chairs and from Germanic feather ticks to coverlets. The dough trough was noted by their father, Jacob, as early as 1749 as being an "English" form.

Pewterware was an *aussteier* item for nearly every girl of this first generation while earthenware was not mentioned until later and wooden plates recorded but once. A clock was given to only one of the daughters—as compared to copperware and ironware which most received. Several daughters received cows, fewer got a horse, and only two received sheep. As Jacob mentioned once, "Now I enumerate some things which Enigen got but which Esther did not get, but for which I gave her cash money." When cash was given, those goods purchased *might* have made the eventual marriage portions or *aussteier* more nearly identical.

Jacob's eldest son, Gerhart, continued similar record-keeping in his father's book. He was a farmer on the original family farm in Lower Salford Township and with his wife raised five children—three daughters and two sons. He died in 1820 and passed the farm (valued at £1500) onto his youngest son, Heinrich, with an *aussteier* or credit of £300 toward its purchase price.

For this second generation several major changes occur that illustrate acculturation—or the mix with another cultural group. Chairs were given to all the girls, two of them getting armchairs as well. Wall mirrors or looking glasses were introduced for the first time as were yarn reels. The drinking of tea was reflected in Sara's tea table, tea set, tea box, and pewter teapot. Forks went from a "flesh" or cooking fork solely to an individual's eating fork or utensil.

Tinware also appeared for the first time starting in 1792 along with the more traditional pewterware, ironware, and copperware. Brass began to be mentioned and cedarware references replaced the more generic "woodenware." Earthenware continued to be recorded for this generation as were coverlets for both sexes. Also, wardrobes and dough troughs continued as prevalent furniture forms while Heinrich, the last son of the second generation, was the first Clemens male to get a desk. Horses, cows, sheep and swine became necessary farm animals for all.

While in both the first and second generations the males got financial credit toward land purchased by their fathers, in the third generation only one male—the youngest—got land; all got more goods. For the second Clemens generation, purchases increasingly were made at stores—sometimes in Philadelphia. Although there were indications that local craftsmen like "the blacksmith" were patronized, increasingly items were storebought. Homespun had begun to be supplemented by mass-produced muslins and calicos.

Raymond Hollenbach did a price analysis of some of the Clemens *aussteier* items. He wrote for Preston A. Barba's column "S Pennsylvanisch Deitsch Eck" in the *Allentown Morning Call* in the late 1960s. He noted then that each first generation girl received a chest made of softwood and one made of walnut and all valued at $3.30 to $5.30. The next two generations of girls got chests of drawers valued at twenty-two dollars each. The beds of the first generation girls cost only $1.85 to $4.00 which made Hollenbach feel that Jacob Clemens might have supplied the wood to a local craftsman. Katherine was the first daughter to get two beds (in 1799). At least one was high-posted (for bedhangings were listed). In the second generation the beds were definitely "roped." Beds had also increased in value, to as much as seven dollars. On the other hand, only one girl got a chair with back valued at 50¢ in the first generation while Gerhart's daughters in the second generation all got sets of chairs and each chair was then 80¢.

Mr. Hollenbach also remarked that the Clemens girls in the eighteenth century also received a simple and inexpensive cupboard valued at two dollars. By the early nineteenth century the cupboard was costing eight dollars and by the last generation it was "with glass" and valued at between ten and sixteen dollars. Tables also went from being a rarity to being more specific like dropleaf. Other woodenware included the household machine—the spinning wheel—which was as much as four dollars. Also, wooden utensils such as butter molds, tubs and buckets and even plates which were relatively expensive or $2.95 for a set of six.

Metalware for the kitchen mostly included iron which partly was replaced in the later generations with tinware; sometimes totaling twenty-five dollars. Pewterware was considerably more expensive than the iron and although listed generically it probably encompassed a variety of tableware forms: basins and plates. Each of the first generation girls received nearly seven dollars worth (which Mr. Hollenbach noted was the price of a cow then). Copper and brass articles were rarely mentioned for the Clemenses, as was the case in all the other families whose *aussteier* records survive. The form most common was the large copper applebutter kettle which cost as much as $12.50 by the third generation. Smaller kettles and also ladles in copper or brass were less frequently mentioned.

The third generation was headed by Heinrich. He married in 1806 and farmed on the family's Lower Salford Township property where he died in 1860. He and his wife had seven children: three boys and four girls. As with other *aussteier* accounts of this mid-nineteenth-century period, entries became very specific and detailed: "31½ lbs. of feathers, home plucked," "a half-dozen large plates with a blue border," or "three buckets, two with iron hoops for $1.00 and one with wooden hoops for $1.25." Even more of the items would have been storebought rather than made by a local craftsman. Although earthenware was still mentioned, more often dishes were now "green-rimmed" or "flowered"; also plates and glass were mentioned. Stoneware was entered for the first time for daughter, Elizabeth (c.1846): "2 stone crocks for cream and two stone jugs $1.62½." Tea drinking with all its accoutrements was well entrenched with tea sets, pots, sugar bowls, creamers and tea cans as contrasted to its mere introduction in the second generation. Brass items, which were mentioned only once in the second generation's outfittings, were still infrequent entries. But Heinrich's cedarware notations become more specific: large and small tubs, washtubs, butter churns, small butter tubs, and buckets.

Chairs and desks which had been introduced in the second generation of the Clemens family became well established furniture types for the third generation: kitchen cupboards or dressers evolved into corner cupboards with glass fronts; blanket chests which had become passé in the second generation were still absent as are wardrobes and in their place were chests of drawers. Bedding types evolved too with the introduction of quilts (in 1834) along with the traditional coverlets (males getting one and the females as many as four). Garden tools such as shovels and hoes are added to a more specialized line of female household utensils: scissors, sweeping brushes, fireplace tongs and shovel, butter scales, molds, boxes and tubs, knives, forks and spoons, waffle irons, rolling pins, graters, and sauerkraut strainers.

Dishes were sometimes pewter, at least once "cedarware," and most likely earthenware for both the first and second generation Clemenses. They appear to have been purchased from a very local source. In the Salford Township area there would have been a few potters from whom to make such purchases: Jacob Scholl, John Leman, and Johannes Neis for example. In the third generation, china or porcelain dishes replaced the earthenware—their new colors and decorations were noted by Heinrich as he bought them.

Finally, the girls also were given horses (with saddles for riding for the first and second generations), cows—an average of over two per girl, and sheep—at least one per girl, and later, pigs.

The first generation of twelve children received about $350 of *aussteier* goods at a time when average wages were about fifty cents a day. By the third generation of seven, their totals were three hundred dollars in goods followed later by a cash sum of three hundred which Heinrich noted "is to be counted as part of her inheritance."

Most of the value of the *aussteier* of the Clemens men was in land or cash, but they also received watches which were listed as being valued from ten to eighteen dollars and a desk which was priced much like its counterpart, the female's chest of drawers, at twenty-four dollars.

In summation, these entries reflect the gift giving patterns and tastes of a somewhat Anglicized prosperous Pennsylvania-German farm family over a long period of time. They had access to both the Philadelphia marketplace as well as to many local craftsmen and they had the ability and inclination to be fashionable.

JACOB KROB'S ACCOUNT BOOK

Jacob Krob (Krupp) was born on September 3, 1712 in Essen, Germany, and as a seventeen-year-old arrived in Philadelphia in 1729. He married Mary Uplinger and settled in Harleyville, Lower Salford Township, Montgomery County. He was

	JACOB CLEMENS 1749-1781	GERHART CLEMENS 1789-1812	HEINRICH CLEMENS 1827-1857
Bedding: bed cases, bolster cases, pillow cases, sheets, bed ticks, feathers, curtains	F, F, F, F, F, F, F, F, F	F, F, F	F, F, F, F, F, M, M, M
Bedsted(s): low post, high post	F, F, F, F, F, F, F	F, F, F, M, M	F, F, F, F, M, M, M
Blanket chest w/ drawers	F, F, F, F, F, F, F		
English baking trough	F, F, F, F, F	F, F, F	F, F, F, F
Cupboard (see line 77)	F, F, F, F, F, F	F, F	F, F, F
Copperware: kettle, tea kettle	F, F, F, F, F, F	F, F	F, F, F
Spinning wheel	F, F, F, F, F, F, F, F	F, F, F	F, F, F
Pewterware	F, F, F, F, F, F, F, F, F	F, F, F, F	
Iron pot	F, F, F, F, F, F, F, F, F	F, F, F	F, F, F, F
Iron spoons: ladle, skimmer	F, F, F, F, F, F, F, F	F, F	F, F, F
Meat fork, flesh fork	F, F, F, F, F	F, F	F
Iron pan	F, F, F, F, F, F	F, F	F, F, F, F, F
Smoothing iron and stone	F, F, F, F, F, F, F	F	F, F
Cow(s)	F, F, F, F, F, F, F, F, F	F, F, F, M, M	F, F, F, F, M, M, M
Horse(s)	F, F, F, F	F, M, M	M, M, M
Seed oats	F		
Cash	F, F, F, F, F, F, F, F, F	F, F, F, M, M	F, F, F, F, M, M, M
Soup pan	F		
Table	F, F, F	F, F, F	F, F
Sheep	F, F	F, F, F, M	
Barrel of brandy	F		
Hay	F		
Wardrobe	F, F, F	F, F, F	M
Tubs and buckets	F, F		F, F
Butter churn	F		F, F
Clock	F		
Table cloth	F, F, F, F, F	F	F, F, F, F, F, M, M
Saddle and bridle	F, F, F, F, F, F, F	F, F, F, M, M	M, M, M
Cake pan	F, F, F, F		
Earthenware	F, F	F, F, F	F, F, F
Wooden utensils	F, F, F, F		
Land	M	M	
Iron light, lamp	F, F		
Wooden plates (6)	F		
Chair(s) with backs (2, 6, 10)	F	F	F, F, F, F
Towels	F		
Coverlet	F	F, F, F, M, M	F, F, F, F, M, M, M
Harness		M	M
Wagon		M, M	M
Silver watch (pocket)		M, M	M, M, M
Pig(s)		F, F, F, M	F, F, F, F, M, M
Tinware (buckets, measures)		F, F, F	F, F, F, F, F
Yarn reel		F, F, F	F, F, F, F
Mirror		F, F	F, F
Tea set		F	F, F, F, F, F
Coffee mill, grinder		F	F, F, F
Sprinkling can		F	F, F, F
Candle stick, candle holder		F	F, F, F
Lamp trimmer		F	
Tea table		F	
Tea pot, kettle		F, F	F, F, F
Cedarware: tubs, churns, wash tubs, butter tubs, buckets, butter boxes		F	F, F, F
Desk		M	M, M, M
Room stove w/ pipe		M	M, M
Butter scale w/ weights			F, F, F, F
Soup spoons, teaspoons			F, F, F, F
China: creamer, saucers, plates, sugar bowl, tea cups			F, F, F, F
Iron taster			F
Sauerkraut strainer			F, F
Wash machine and tub			F
Pepper box			F
Butter mold			F, F
Grater			F, F, F
Rolling pin			F
Straw baking baskets (6)			F, F, F, F
Waffle iron			F, F
Tankard			F, F
Knives and forks			F, F, F
Dough tray scraper			F, F
Brass kettle			F, F, F
Corner cupboard w/ glass front			F, F, F, F
Scissors			F, F

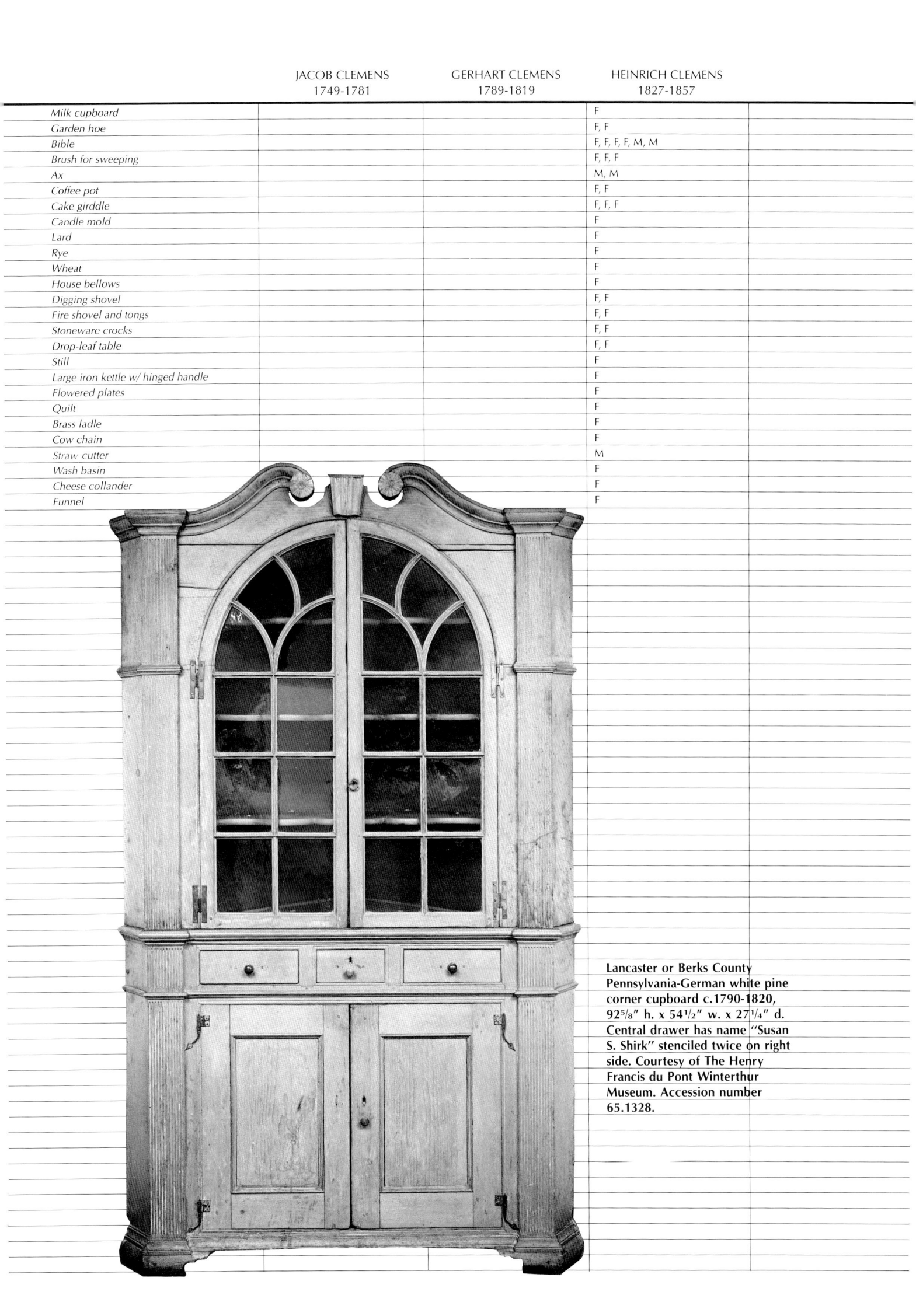

	JACOB CLEMENS 1749-1781	GERHART CLEMENS 1789-1819	HEINRICH CLEMENS 1827-1857
Milk cupboard			F
Garden hoe			F, F
Bible			F, F, F, F, M, M
Brush for sweeping			F, F, F
Ax			M, M
Coffee pot			F, F
Cake girddle			F, F, F
Candle mold			F
Lard			F
Rye			F
Wheat			F
House bellows			F
Digging shovel			F, F
Fire shovel and tongs			F, F
Stoneware crocks			F, F
Drop-leaf table			F, F
Still			F
Large iron kettle w/ hinged handle			F
Flowered plates			F
Quilt			F
Brass ladle			F
Cow chain			F
Straw cutter			M
Wash basin			F
Cheese collander			F
Funnel			F

Lancaster or Berks County Pennsylvania-German white pine corner cupboard c.1790-1820, 92⅝" h. x 54½" w. x 27¼" d. Central drawer has name "Susan S. Shirk" stenciled twice on right side. Courtesy of The Henry Francis du Pont Winterthur Museum. Accession number 65.1328.

IT'S IN THE ACCOUNTS

Once "English" wall mirrors or looking glasses were added to the Pennsylvania-Germans *aussteier* toward the end of the eighteenth century, they became a commonly listed home furnishing. This black walnut example with gilded pewter trim measures 36" h. x 17³⁄₄" w. x 1¹⁄₂" d. Courtesy of The Henry Francis du Pont Winterthur Museum. Accession number 64.1528.

a farmer and weaver and at least two of his sons—Abraham and Isaac—became weavers also. Jacob Krob could neither read nor write but an *aussteier* book was kept in German for him by his eldest son and it recorded the gifts to eight of his twelve children from 1764 to 1785 (when he died). The entries were quite detailed until 1782 when the children's portions reflect cash gifts primarily. Jacob's will (dated 2/25/1785 and probated 1/13/1786) left his wife Mary "a chest with all the cloths and linen and what is in the chest without any opening to search the same."

He gave his first-born child and eldest daughter, Cadarina, the most detailed "outfit" as it was called and cumulatively the most valuable one also: household items at £5; a doughtray, chest and bedstead at £3, 7 shillings and 6 pence; a cupboard at £1, 10 shillings; four beds ranging from £5 to 4 shillings each; a spinning wheel for 12 shillings; a wagon full of hay for £1, £4 cash, and £4 for her wedding or a total of £33, 17 shillings and 6 pence. His other daughters received from £20 to £28 of goods. Each female entry was recorded having "outfitted my daugher . . . " in contrast to the male entries which omitted that wording. The males received goods, including looms for Isaac and Abraham but more often £50 cash.

JOHN AND JACOB BACHMAN'S ACCOUNT BOOK

John Bachman II (b. 1746, d. 1828) was a joiner who worked in Conestoga Township, Lancaster County, on his small farm on which a separate shop had been erected. Two of his sons worked with him as well as eight others from 1775 to 1810. His eldest son, John III, set up shop in Pequa Township while another, Jacob, went to Lampeter. This book includes the output of John from 1769 and of Jacob starting in 1822.

John was a Swiss Mennonite who did house carpentry and coffinmaking in addition to making over 400 bedsteads, 185 chests as well as other Pennsylvania-German forms: tables, doughtrays, kitchen cupboards, wardrobes, clockcases and cradles; also, newer English forms: chest of drawers, desk and bookcases, corner cupboards, tea and breakfast tables. The furniture was made in unpainted hardwood (walnut and later, cherry) or of painted pine and/or poplar. Jacob charged $14 to $16 for a kitchen cupboard in softwood as compared to $24 for one in walnut (for Jacob Rohrer in 1823). One *aussteier* outfitting appears to have been made by Jacob for Christian Bachman and entered in April 1824: one poplar kitchen dresser ($16), one walnut dining table ($6), one high post bedstead ($7.50), one open dresser ($2.50), one doe-trough [sic] ($1.50), two benches ($1.50), boxes and lampstand ($1.25), and five months later—a corner cupboard.

ABRAHAM OVERHOLT'S ACCOUNT BOOK

Abraham Overholt was a Mennonite farmer and joiner who was born in February 1765 and died in March 1846. He was a sixth-generation Pennsylvania German whose account book reflects his work as a turner and joiner although he was a farmer primarily. In his work as a joiner he made many spinning wheels—eighty-five from 1790 to 1814. His work was more diversified than that however, and several times he recorded making small typical dowry groupings, for example: the bedstead, walnut table, kitchen cupboard, spinning wheel, and reel for Jacob Lederman in December 1790; a bedstead, pine chest with three drawers painted brown; a walnut chest with nine drawers and a kitchen cupboard without the hardware for Philip Kratz in the fall of 1792 and then in the spring of 1794, a kitchen cupboard painted brown, a walnut table with two drawers and a doughtray table for William Godschall as well as a kitchen cupboard with twenty-four panes and painted red, a varnished breakfast table and a red doughtray table for Magdelena Gross in April, 1827.

PETER RANCK'S ACCOUNT BOOK

Along with his older brother, John, Peter was a joiner in Jonestown, Lebanon County, and his account book covers the period 1794 to 1817. Peter's work as a furniture maker and decorator, particularly on his blanket chests, has been recognized since it was featured in an article, "Pennsylvania German Dower Chests" by Esther S. Fraser in *Antiques*, 1927. Although he recorded sixty blanket chests in his account book he made more bedsteads (over eighty) as well as forty-five tables, twenty doughtrays or troughs, ten kitchen dressers, four desks, four corner cupboards, three chairs, two salt boxes and single line entries for a chest of drawers, a picture frame, a wax chest, and a clothes press.

As Frederick Weiser, who translated and edited Peter Ranck's book, noted: "the fact that several groups of furniture were sold to one person—a bedstead, a table, a doughtray, a chest for instance—probably reflects a father's wedding gift to a child. In one case we can affirm that newlyweds purchased a chest for their home (George Bross and Elizabeth Winter)." Dowry-type groupings that appeared in the account book were for a chest, bedstead, table and dough trough (£4, 11 shillings and 10 pence) for George Uhland on March 29, 1798; for three bedsteads, three tables, two chests and a dough trough (£8 and 4 shillings) for John Leman on January 25th, 1800; for a chest, bedstead, table and dough trough as well as mending a dresser (over £5) for Valentine Schaufler on May 11, 1800; for a chest, bedstead, kitchen dresser, table and dough trough (£6, 16 shillings and 3 pence) for Henry Winter on October 15, 1804; for one chest of drawers, a bedstead, table and three chairs (£6, 7 shillings and 6 pence) for Phillip Krebs on November 17, 1804; for a table, bedstead, dough trough, kitchen dresser and frame for a bedstead (£2, 2 shillings and 3½ pence) for John Eshelman on April 5, 1811, and a chest of drawers, long- and short-posted beds, and a dough trough for George Merk on January 21, 1811.

ABRAHAM WISMER SR'S ACCOUNT BOOK

From 1798 to 1818 Abraham Wismer, a weaver who lived in Bedminster Township, Bucks County, recorded gifts to his eight children: four boys and four girls. Each child's entries were noted in pounds, shillings, and pence but the totals are always converted to dollars and cents, the pound being equal to $2.67 at that time.

On May 28, 1798 Abraham stated that "this Book gives a true account of what my children got of their father Abraham Wismer his Book and Hand" (translated by Raymond Hollenbach in 1968). The girls consistently were given more—about $350 of varied goods—while the sons received from $170 to roughly $350 of varied farm goods and implements (except for Isaac who after his marriage in 1802 left Pennsylvania. He received cash and a new wagon, body, gears and cover along with some sundries instead. Certain items such as the testament and psalm book, a saddle and bridle, hogs, cows and sheep as well as cash were given to both sexes while other goods were sex-linked: looms, wagons, harrows, plows, axes and harnesses for the men; beds and bedding, chair sets, tables, dressers, drawers, looking glasses, spinning wheels and bread baskets as well as cedar-, iron-, pewter-, brass-, and earthenware for the women only.

WILLIAM AND SAMUEL SCHULTZ'S ACCOUNT BOOK

William and Samuel Schultz were farmers in Hereford Township, Montgomery County. Samuel also did carpentry according to the surviving account books from 1812 to 1871. In 1815, mentioned along with single line entries for roll-away beds, bedsteads, a doughtray, a kitchen cupboard, a salt box and a corner cupboard, there was a furniture grouping made for Anna Bechtel that is not unlike many *aussteier* furniture groupings: a cupboard ($21), a dropleaf table ($10), a bedstead ($6), a table ($5), a water bench ($3.50) and a doughtray ($1.50), all in a single entry. A year later he made two desks (a typically male item) for $54 for Killian Weis's sons, probably John and Jacob. Two other single group entries in 1816 are similar to furniture goods assembled for females' "outfitting": Abraham Heistand is charged for a kitchen cupboard ($25), a table ($6.25), a bedstead ($5), a bedstead and doughtray ($5) in addition to a spice drawer and a salt box while Johann Feringer is charged for a cupboard ($19), a bedstead ($6), a table ($5), and a doughtray ($1.50). Most likely both were fathers buying dowry items for daughters.

PETER KNAB'S ACCOUNT BOOKS

Peter Knab, a farmer living in Oley, Berks County, wrote in his first account book, "The 22nd of July 1795 a little daughter was born to us her sign was under Libra and was baptised the 15th of August. Her godparents were Julius Knab and his wife Mary Elizabeth and she was named Susana in holy baptism [translation]." In a second account book Peter Knab continued, "Bought a family book and paid for the household goods to start with for her file (October 28, 1818 Susana)" and he listed $450.50 worth of goods as well as $180 given to Susana's husband seven years later. In 1827 another $400 was given, presumably to the husband, "on his wife Susana's inheritance." At the bottom of that page farmer Knab noted: "I wrote everything in my family book."

Other entries follow for daughter Sara in 1819 (again $450.00 in goods and $180 in cash and later $400 for Sara's inheritance); later, those for his sons Jacob, William, and Nathan who receive from $508.25 to $730.59 apiece. All goods seem to have been accumulated in a short space of time for each child.

Unlike most other *aussteier* listings, Peter Knab was often specific in noting from whom he had purchased the crockery, tinware or who made the chairs (Eiler), the bureau (Weimert), or the baking baskets (Schmit). His attention to detail included descriptions of beds sometimes as "old" or the horse as "fox colored." He also noted when the dishes were tin or cedar, and that the small cupboard for Sara was for kitchen dishes.

CHRISTIAN MYERS'S ACCOUNT BOOK

Christian Myers (Meyers) was born in Bucks County on April 24, 1772; he was a farmer and blacksmith as had been his father before him. Of his seven boys and one girl, five were mentioned in his account book (1809 to 1845) starting on April 22, 1827. He first gave to his only daughter and third child Catharine for her "outsetting": a lot of crockery, three tubs, two buckets, a churn, a pigen, two iron pots, and a fry pan along with two dozen knives and forks, two flat irons, two dozen tablespoons, a coffee mill, sundries and an iron kettle for the kitchen. The most expensive line items were the beds, bedstead and bedding for $40.00 followed by a case of drawers and a bureau for $24.00. Along with a set of twelve chairs (and a small one), cows, sheep, a hog, a teakettle, two ladles and his own work at putting a bail on a kettle and getting two pot lids, her *aussteier* totaled $167.08. Six years later, Catharine was advanced one hundred dollars interest free and then in 1844 another one hundred dollars or a total, as her father records, of $367.08.

Catharine's brothers Michael, Charles, Samuel, and Isaac are similarly "outset" with the more typical male furnishings of wagons, harrows, wheelbarrows, and smaller tools like grubbing hoes, axes, shovels, wedges, and cutting boxes with knives. All his children regardless of sex, were provided with a bed, bedstead and bedding and the sons were advanced one or two hundred dollars without interest always on the first of April. Except for one child's entry, they were nearly identical total dollar amounts, made up of different goods ($167.08, $160.20, $147.35, $98.13, and $176.25). Samuel, the fourth child in the accounts, got the lowest "outsetting" and never was given a lump money sum, while Isaac died before getting his second one hundred dollars. Otherwise there is a real attempt to be equitable regardless of sex or age.

CHRISTIAN HOWSER'S ACCOUNT BOOK

Over a six-year period (1827 to 1833) Christian Howser of West Lampeter Township, Lancaster County, recorded the outfits of five of his eight children. While the entries for Jacob (1827 to 1828), Anna (1828 to 1829), and Isaac (1832) were fairly detailed and not unlike others of this time period, the last two entries made for Elizabeth and Barbara both allude to their accounts continuing in another book. Missing from this family book, but not from his will, were accounts for his eldest son John and for other daughters, Mary and Susanna.

As is sometimes the case, Christian Howser's will clarified the responsibilities of the children to their father and set forth his responsibilities to them referring at times to "my book" and advancements:

I give and bequeath four hundred and fifty dollars to each and every of my three daughters Elizabeth, Barbara and Mary Howser.

I give and bequeath to my said three daughters all my linen, my table cloths, napkins, blankets, coverlets, two stoves and pipes, corner cupboard and its contents and clock and case their choice and to each and every of them two good beds and bedsteads with the necessary bedding.

I bequeath to my three sons Jacob, John and Isaac, my cider press and its apparatus at thirty dollars; and to my sons Jacob and John all my smith tools, bellows at forty dollars to be accounted for by them.

I bequeath my dearborn wagon and a horse their choice, and two cows their choice to my three daughters Elizabeth, Barbara and Mary.

All the residue of my estate, real personal and mixed including all the valuation moneys aforesaid of the land devised to my children and the purchase money of the land directed to be sold; and including all advancements which I have made or shall make to my children as will appear by my book or otherwise I give, devise and bequeath in equal shares and parts to and among my eight children Jacob, John, Isaac, Elizabeth, Barbara, Mary, Susanna, the wife of Daniel Weaver, and Ann, the wife of John Gordon their heirs and assigns each and every of them accounting for his or her advancement; and those to whom I have devised land shall account for said valuations thereof respectively and those whose valuation moneys shall exceed their shares shall pay to the rest such excess in three equal annual consecutive instalments without interest the first instalment to be paid in one year after my death; and the final available moneys of my estate after the payment of my debts, expenses and specific legacies shall be paid to such of my children as to whom most shall be coming of their share until they shall be equalized.

In the disposal of my estate by this my will I have considered all services rendered to me by my children or which any of them may render to me: and therefore none of them shall bring any claims against my estate for such services.

In addition to these items, Christian also gave farms to his three sons and tenancy in his home in Lampeter Square to his three unmarried daughters.

MICHAEL ALBRECHT'S ACCOUNT BOOK

A farmer and weaver by trade, Michael Albrecht lived in New Hanover Township, Montgomery County. Born on June 5, 1780, in Douglas Township, he married Susannah Kurtz (b. 1782, d. 1860) on December 15, 1805 and they had seven children. Along with a book for his weaving accounts, he kept another which was his family book. On its cover was written "My life story/Michael Albrecht/ and of my family/ written the 14th day of June 1807." The pages that followed cited the circumstance of each child's birth, baptismal date, the minister's name and those of the godparents. The dowries of three of his four daughters: Judith, Salome, and Rebeca were included.

"All this which I wrote down in this book for my children shall be regarded such that the others for whom nothing is written shall have so much that they are even with the older ones out of my estate, but it shall never be taken in one _____ what I wrote down for them. So much from Michael Albrecht" [translated from his German script.]

From March 25, 1831, when he started with "a listing of my daughter Salome's household goods"—until April 15, 1837 with Rebeca's list (she married on February 12, 1837), he purchased as full, detailed, and consistent a complement of home furnishings as any father. He spent nearly the same on each of the three girls—from $111.30 to $117.30 for over two dozen basic items: wooden tubs and churns, porcelain, earthenware, cedar and tin dishes, cake plates, eating knives and spoons, iron cooking ladles and flesh forks, footed hearth pans, iron pots with lids, fireplace tongs and shovels, coffee mills, baking baskets, tea kettles, candlesticks, flat irons and oil lamps. Their furniture included sets of chairs, dropleaf tables, corner cupboards, dough troughs, bureaus, bedsteads and for the first time—bed quilts with accessories—as well as coverlets. Tools used outside the kitchen were limited to garden shovels or spades and hoes. Their animals were sheep, lambs, and pigs but not cows or horses. Rebeca alone received a mirror and a brooch.

On May 6, 1840 Michael Albrecht concluded this record. "I have given my daughters' husbands Johannes Schweissfort, Heinrich Hollenbusch, Peter Schweissfort to each of them $25.00 from the inheritance of my deceased son Frederich. Ephraim Albrecht's $25 I hold in hand. If I should live so long until he is twenty-one, then I will give it to him myself. If not, he shall have it from my estate beforehand with interest of five percent. So much from Michael Albrecht." As it turned out Ephraim predeceased his father. In fact, neither son lived long enough to have set off on their own and two other daughters had died earlier, so one is unable to see what he would have given to his sons other than cash.

JOHAN BOMBERGER'S ACCOUNT BOOK

Johan Bomberger, a Mennonite farmer in Warwick Township, Lancaster, kept a family account in which he recorded the marriage portions as well as the continuing inheritance for his five children from 1832 to 1861: Christian, Jacob, Maria, Anna, and Fronica. There is a similar family account book in existence kept by his first son Christian (from 1860 to 1909) for Christian's ten children.

Johan was a fourth generation Pennsylvanian who inherited the original family farm and homestead. He was born in 1780 and died in 1861. Starting in 1832 he outfitted his daughter Anna, his fourth child, who was the first to marry. Portions to Maria (starting in 1836), Christian (starting in 1840), Fronica (starting in 1841), and finally Jacob (starting in 1846) were very complete and detailed. Their marriage dowries began each individual's account and varied in their totals though they are similar in the type of goods given. The *aussteier* portions were followed by additional cash amounts given to each child over a period of a decade or more. Some of the cash was most likely from the sale of the farm to the youngest son Jacob for $4,700. He repaid his father from 1850 to 1861 and it is during that time that cash was given to his siblings as well as to Jacob, himself.

Except for Christian, the oldest son who is recorded as receiving $1760.21 plus $54.00 in final settlement, the total amounts in goods and cash to the other four children are nearly identical: Anna $4,450 plus $54, Maria $3,350, Fronica $3,450 plus $54, and Jacob $4,435.50 plus $54. (Most likely there was a transaction between the father and his son, Christian, that accounts for the large difference in his account.) All children had cash entries from their father's estate sale in 1849 and Jacob, the youngest, showed the major part of his goods coming to him just prior to that sale: numerous wagons, ploughs, harrows, cows with calves, horses, various hoes, shovels and forks, a curry comb, hay knife, sieves, grinding wheel, cow chains, and earthenware. The goods given to both sons were similar and include sacks, oxen, the bed, bedstead and chest as well as a desk ($20) a house clock ($31), a writing book (25¢), wheelbarrow ($3), wood saw ($1.25), an axe ($2.25), a windmill ($15) in addition to pigs, sheep, and grains: wheat, corn and oats for Christian.

The girls' household items were more varied and they are typical of other female marriage portions of the period. Some new and different items mentioned were oven peels, flour boxes, rolling pins, wash tubs ($3.75), butter churns ($3.00), copper and brass kettles ($15.50 and $2.87½), Dutch ovens ($1.40), oven pans (75¢), bellows (40¢), dough scrapers (31½¢), soap stands ($1.15), wash lines (45¢), butter scales, watering cans ($1.00), scrub brushes and tin plates, bowls and platters.

The girls received spinning wheels and yarn winders, usually high and low post beds, dough troughs, sometimes several kitchen cupboards, tables, and chairs as did earlier generations of Pennsylvania-German women. But, the Bomberger girls no longer received a blanket chest; rather a bureau or two. They also got a rocker as well as chairs and the youngest girl, Fronica, got a clock and case ($31.00) and a clothes press ($14.50) in 1841. Tinware had replaced pewterware for these nineteenth-century women but earthenware was still the pottery of choice. These female *aussteier* entries indicate some changes in the form or material of traditional pieces in the first half of the nineteenth century, but also a lot of consistency with what had been given to females for decades past.

JOHANNES HELM'S ACCOUNT BOOK

The account book of Johannes Helm, a farmer in East Hanover Township, Lebanon County, spanned a long period of time, 1792 to 1855, but among many general entries there is only one short dowry entry: "I, Johannes Helm have given my daughter Magdalena when she married a cow for the price of eleven Dollars."

JOHANNES GEHMAN'S ACCOUNT BOOK

John Z. Gehman's family records were compiled and transcribed by Raymond E. Hollenbach in 1971. They include his daily expenses, a diary, an inventory of his farm equipment, the costs of building a schoolhouse, recipes and remedies, as well as marriage records and family wills.

Included in these records are lists of goods for setting up house that John gave his sons Abraham and John as well as his daughter Barbara. Abraham's accumulation began first in 1835 more than five years prior to his marriage on April 13, 1840 and six years before he would move out of the family homestead.

Like his siblings, Abraham's list is a very complete listing and often cites not only the items and their cost but also the exact date of purchase and from whom. His brother John received many of the family home's furnishings: a bed and chest from the boys' room; a bed and corner cupboard from the stoveroom, and a case clock, corner cupboard, wooden chest, benches, and table from the parlor. All the children received land as a substantial gift; John's being $6,900 on one piece of land and $81.30 for another plot bringing his total including tools and furniture to $7,905. It was noted that he had an obligation of $2,312 for a dower—perhaps his mother's.

The John Z. Gehmans lived in Upper Hanover Township, Montgomery County, just across the Berks/Montgomery line, about a mile and one half east of Bally.

LEDERACH STORE RECORDS

In the early 1970s Raymond E. Hollenbach transcribed the Lederach Store records (begun in 1828). They were written primarily in English but the spelling was phonetic and showed the influence of the Pennsylvania-German dialect as spoken in Lederachsville, Lower Salford Township, Montgomery County.

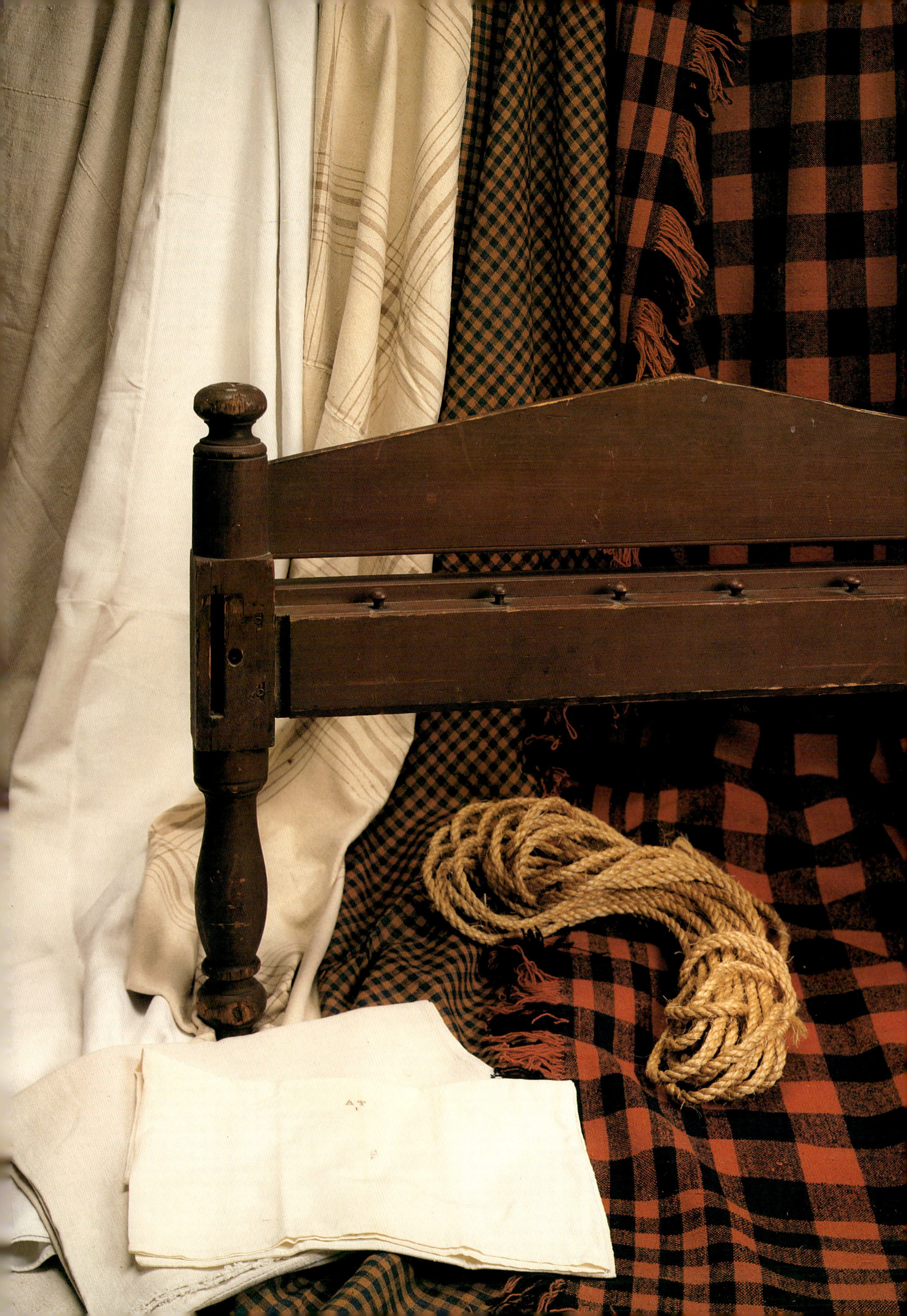

One or more beds complete with bedding were nearly always given to both males and females with the females often getting more than one. This tradition persists today in the Amish communities of Pennsylvania. Informants in Lancaster, Mifflin, Clinton, Centre, and Union counties tell of currently giving bed(s) with several sets of linens for each child. The range of bedding needed for a bed of the late eighteenth century is shown here (from left to right in the order in which the pieces would have been put on the bed once set up: handwoven chaff bag, courtesy of Robert and Shirley Kuster; handwoven linen sheet, handwoven fustian feather bag, handwoven check coverlet (topmost covering) all courtesy of Dr. and Mrs. Donald M. Herr; woven bolster bag, courtesy of Dr. Paul M. Corman; handwoven linen pillowcase with cross-stitch initials, courtesy of Charles and Tandy Hersh) and painted footboard of four-piece bed and handturned rope, courtesy of William and Jeannette Lasansky.

Mr. Hollenbach noted that on August 11, 1837 a long list of small household goods was purchased by Abraham Geres Sr. for $55.63 and he felt that "someone in his [Geres] family had just gotten married and was starting out housekeeping." Included was a watering pot (75¢), a water kittel [kettle] (45¢), a coffee pot (35¢) a coffee mel [mill] (85¢), a bucket (70¢), a funnel (8¢), two tin cups (12½¢), a tin crupper (8¢) a cantel mold [candlemold] (36¢), two latels [ladles] (37½¢), 2 fancy plates (60¢), ½ dozen plates (40¢), a bowl (30¢), two bowls (25¢), ½ dozen teaspoons (15¢), pind [pint] tumbler (12½¢), ½ dozen knives and forks (75¢) and 21 pounds of feathers ($12.60). Also, two wine tumblers (14¢), ½ dozen plates (50¢), ½ dozen fine plates (62½¢), four large sups [soups] (50¢), ½ dozen sups (45¢), a basket (12½¢), ½ dozen fine plates (55¢), ½ dozen tees (26¢), 1½ dozen tees ($1.50), a pitcher (28¢), two sets of teaware ($2.50), a swepen brush (56¢), three iron kittel @ $1.10 per hundred pound ($4.40), two flatirons (75¢), 1 dozen spoons (56¢), a frying pan and two candlesticks (50¢).

An even more extensive entry was for Mary Care who also appeared to be buying all the small goods for setting up a house on February 28, 1839. She spent $61.75 which as Mr. Hollenbach noted was a large amount since average daily wages were 50¢/day or less. In addition to the range of goods that Abraham Geres purchased she got a wash basen (46¢), a stone picher (18¢), lots of comen [common] plats, boles and cups, ½ dozen wein [wine] classes (48¢), two decanters (37¢), a shufel [shovel] and tong (62½¢), a copper kittle @ 13¢ a pound or $13.00, and a copper kittle ($2.62½).

Although the types and numbers of household dishes seem considerable, especially in the instance of Mary Care, (and when compared to earlier family account listings of pottery) this may be explained by the fact that this is a store's ledger and every different type of item is noted (almost like inventory control) rather than lumped in a single category entry like "earthenware" or "porcelain dishes" as seen in the family account books.

HENRY MOYER'S ACCOUNT BOOKS

A carpenter, Henry Moyer, who lived and worked in Hereford Township, Montgomery County, had one grouping of *aussteier*-type furnishings in his first account book: a corner cupboard for $11.00, a table for $5.25, a bedstead for $4.50 and dough tray for $1.25, or a total of $22.00 in 1837; and a second grouping labeled "Joseph Butterweck's household goods": a corner cupboard $14.00, a bureau $16.00, a table $5.00, a doughtray $1.00 and bedsteads in 1846.

JACOB SCHOLL'S ACCOUNT BOOK

Jacob Scholl, a potter and son of potter Michael Scholl, was born in Upper Salford Township, (then Philadelphia County, later Montgomery County) in 1781. Only two of nine children he had with Catharine Leidy (daughter of potter, Jacob Leidy) are mentioned in his account book—Jacob and Samuel. (It is known that Samuel married Mary Ann Wambold three years later.)

Both sons received virtually identical and also typical male marriage outfits. Since there was reference made to Jacob being given meat "like Tobias" (the first son), one might conclude that similar goods were given to Jacob Scholl's other children. Potter Scholl's accounts indicate a greater concern for provisions (seed, food, and grains) than mentioned by most other parents previously.

JACOB LEIBY'S ACCOUNT BOOK

Jacob Leiby, a farmer living in Perry Township, Berks County, kept a family book from about 1855 until close to his death in 1884. He wrote in German that "the contents of this book is what each one has received for outfit who have worked until they attained their majority [translation]." In the book are listed very long "outfits" for his daughter Esther and his son Jacob with what appears to be the start for his son Ephraim's outfit. As the father noted about another child, "John, who was away three years before his majority, therefore he is charged one hundred dollars for the three years [apparently his labor's worth to the Leiby family]." He continued, "For that which is charged in the book, no interest shall be reckoned, excepting what is more than 900 dollars, then they shall be reckoned." Esther's dowry totaled $985.99 as of April 1, 1880 while Jacob [Jr] had received $2,733.17 in goods and cash by that same date. It was then that Jacob drew up a will that would be contested by some of his descendants (see pp. 17, 18).

The very complete listings for these two children reflect both long-standing traditional goods such as doughtrays, beds, coverlets, and earthenware with the addition of entirely new entries like an umbrella and an accordion. He also set up both of these children with tools of a trade in addition to the typical sex-related paraphernalia: charged against Esther's account are lessons from Mrs. Gehr for bonnetmaking as is a hat press, hats and "a box to make hats white," as well as quilting frames and four quilting frame screws; while Jacob [Jr's] was a blacksmith's anvil, bellows, tongs and hammer for $86.50. Both Esther and Jacob received many provisions like wheat, rye, corn, vinegar, and meat as well as a greater range of furniture than was noted in earlier family books: salt and spice boxes, a sink, corner cupboard, a closet, drawer, chests, chairs, tables, a looking glass, beds including a trundle bed, benches, a bureau, a flour chest, a doughtray, and clocks. Specificity was important and is reflected not only in listing the traditional bake basket (*bak korb*) but also a bushel basket, straw basket, and willow basket (*ein Weitken korb*). Not only are the entries very detailed and numerous in this family book but there are also some that indicate the father's relative affluence: $75 for a horse, $20.00 for silk for Esther, $20.00 for each cow, $18.00 for a bed and bedstead, $13.00 for a drawer, $12.50 for a corner cupboard, $11.00 for a wagon full of corn, $10.00 for a stove, $6.00 for a woolen coverlet, $6.00 for each clock and $5 for each blanket chest, for instance. The copper utensils were the most expensive kitchenware: $2.50 for a small copper kettle and $2.25 for a copper skimmer and ladle. There were no entries for silver or fancy dinnerware, however.

CHRISTIAN BOMBERGER'S ACCOUNT BOOK

Like his father before him, Christian Bomberger (b. 1818, d. 1898) was a farmer in Warwick Township, Lancaster County. He also became a minister (1848) and later a bishop (1860) for the Mennonites of the Lancaster Conference. At the age of twenty-one he married Catherine Hess and they were parents of ten children who are listed in the family account book. Christian's book was kept even after his death to account for the parceling out over time (until 1909) of the children's legacies. Christian's accounts emphasized equality over time. All but Fanny (who died in 1862) got $9,031 in goods and in cash. The heirs of Fanny and Nancy (who died in 1901) received cash gifts after their mothers' deaths. In October 1887 Christian's estate had vendue even though he was to live for another eleven years (his wife had predeceased him in 1876). Each child got a portion of the estate sale and Henry, the youngest son who appears to take over the family farm, gave an account of the farm goods retained in March 1888.

This second Bomberger family book yields information on the gifts to ten children, double the number of the first generation. However, some of the specificity of goods is lost when many entries, especially those for the females, are for store bills: Lehn's Store, Sprecher's Hardware Store, Hollinger and Fahnstock Store, Bricker and Tshudys', Wolleys', Reists' and Steinman's Hardware Store. Some entries though are for Lancaster County craftsmen: to James Miksch for tinware, to Augustus Hall for furniture, and to Conrad Gast for earthenware. Nonetheless, when there is specificity on entries, traditional goods as well as evolution in materials are both present. All the girls still got feathers for their featherbeds as well as beds, kitchen dressers, cupboards, grainbags, copper kettles, cows and hogs. Earthenware was no longer the only pottery listed; rather, chinaware and queensware. A stove was now bought from the tinsmith or hardware store and carpet was now mentioned (ninety-five yards @ 68¢/yd for Barbara in 1874) as was a sewing machine, a washing machine with a wringer ($33 and $15) and a sideboard ($14.00) for Martha. The girls' wedding dresses were usually the first item mentioned in their entries and they cost from $29.50 for Fanny's in 1860 to $60.00 for Barbara's in 1874.

The males were also given wedding suits, (usually $75 to $85), sometimes "traveling expenses," and all the traditional goods: bed, bedding, and a desk or bookcase as the only household furniture. The bulk of their outfits was livestock, buggies, sleighs, and wagons, grains, and farm tools: mowers, reapers, corn shellers, grain fans, separators, ploughs, harrows, and threshing machines. The horses and vehicles tended to be big money items. Amos was noted as getting a second watch ($25.00).

PETER ZIMMERMAN'S ACCOUNT BOOK

Peter Zimmerman, a Mennonite farmer in Earl Township, kept a meticulously detailed "Family Account Book" concerning the "Advancements to his children" from 1862 to 1885. He was born in 1817 to Christian and Elizabeth (Wenger) Zimmerman. He in turn married Anna B. Weaver and they had nine children who were born between 1840 and 1863. His wife, Anna, died in 1871 and Peter remarried widow Elizabeth (Landis) Weaver, who outlived him by eighteen years.

Eight of Peter's children had their advancements listed by their father in an account that was "Entered by F.S. Stover, and directed and approved by me, Oct. 9, 1885. Peter Zimmerman." The first account was for his first-born, Franklin, and began April 1862 with subsequent entries each April 1st (the custom practiced by a number of these farming fathers who kept such advancement records). The last and most detailed record for Franklin was made in April 1864 when his total in goods had reached $604.90. He died the following September so his advancement was incomplete. All the other children except Lydia and John (who also died in the fall of 1864) Elizabeth, Mary, Christian, Henry, David, and Anna received equivalent amounts. Lydia who was entered last (in 1881) fell shy of the total of $4,000 in goods, land and cash only because she had not received her cash when book was written in 1885.

The females, similar to entries in other family records, got a wide range of goods while the males got less in the number of items but made up for it by having higher priced goods. For example, Elizabeth, who married David Hoover, received $792.51 of home furnishings and tools over the course of the three months (January to April 1869) with a sewing machine ($67.50) and cash ($3,140.00) being given ten years later for a total of $4,000. In contrast her brother, Christian got $797.45 worth of seeds, tools, a few household goods including a desk, a new and an old bed ($30.00 and $7.00 respectively), a dozen homemade bags, two brooms, and some cash with the balance of his $4,000 being made up in "legacy allowed him when I gave him the farm." Very small amounts of cash ($2.55 in Christian's case) were used to equalize the advancements amongst the siblings.

The entries when numerous, are very detailed and specific with merchants often being listed. Items not delineated before include a soap dish ($.08), a ball of twine ($.37), a spring balance ($.40), 1⅞ yds. table oilcloth ($1.13), a handbell ($1.50), a pair carving knife and fork ($1.62½), and a crout [sic] stand ($1.88) for example. The cookstove at $30.00, the sewing machine at $67.50, the carpeting at

$32.50, the feathers at $36.66, the cows at $50.00 each and the 560 pounds of pork at $56.00 were the most expensive items for the women while those of high cost for the men include a wagon at $92.50, the saddler's bill for horse gears at $66.75, a desk at $24.00, a bed at $30.00, forty bushels of corn at $30.00, and 392 pounds of pork at $39.20.

The abundance of detail in Peter Zimmerman's account book makes it a particularly wonderful record of family giving in the last third of the nineteenth century among Mennonite farming families of means. The furniture bill for daughter Anna in 1878 is typical: six brown chairs, six open back chairs, a nurse rocker, six cane seat chairs, a large cane rocker, a ten-foot ¾ extension table, a cane bedstead, a French bedstead, an open washstand, a walnut (bedroom) suite, a sideboard with glass (mirror), a cupboard, a sink, a flour chest, a doughtray, a bench, a lounge, two looking glasses, two bureaus, three tables, a bedstead, a chest, and a wood chest. The Zimmermans were also giving clocks to their children, sometimes noted as "eightday," other times just as "clock."

The Mennonite farmer Peter Zimmerman recorded the widest variety of goods given by any father. In particular his daughters received items that were listed in such detail that had the book surfaced earlier in the research, it would have been charted differently. All items were charted but the many tin, iron, glass or ceramic forms, for example, were often grouped in generic and comprehensive categories like tinware rather than listed separately by their very specific names. That would have been preferable. Even so, nearly three dozen new line items were added to the chart's vertical listing.

To indicate the profusion of items given and the detail of Zimmerman's listing, here are several illustrative examples. Lydia, his last daughter, got the following amounts and types of flooring: 36¼ yards of rug carpet at 55-60¢/yard, 26½ yards of chain carpet at 75¢/yard, 17 yards of hemp carpet at 25¢/yard, 25 yards of ingrain carpet at 55¢/yard, and one rug at $1.00. She also received the following chairs: ½ dozen fanback chairs at $5.00, ½ dozen caneback chairs at $7.00, ½ dozen corn chairs at $5.50, ½ dozen closed chairs at $7.00, as well as a nurse rocker at $2.25 and a horse shoe arm chair at $2.25. Mr. Heilig from whom most were purchased gave Peter Zimmerman two footstools gratis which were given to Lydia. She also got "an open wash stand," "an extension table," "a sink with four drawers," "a corner sideboard," and "a marble table." Such detailed itemization was seen throughout this family's records and yielded information on new forms of ceramics (jelly mugs, wash bowls and pitchers, scallop dishes, meat plates, deep plates, long dishes, soupbowls, cream jugs and butter dishes), tinware (match safe, dustpans, cake cutters, swill dippers, basting spoons, egg dippers, breadboxes, and coffee boilers) and brushes (wall, scrub, dust, hair, cloth, shoe, and stove) for example.

CHARLES DAUB'S ACCOUNT BOOK

Daub was a cabinetmaker, carpenter and undertaker born in 1809 and first recorded as working in Upper Salford Township, Montgomery County; later outside of Souderton in Franconia Township, Montgomery County. In one of his account books, there appears to be two *aussteier* furniture groupings, the first was a bedstead $5.50, a sink $7.00, a washstand (*wachstend*) $2.50, a stand (*ein stend*) $2.00 and a dough trough (*ein back drok*) $1.50 debited against Pieter Rautenbusch on March 19, 1864 and later, a sideboard $22.00, a bureau $24.00, a "hingen" sideboard $12.00, two bedsteads $10.00 and $7.00, a table, a stand, washstand, and a doughtray debited against Samuel Berge in 1869 possibly for Samuel's daughter Sarah (b. 1849).

ERASTUS D. RHOADS'S ACCOUNT BOOK

Erastus Rhoads, a schoolteacher and organist from Unionville, Lehigh County, had three daughters. Two lived to maturity and were listed with their advancements among miscellaneous account book entries in his slim "Ledger C" which covered the years 1867 to 1870. An "Account of furniture and articles given to Alice 1867-8" was made when she was eighteen or nineteen and prior to her marriage to Lewis F. Kuntz. Sabina, his second child, was given very similar articles in 1870. Their totals were $371.71 and $410.63 respectively.

The entries were clustered for both girls in the following categories: textiles, furniture, small housewares, and staples with some variation particularly in the textile area. For instance, Alice was given seven yards of muslin for pillowcases at thirty cents a yard, eighteen yards of quilt calico at twenty cents a yard, twenty-four bales of cotton at ten cents a bale, twenty-four yards of calico for comforts at eleven cents a yard, as well as finished goods like a fine quilt $12.00, a white coverlet $6.50, and a linen tablecloth $3.37½. Sabina did not get a fine quilt but did receive two coverlets, one colored and one white each at $4.50, and also six yards of lace for pillowcases. Both girls got bed ticking and feathers but Alice got nine pounds as contrasted to one pound for Sabina as well as bed rope and clothesline. Both received similar furniture: a dressing bureau ($40), sideboard ($27), bedsteads ($7.25 to 13.00), sink ($10.00), washstand ($8.00 to 9.50), table ($7.00 to 10.25), sewing table ($2.25 to 2.50), cane seat chairs, a rocking chair ($6.50 to 7.00), baking trough ($3.00 to 3.75), and window shades. Sabina also was given a cradle ($5.00).

While many of the surviving Pennsylvania-German *aussteier* accounts were of Mennonites, it is known that Erastus was a member of the Reformed Congregation.

HENRY H. DIETZ'S ACCOUNT BOOK

The accounts of Henry H. Dietz, a farmer and carpenter in York County, covered a period from 1854 to 1870. In 1868 he records that he gave his daughter, Rebeca $50.00 worth of house fixtures. No other dowry entries are listed. Though he is not specific as to what comprised these household goods, nor if he made them himself, one can assume that they would have been varied and numerous when one sees what Dietz charged for making typical household furniture at that time: chest $2.00, a "flower" chest $1.25, a wood chest $2.40, a small bench 25¢, and to "peasing" a quilt $2.00 and to "soeing" a quilt 37½¢.

DANIEL S. BURKHOLDER'S ACCOUNT BOOK

Daniel Burkholder's account book began in 1858, which is, for practical purposes, when he began his household having married Anna Weaver on December 1, 1857. Indeed, they moved onto their own farm on April 1, 1858. Strict equality

	KROB 1765-1785	WISMER 1798-1818	KNAB 1818-1829	HOWSER 1827-1833	MYERS 1827-1845	ALBRECHT 1831-1840	J.BOMBERGER 1832-1861
Household items (furniture)	F, F, F, F		F, F				
Dough trough	F, F		F	F		F, F, F	F, F
Chest	F	M		F			M,
Cupboard (dresser)	F	F, F, F	F, F	F	F		F, F
Bed(s), bedsted(s)	F, F	F, F, F	F, F, M, M, M	F, M, M	F, M, M, M, M	F, F, F	F, F, F, M, M
Spinning wheel (wool)	F, F			F			F, F, F
Cow(s)	F, F	F, M, M, M	F, F, M, M	F, M, M	F, M, M, M	F, F, F	F, F, F, M, M
Wagon and wagon gears	F, M	M, M	M	M, M	M, M, M, M		M, M
Buckwheat or wheat	M			F, M, M			F, M, M
Cash	F, F, M, M, M	F, F, F, M, M, M		F, F, F, M, M	F, M, M		F, F, F, M, M
Sheep, lamb(s)	M	F, M, M, M		F	F, M, M, M	F, F, F	F, F, M
Sow, hog, pig(s)	M	F, F, M, M, M	F, F, M, M	M, M	F	F, F, F	F, F, M
Corn	M			M			M
Loom	M, M	M, M, M					
Horse(s): foal, mare, nag		M, M, M	M, M	M, M	M, M, M		F, M, M
Grain bags (6, 12, 24)		M, M, M		F, M			F, F, F, M, M
Harrow		M, M, M	M	M, M	M		F, M, M
Plough		M, M, M	M, M	M, M			M, M
Axe		M, M, M		M	M, M, M, M		M
Bible (catachism)		F, F, F, M, M, M	F, F, M, M, M				
Harness		M, M, M	M		M		M, M
Saddle and bridle		F, F, F, M, M, M, M	F, M, M	F	M		
Log chain, chain		M, M	M, M	M			
Drawers, bureau		F, F, F	F, F	F, F, F	F	F, F, F	F, F, F
Table		F, F		F			F, F
Chair(s) (4, 6, 9, 12)		F, F, F	F, F	F	F	F, F, F	F, F, F
Bread baskets (6)		F, F, F	F			F, F, F	F, F
Coverlet		F		F		F, F	
Earthenware		F, F	F	F		F, F, F	F, F, M
Bedding: sheets, curtains, bags		F, F, F		F	F, M, M		F
Feathers		F, F					
Cedarware		F, F	F, F			F, F	
Ironware, hardware		F, F		F	F		
Pewterware (basin, plates)		F, F		F			
Brassware		F	F				F
Check reel, reel		F, F, F		F			F
Tinware: dipper, grater, etc.		F, F	F, F	F		F, F	F, F
Looking glass, mirror		F, F	F	F		F	F, F
Iron kettle		F	F, F	F		F, F	
Spoons, silver teaspoons			F, F				
White earthen dishes			F				
Desk			M, M	M			M
Watch			M				
Straw cutter or bench			M, M		M, M		M
Gun			M				
Dung fork			M		M		M
Wheelbarrow			M		M		F, M
Lamp, oil light				F			
Frocks				F			
Delftware				F			
Twill				F			
Spreader				M			
Barrels: cider, vinegar				M			
Hand screws				M, M			
Fish				M			
Candle holder, candle stick				F		F, F, F	
Meat: pork, beef, dried beef				M			F
Rocking chair				F			F, F, F
Wash or clothes line				F			F, F, F
Basket: sewing, clothes				F, M			F, F, M, M
Vendue bill				M, M			F, F, F, M, M
Wool				M			F
Clock, and case, 8 day				M, M			F, M
Hay ladder, hay rack				M			M, M
Halter chain				M			
Room stove, piping				M			
Coffee kettle, pot, boiler				F			
Rye				M			
Oil cloth (floor)				F			
Stands: sausage, fat, lard				M, M			
Rope, bed ropes				F			
Blanket(s)				F			
Ladles					F		
Tea: kettle, set, pot					F	F	
Hay knife					M, M		M, M

GEHMAN 1835-1847	LEIBY 1855-1884	C.BOMBERGER 1860-1909	ZIMMERMAN 1862-1881	BURKHOLDER 1880-1902	DERSTEIN 1883-1888	KAUFMAN 1901-1945
F		F, F		F, F, F	F	F, F, F, F, F
M	F		F, F, F, F			
M	F,, M M	M,M	F, F, F	F, F, F, F	F,M	
		F	F, F, F, F			F, F, F, F
F, M, M	F, M, M	F, F, M, M, M, M	F, F, F, F, M, M, M, M	F, F, F, M, M, M, M, M	F, M	F, F, F, F, F, F, M, M, M, M, M
F, M, M	F					
F, M, M	F, M, M	F, F, F, F, M, M, M	F, F, F, F, M, M	F, F, M, M, M, M	F, M	F, F, F, F, F, M, M, M
M, M	M	M, M, M	M	M, M, M	M	
	F, M	F, F, M	F, F, F, M, M, M	F, F, F, M, M		M
M		F, F, F, F, M, M, M, M, M	F, F, F, M, M, M, M	F, F, F, F, M, M, M, M		F, F, F, F, F, F, M, M, M, M, M
F, M			M			
F, M, M	F, M, M	F, F, F	M	M, M	F, M	F, F, F, F, M, M, M, M
	M	M, M, M, M	M, M			
				M, M, M		
F, M, M	F, M	M, M, M, M, M		F, F, M, M, M	M, M	M, M, M
M		F, M, M	F, F, M, M, M			
M		M, M, M, M		M, M		
M		M, M, M	M	M, M		
M		M				
	F, M					
M	M	M, M, M, M			M	
M, M			M	M, M, M, M, M		
M					M	
	F		F, F, F, F	F, F, F, F	F, M	F, F, F, F, F, F
M	F, M	F	F, F, F, F	M		
F	F, M	F	F, F, F, F		F	
	F					
	F, M, M	F	F, F, F, F	F, F, F, M		
F, M	F	F, F				
			F, F, F, F	F, F, M	M	F, F, F, F, F, F, M, M, M, M, M
F, M, M		F, F, F, F	F, F, F, F	F, M	M	
F			F, F, F, F			
F		F	F, F, F, F	F, F, F, M	F	
			F, F, F, F			
F, M						
F	M	F, F	F, F, F, F	F, F		
	F	F, F, F	F, F, F, F		F	
M, M	F		F, F, F, F			
	F, M		F, F, F, F	F	F	
			F, F, F, F			
M, M		M, M, M	M, M	M, M, M, M, M, M, M		M, M, M, M, M
M, M		M				
M						
M	F, M			M		
M	M, M	M, M				
			F, F, F, F			
M	F, M	M, M	F, F, F, F, M, M			
	F		F, F, F, F, M, M			
M, M	F	F, F, F, M	F, F, F, F	F, F, F, F, M, M, M	M	
	F		F, F, F, F		F	F, F, F, F, F, F
			F, F, F, F			
M	F, M	F	F, F, F, F	M		
		F, F	M	M		
	F, M, M	M, M		M		
M, M		F, F, F	F, F, F, M			
M, M			M	M, M, M		
M						
M, M			F			F, F
F	F, M		F, F, F, F			
	F, M, M		M			
		F	F, F, F			
M		F, F	F, F, F, F			
			F, F, F			
			F, F, F, F	F, F	M	
	F	F, F	F, F, F, F			
M			F, F, F, F	F, F		

	KROB 1765-1785	WISMER 1798-1818	KNAB 1818-1829	HOWSER 1827-1833	MYERS 1827-1845	ALBRECHT 1831-1840	J. BOMBERGER 1832-1861
Leather lines—pair; halter					M		M
Grubbing hoe					M, M, M		M, M
Wedges					M, M, M		
Work fork					M, M, M		M
Leather collar, traces					M, M, M		
Shovel, spade					M	F, F, F	F, F, M
Pitch fork					M		M, M
Woodenware: tubs, buckets, butter churn, mold						F, F	F, F, F
Porcelain dishes						F, F, F	
Eating knives and spoons						F, F, F	F
Fire tongs and shovel						F, F, F	F, F
Coffee mill						F, F, F	F
Iron pots w/ lids						F, F, F	F
Cake plate						F, F, F	
Corner cupboard						F, F, F	
Table: drop-leaf, extension						F, F, F	
Bed quilt (& accessories)						F, F, F	
Iron spoon and flesh fork						F, F, F	F, F
Pan: fry, dish, w/ legs, skillet						F, F	F
Broach						F	
Flat iron, sad iron						F	F
Garden hoe, rake						F	F
Oven peel							F, F, F
Wash machine							F, F, F
Bellows							F
Dough scraper							F
Soap stand, dish							F
Watering can							F
Candle mold							F
Cow chain							F, F, M
Oats							F, M
Eating forks							F
Flour chest or box							F, F, F
Brush: shoe, clothes, wall scrub, stove, dust, hair							F
Scale, spring balance							F
Rolling pin							F, F, F
Salt box							F, F
Copper kettle							F, F
Clothes press							F
Sled							F
Curry comb							M, M
Writing book							M
Oxen							M, M
Grindstone, grinding wheel							M, M
Grain cradle							M
Windmill							M
Carpet, tacks, hammer							F, F
Fanning mill							
Blacksmith work							
Carpenter work							
Umbrella							
Lantern, glass lantern							
Flax hackle							
Flax brake							
Clover seed							
Hay stool							
Apple mill							
Hay							
Potatoes							
Mason tools							
Land							
Rope maker							
Planing bench							
Sausage grinder & stuffer							
Small table, stand							
Table cloth, towels							
Glasses, glassware							
Accordian							
Chickens							
Wash board							
Copper ladle and dipper							
Slaw cutter							
Milk closet							

Pennsylvania-German red oak, cherry and walnut flax brake 27" h. x 48" l. x 18" d. Courtesy of the Philadelphia Museum of Art, gift of Mrs. William D. Frishmuth. Accession number '02-289.

Lancaster County Pennsylvania-German black walnut armchair upholstered in leather 47" h. x 22 1/8" w. x 18 1/4" d. Courtesy of The Henry Francis du Pont Winterthur Museum. Accession number 58.65.

GEHMAN 1835-1847	LEIBY 1855-1884	C.BOMBERGER 1860-1909	ZIMMERMAN 1862-1881	BURKHOLDER 1880-1902	DERSTEIN 1883-1888	KAUFMAN 1901-1945
M	F, M					
M, M	M			M		
M, M			F, F, F, F		M	
M, M	F	F	F, F, F, F	F, F		
F	F, M, M	F, F, F, F	F, F, F, F			
M, M	F, M		F, F, F, F	F	F	
	M, M					
	F		F, F, F			
M			F, F, F, F			
M						
M	F	F				
			F, F, F, F			
		F, F	F, F, F, F			
	F		F			
	F, M		F, F, F, F	F		
	F		F, F, F, F			
			F, F, F, F	F		
			F, F			
		F, F				
			F, F, F, F			
		F	F, F, F, F			
			F, F, F			
			F, F, F, F			
M, M	M, M			M		
M, M		M, M, M				M
M, M	F		F, F, F, F, M			
	F		F, F, F, F			
			F, F, F, F			
			F, F, F, F			
	F, M		F			
F		F, F	F, F, F, F	F, F		
		F				
M	M					
M						
M, M						
M, M	M					
M				M		
	F, M	F, F, F	F, F, F, F	F	F, M	
M						
M						
M						
M	F, M					
M			F, F, F, F			
M						
M, M						
M, M		M		M, M		
M, M						
M, M						
M, M						
M, M		F	F, M	F, F, F, F, M		
M						
F, M, M			M, M			
M						
M						
M						
	F, M		F, F, F, F			F, F, F, F, F, F
	F, M		F, F, F, F, M, M	M		
	F		F, F, F, F			
	F, M					
	F	F, F, F, M	F, F, F, M, M	F, F, F, M, M	F	F, F, F, F, F, F, M, M, M, M
	F, M		F, F, F			
	F					
	F		F, F			
	F		F, F, F			

	KROB 1765-1785	WISMER 1798-1818	KNAB 1818-1829	HOWSER 1827-1833	MYERS 1827-1845	ALBRECHT 1831-1840	J.BOMBER(1832-186
Sink (w/ 4 drawers)							
Bench							
Patty pans							
Lard, lard can							
Broom, broom corn							
Hatmaking lessons							
Silk							
Hats							
Quilting frame and screws							
Blacksmith tools							
Planes, handsaw							
Scythe							
Draw knife							
Kettle hanger, pot rack							
Spice box							
Geese							
Closet							
Wedding dress or suit							
Sideboard (w/ glass)							
Flour barrel, flour chest							
Crocks							
Store bill, sundries							
Queensware							
Threshing machine							
Buggy							
Cultivator							
Reaper and mower							
Sleigh							
Carriage							
Sewing machine							
Separator							
Traveling expenses							
Bookcase							
Corn planter							
Grain fan							
Corn sheller							
Window shades and fixtures							
Sewing table							
Meat saw							
Snuffer							
Comforts							
Doubletree							
Wood for ...							
Binder							
Grain drill							
Corn marker							
Wash stand							
Round table							
Coffee can, box							
Pick							
Shed at Franconia Meeting							
Incubator							
Boarding/washing							
Scissor, shears							
Tallow candles							
Match safe							
Coal bucket & shovel							
Salts and peppers							
Chamber set							
Granite dishes							
Curtains							
Cook stove, range							
Carving knife & fork							
Sofa							
Settee							
Wood chest							
Nurse chair, rocker							
Clothes pins							
Knitting needles							
Waffle iron							
Pie wheel							
Spittoon							
Hand bell							
Cord, ball twine							
Shroats							

Vehicles, most frequently wagons, and later—sleighs and carriages, appeared in male *aussteirs*. This example was made by John Gutelius and Son c. 1905 in Mifflinburg, Union County. Courtesy of David W. Reed.

GEHMAN 1835-1847	LEIBY 1855-1884	C.BOMBERGER 1860-1909	ZIMMERMAN 1862-1881	BURKHOLDER 1880-1902	DERSTEIN 1883-1888	KAUFMAN 1901-1945
	F		F, F, F, F			
M	F, M, M		F, F, F, F			
	F, M		F			
	F		F, F, F	F, M, M, M		
	F, M		F, M, M			
	F					
	F					
	F					
	F					
	M					
	M, M					
M	M	M				
	M					
	M		F, F, F			
	M		F, F			
	M					
	M					
		F, F, F, F, M, M, M				
		F	F, F, F, F			
		F, F	F, F, F, F			
		F, F	F, F, F, F	F, F, M, M, M		
		F, F, F, M	F, F, F, F, M	F, F, M		
		F, F, F	F, F, F, F	F, F	F	
		M		M		
		M, M, M, M, M		M		
		M		M		
		M, M, M		M		
		M, M, M			M, M	
		F				
		F	F, F, F, F		F	
		M				F
		M, M, M, M				
		M				
		M				
		M				
		M				
			F, F, F			
M			F, F, F			
			F, F, F, F			
			F, F, F, F	F		
				M, M		
				M, M, M		
				M		
				M		
				M		
			F, F, F, F		F	
					F	
			F, F, F, F		F	
					M	
					F, M, M	
						F
			M			
			F, F, F			
			F, F			
			F, F, F			
			F, F, F, F			
			F, F			
			F, F, F			
			F			
			F			
			F, F, F, F			
			F, F, F			
			F			
			F			
			F, F, F			
			F, F, F			
			F, F			
			F			
			F			
			F, F, F			
			F, F, F, F			
			F, F			
			F, F			

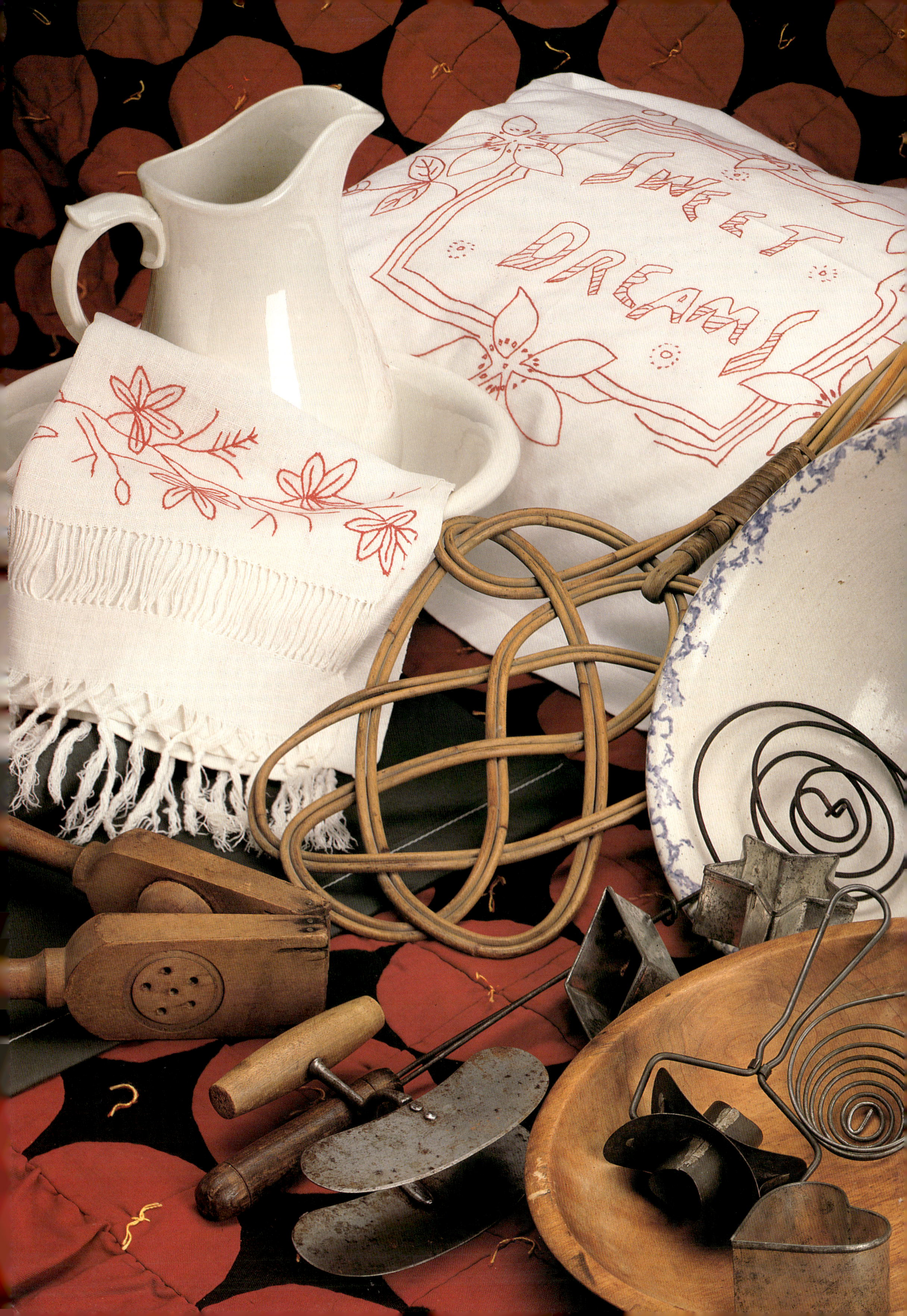
SWEET
DREAMS

was an important matter to him. He recorded the *aussteier* settlements for his twelve children starting in the 1880s and running through to 1902 when his last child Daniel, Jr. was preparing for marriage. A farmer living in Earl Township, Lancaster County, the senior Burkholder provided essentially the same items (as determined by his child's sex): the girls all received a bureau, a bedstead and a chest; the boys a desk, all but one a bed and bedstead, and the first four of seven—a saddle and bridle—goods that had typically been set aside for young Pennsylvania Germans for decades.

In Daniel's book the children's "advancements" as they were called, are listed in the order of their birth and this was almost synonymous with the sequence of marriage. The exceptions were Fannie and Lydia who both married earlier than some older siblings while Mary married much later. Only the first child, Martha, did not marry having died in a snowstorm, but her "advancement" nonetheless is the first recorded. Ten of the children got $371 of goods with cash sometimes being added to make one's amount the same; two received $354 and $361 each.

Late nineteenth-century "outfittings" were greatly changed in appearance. Bedding and other household textiles, some still homemade, reflected new ideas of fashion such as this Turkey red embroidered outline work, which was heavily promoted in the ladies' periodicals. Quilts ranged from impractical silk and velvet "Crazy" designs to the more traditional heavy comforts or haps. Ironstone, spatterware and cobalt blue decorated stoneware replaced earlier slip-decorated red earthenware. Iron and tinware were as likely to have been mass-manufactured and store-bought as to have been made by a local blacksmith or tinsmith. Tools were no longer for hearth cooking but for use on or in a cast-iron cookstove as seen in the wire stovetop toaster. Carpets and their carpetbeaters were entirely new listings. Collection of the Heiss House of the Mifflinburg Buggy Museum.

Amos B. Hoover, a grandson of Daniel Burkholder, writes: "Daniel Burkholder (b. 1833, d. 1915) was from a strong Mennonite family. He was totally given to agriculture and he had the ability to craft his own tools and implements used on his farms northwest of Martinsdale in Earl Township, Lancaster County. In 1863 he was chosen as a deacon which office he served faithfully for over 50 years. He was a craftsman in smithing and woodworking and excellent as a businessman and his advice was sought by the church and community [letter to author, July 13, 1989]."

ABRAHAM F. DERSTEIN SR'S ACCOUNT BOOK

The most recent Pennsylvania *aussteier* book seen was that of Abraham Derstein, a farmer who lived in Franconia Township, Montgomery County, from 1836 to 1912. His accounts were recorded for all of his three children and he starts each page as "An account of merchandise bought for . . . . by Abraham F. Derstein Sr. to be deducted from . . . . inheritance." Although these are late entries (1883 to 1888) they are not unlike dowry entries in other account books which were made a full century earlier, except for those for a sewing machine, carpet, sleigh, rocker, and a shed at the Meeting.

MOSES A. KAUFMAN'S ACCOUNT BOOK

Moses A. Kaufman's parents moved from Somerset County, Pennsylvania to Walnut Creek Township in Holmes County, Ohio prior to his birth in 1857. He was an Old Order Amish man, whose accounts for his twelve children are the most recent we studied. They reflect both the long-standing outfittings for Pennsylvania-German males and females and are not unlike today's *aussteier* as practiced among some of Pennsylvania's plain sects.

Moses's six girls were each given a chest of drawers, three of which have been located. Sarahann (b. November 3, 1881 and married January 11, 1906) was also given one cow $35.00, fourteen chickens $5.60, a bureau and stand $18.50, a stove $25.00, kitchen and stove furniture $9.00, a bed and bedding $15.00, a cupboard $18.00 and the remainder in cash, all totalling $1259.80. Her bureau or chest of drawers has been located. It is dated "1901" as is her next sister's, Maryanne (b. 1884 and married 1911). The third chest found was Katie's (who married last in 1942) but it is not dated.

Other items that were sex-linked were the desk/secretary for all the males as well as a horse. Moses's daughters as well as his sons received a bed and bedding, cows, hogs, chickens and cash but only the girls got the bureau and stand, a stove, kitchen furniture, and cupboards. With the exception of one child, all their accounts were equal. When they got chickens there were always fourteen.

Moses Kaufman's last son, Moses, had the briefest account—just cash and a "secontary" which is still in the family—a golden oak secretary with glazed doors, dropleaf writing surface, and drawers. One of his cash entries ($353) was for a horse and buggy—a traditional gift for a sixteen-year-old Amish male.

Initialed and Dated Objects

The largest groupings in the dowry or *aussteier* were household goods as well as garden tools for women; some household goods, farm tools and vehicles for men. Over time these articles—whether furniture or kitchen tools—reflected both cultural and technological changes in our society. There were numerous instances where Pennsylvania Germans adopted furniture forms or adapted construction methods used earlier by their English neighbors and vice versa. (See Benno Forman's article, "German Influences in Pennsylvania Furniture," *Arts of the Pennsylvania Germans*, New York: W.W. Norton, 1983, for an in-depth discussion of cultural transfers.)

However, some forms were abandoned, for instance the Germanic wardrobe or clothes press (*kleiderschrank*) and the blanket chest (*kist*). The wardrobe succumbed early while the blanket chest persisted as a traditional piece for some families well past 1850. Many Pennsylvania Germans replaced their wardrobes and blanket chests with the "English" chest of drawers and desk in the nineteenth century. Germanic built-in furniture such as benches and cupboards gave way to moveable pieces by the second half of the eighteenth century; their open kitchen dressers evolved into cupboards with doors. Corner cupboards and sideboards were added in the early and mid-nineteenth century respectively.

More Anglicized and prosperous Germanic families bought "English" doughtroughs and chairs as early as the 1740s. In the first third of the nineteenth century, they purchased tea tables, dropleaf tables, various stands as well as looking glasses or mirrors—all of which were added to the standard Germanic *aussteier*.

The charts (pp. 46, 54, 55, 64-69) show when these furnishings were first mentioned in the family account books that we analyzed. Earlier dates might be established when other account books are found, but there probably will not be major changes for already the consistency of these forms in the *aussteier* has been pronounced.

Some household furnishings collected by museums and individuals or retained by families are noteworthy for the number of inlaid, engraved, or punched initials and dates on their surfaces. Where provenance is established, dates usually are those of manufacture rather than commemorative in nature. The names and/or initials are usually those of the owner(s). When one compares the frequency with which some of these "initialed/dated" forms are or are not listed in family dowry accounts, one might be able to make the supposition as to which were dowry or *aussteier* goods. For example: blanket chests, desks, and wardrobes so marked could well be from dowry portions, while clocks are more problematic and spice boxes (popular in both cultural groups) do not appear to be because they were rarely given before or at time of marriage. When signed and dated one might best presume a post-marriage date.

In examining a group of Germanic wardrobes or clothes presses this form emerges as a pre- or close-to-marriage piece for males or females. They are mentioned specifically in the first section of the Clemens account book as being given to three of the nine daughters. The Philadelphia Museum of Art owns a walnut clothes press from Lancaster County with "17•PT•BR•75" executed in maple inlay below its cornice. Two others in that collection have a male's name and date: "GEORG/ANNO" and "HUBER/1779" in sulphur inlay on the wardrobe's black walnut doors (made in Warwick Township, Lancaster County, by Peter Noll and Christian Huber), while "17 MARTIN EISENHAUER 94" is painted below the cornice of a multi-colored pine and poplar piece (made in Greenwich Township, Berks County). This latter piece is related to another sponge-painted wardrobe (in a private collection) with "JACOB•17•92•BIEBER" also painted below its cornice.

Three related Lancaster County wardrobes all have matching pairs of male and female initials or surnames: "EMANUEL•HERR/FEB•D•17" and "MAG•HER/1768" inlaid in sulphur paste on the doors of one owned by Winterthur Museum (on right); "I.M. A.M. KAUFFMAN/1776" is on the second at the State Museum of Pennsylvania; "ABRAHAM ELIZABETH REIST MARCH 18 1776" is on the third in a private collection.

Another walnut clothes press (in a private collection), with "M•L/E•M•L/ 1•7•7•1" inlaid in sulphur paste on a central panel below the cornice, was made for Michael and Eva Magdalena Ley who lived in the Tulpehocken Manor located near Myerstown in Berks County. While a Berks County wal-

INITIALED AND DATED OBJECTS

Detail: Lancaster County Pennsylvania-German walnut wardrobe 76½" h. x 71" w. x 22" d. with maple inlay dated "1775". Courtesy of the Philadelphia Museum of Art, purchased by Special Museum Fund. Accession number '16-332.

Lancaster County Pennsylvania-German walnut wardrobe 89½" h. x 85¾" w. x 30⅝" d. with sulphur paste inlay dated "1768". Courtesy of The Henry Francis du Pont Winterthur Museum. Accession number 65.2262.

73

nut wardrobe, even more Germanic in form is inlaid in wood, above its doors, "DVAD/1781/HS." This now belongs to Winterthur Museum. It was listed in David Hottenstein's inventory in 1802 as a "cloath dresser," valued £5, 5 shillings. Like some of the others, it has the initials of a male recipient—David Hottenstein. The date "1781" predates the move by David and his bride Catherine to their new stone house in Maxatawny Township, Berks County in 1783. These examples fairly firmly establish that wardrobes were primarily, though not exclusively, a male *aussteier* furnishing or a piece made for a couple close-to-their-marriage date. The Clemens account book suggests that they were given to females as well.

Blanket chests (*kists*), sometimes mistakenly called "dower chests" (see p. 23), have long been associated with the *aussteier* or dowry and correctly so. They were not just female items although a greater number exist with females' names on them. Often the name is in the Germanic form indicating the recipient's feminine status as in the chest made for Sarah Schupp ("Schuppin") in 1798 (below). Other examples have male provenance either in the family's oral tradition (see cover and p. 13) or, in written form as in Jacob Dres's chest (on right): the chest has the painted declaration *Dise Kist Gehert Mir Jacob Dres 1791 JF*, or "This chest belongs to me Jacob Dres" and it is attributed to John Flory, a cabinetmaker in Rapho township, Lancaster County. Both chests are in the Philadelphia Museum of Art and are representative of hundreds of others held in both public and private collections.

In time, the Germanic wardrobe or clothes press was replaced by chests of drawers for young women and by desks for young men. These newer furniture forms are rarely found signed and dated except for case pieces made by Pennsylvania-German craftsmen in the Schwaben Creek area of Northumberland County. Jacob Maser's desk (see p. 76) is an example of this as are four bureaus—two of which were made for the Tryon sisters in 1829. (See Henry M. Reed's *Decorated Furniture of the Mahantongo Valley*, Lewisburg, PA.: Center Gallery, Bucknell University, 1987. Mr. Reed states, not surprisingly, that when the age of the recipients is known, they were usually fifteen to eighteen years old.)

A small furniture form that was made for both Pennsylvania Germans and English Quakers is the table chest or Bible box. A number of these have initials and sometimes dates such as one in the Philadelphia Museum's Titus C. Geesey Collection. It has inlaid in maple "S + 17 S + 69". Some of those made for Quaker recipients are now documented to have been made for single young women as a result of recent research by Lee Ellen Griffith ("The Line-and-Berry Inlaid Furniture of Eighteenth-Century Chester County, Pennsylvania," *Antiques*, May, 1989. pp. 1202-1211). Two Bible boxes are illustrated in her article, the one (see p. 77) is walnut and yellow poplar with locust and holly inlay including the initials "S T" for Sarah Thomas, a third-generation Welsh Quakeress, who married Joseph Walker in 1752. The other walnut box is inlaid in red cedar and holly with "S C" for Chester Countian Sarah Carpenter who married Michael Gregg in 1755. As Ms. Griffith noted, "More than half of the pieces

Pennsylvania-German painted poplar blanket chest 22½" h. x 47" w. x 22½" d. dated "1798". Courtesy of the Philadelphia Museum of Art, gift of Thomas Skelton Harrison. Accession number '13-111.

A HATCHING CHEST FOR GIRLS

IN Germany they have a pretty fashion when the stork comes down the chimney and brings a girl baby to make the house glad, to begin on her first birthday to form her trousseau. Her godmother gives the big, handsomely-carved hatching chest, and in this goes gradually the bed-linen, the napery and the silver that, as an industrious fraulein, she is to carry to her new home. The American mother is beginning to see the value of this custom, and the hatching chest now makes its appearance and is carefully filled. Grandmamma, wisely enough, begins a set of tablespoons, and when the little girl is twelve years old she will have a full dozen of then, each bearing her initials. From an adoring aunt will have come the teaspoons, from an uncle the forks, and from mamma the handsome napery. Now, these things cost a lot of money, but as they are given so gradually on birthdays, not one feels that they are any great expense. After the twelfth year come the bed-linen and some heavier pieces of silver or fine ones of china. Suppose she should never marry? O, but she will keep a home for herself and in it she will want to have her own belongings: or if she should sink into the position left vacant by mamma and the contents of the hatching chest should never be used, don't you think it will be a pleasure to her to give them to one for whose future there has not been so much care taken? American women are not, as a general thing, accumulative. Something is bought to-day, discarded to-morrow and forgotten at the end of the year. She who keeps things always has a stock from which she can be generous, and it is pleasant, even after death, to live in the memory of one's friends, even if the thought comes with the fragant tea out of the fat, silver teapot which has been yours, or the delicate-handled old-fashioned spoons from which the preserves are eaten, and to which you devoted so much thought in designing. Don't you remember Mary Washington leaving to her son George her best feather bed? That showed a thought for the future, and a looking after his comfort that is much to be commended. However, without thinking of what one will do about willing things, start a hatching chest for your small girl and conclude that she will use its contents in her own household.

Ladies Home Journal, April 1890, p. 23

studied in this survey are inlaid with an owner's initials, and many of them with a date as well. The initials often proved to be those of a woman before marriage. (In his will of 1727 Jonathan Ogden of Chester left his daughter 'one walknut [sic] Chest marked with the Two letters of her mother's name [Anna Robinson] before marriage')."

In her unpublished thesis, Line and Berry and Inlaid Furniture: A Regional Craft Tradition in Pennsylvania 1682-1790 (University of Pennsylvania, 1988), Ms. Griffith is more specific as to marked Chester County pieces with owners' initials and/or dates of manufacture: forty-five of those with dates have initials also. The initials on the pieces she researched indicated ownership—sometimes jointly for husband and wife, and often for single women. She notes that when marked for married couples the initials arrangement often appeared in the same configuration as on carved datestones and engraved silver of the period: the surname's initial appears somewhat above and between the husband's to the left and the wife's to the right.

Ms. Griffith concludes that dates on house capstones, ceramics, needlework including samplers, quilts, show towels, bed linens and pocketbooks, are generally those of manufacture and sometimes "fiat" or "fecit" (the Latin for "made" or "was made") is included. Ceramic inscriptions are probably the most explicit in this regard. Also, one furniture piece so marked is a William and Mary dressing table made in Pennsylvania and on its top is inscribed: "Anno/1724/Fiat", as cited by Lee Ellen Griffith.

Detail: Lancaster County Pennsylvania-German painted poplar and white pine blanket chest attributed to John Flory 25½" h. x 50" w. x 24" d. and dated "1791". Courtesy of the Philadelphia Museum of Art, Titus C. Geesey Collection. Accession number '58-110-1.

INITIALED AND DATED OBJECTS

In Pennsylvania-German male dowries, the desk replaced the blanket chest as the primary piece of furniture in the early nineteenth century. In the dowry listings reviewed, Peter Knabb of Oley, Berks County, was the first father to give his sons desks instead of the earlier chests (1818 to 1829). Others like Johan Bomberger, a Mennonite from Warwick Township, Lancaster County and Johan Gehman, a Mennonite from Upper Hanover Township, Montgomery County, did likewise. The desks that Bomberger and Gehman purchased for their sons were fairly expensive items at the time—$20 and $22 respectively (1835 to 1846). Later in the nineteenth and into the twentieth century, the tradition was even more prevalent. Daniel Burkholder, a Mennonite from Earl Township, Lancaster County, gave each of his seven sons a desk as did Moses Kaufman, an Amish man from Holmes County, Ohio. Women never received desks.

The desk pictured here, 49 1/8" h. x 39" w. x 19 3/4" d., of tulip wood was made for if not by Jacob Maser and is inscribed "JACOB 1834 MASER". That is the year he married Catherine Christ in the Schwaben Creek Valley of Northumberland County. Its colors and decoration are typical of other pieces made in this German Lutheran and Reformed settlement area and are colloquially called "Mahantongo" for the creek flowing between the Line and Hooflanders mountain ridges. Courtesy of the Henry Francis du Pont Winterthur Museum. Accession number 64.15.18.

An important reason for initialing a furniture piece might well have been for ownership identification purposes, much in the same way numerous textiles were marked and sometimes numbered—whether grainbags or pillowcases. Subsequent bequests of such marked pieces can illustrate kinship ties or the relationship of namesakes, which is an important reason to keep objects according to Lancaster Amish informants we interviewed.

Ms. Griffith gives several examples of namesake or kinship giving in her thesis which drew primarily upon early Chester County inventories and wills. For example, Thomas Garrat's estate (1748) included the dowry textiles of his wife Rebecca Sykes (m.1744, d.1745) such as "Table Linnen Marked RS," as well as "feather Bed & furniture Marked RS, 6 Teaspoons & Tongs marked R.S." Childless by her, Thomas Garrat left those articles to Rebecca's sisters. Also, Mary Smedley in her will of 1772 gave "a Pewter Dish marked IS which was his Mother's" to son-in-law Joshua Smedley, while James Trimble left to his daughter, Mary Dowing, one

INITIALED AND DATED OBJECTS

Chester County English Quaker table chest of walnut and yellow poplar inlaid in locust and holly 8³/₈" h. x 20½" w. x 5⅛" d., c. 1750-1752. Courtesy of the Henry Francis du Pont Winterthur Museum. Accession number 58.552.

of seven children, "The little walnut Table Marked with the letters MP" [probably made for her mother Mary Palmer]. Finally, Ms. Griffith notes that in the Reifsnyder auction catalog (1929) is mentioned an inlaid Bible box and matching chest of drawers: "The above was part of the wedding dowry furniture of Sarah Smedley in 1737 and 'descended to a Sarah in each of several generations' before its purchase by Mr. Reifsnyder from Mrs. Henry M. Jones, the last of them."

Chester County wills cited by Ms. Griffith show husbands giving back marriage portions. George Jackson in 1805 returned to his widow those things brought by her: "two feather Beds and furniture $44.00, Case of Drawers Marked DI $6.00, all the Pewter and Teaware $7.00, Six Silver teaspoons & Brass kettle $5.50, and three Chairs her choice $.75.," while George Gilpin, Sarah Sharpless' second husband, in 1773 left his wife "One Case of Drawers Markt S:S: along with the feather Bed & furniture I had with her, Six Blue painted Chairs & One Arm [Chair], my old Black mare, one Best Cow" and cash. These wills not only show that certain furniture pieces were often "mark'd" for the original female recipient; they also show these pieces within the context of other dowry items.

*S*ome furniture with initials and dates should not be associated with *aussteier* or dowry, however. For example, Quaker spice boxes were not dowry pieces. Only one of those inlaid with initials and dates corresponds to a marriage date (see p. 77) and it happens to be a revival piece. All the others for which Ms. Griffith has found genealogical provenance have dates of manufacture that are several years after the owners' wedding. For example, one spice box (illustrated in her article) was "P/GM/1744" in holly and cherry inlay and this represents George and Margaret Passmore of London Grove, Chester County who married in 1742. Other examples of spice boxes which are signed, dated, and made after the marriage appear in Ms. Griffith's book, *The Pennsylvania Spice Box* (West Chester, PA.: Chester County Historical Society, 1986).

Spice boxes or chests were generally a piece of furniture acquired after a couple's marriage. This example, 21¼" h. x 15" w. x 11¼" d., is an exception. It was made in Chester County for Mary Hutton at the time of her marriage to Nicholas Hurford and has a cherry and maple inlay in its walnut body commemorating this: "MH/1788". According to Lee Ellen Griffith in her book, *The Pennsylvania Spice Box* (West Chester, PA: Chester County Historical Society 1986), it is the only one of those six personalized spice boxes she found that was made at the time of marriage (at the New Garden Quaker Meeting in 1788). Ms. Griffith said it was a *revival* piece inspired by the similar inlaid spice box made for Mary's uncle and aunt, Thomas and Elizabeth Hutton in 1744. Courtesy of the Chester County Historical Society, West Chester, PA. Photo: George J. Fistrovich. Accession number 56/77F SP85.

77

Likewise, a settle made by Quaker cabinetmaker Abraham Darlington for his sister and her husband is initialed and dated "P/IE" and "1758" on its crest rail. It is an "after marriage" piece confirmed by the fact that the owners, Elizabeth and Isaac Pyle were married in 1750. In fact, neither settles or settees were ever listed in *aussteiers* and dowries. The only seating noted in accounts are armchairs, sets of chairs, or rocking chairs and they are not found marked.

Small woodenware such as butterprints are sometimes seen with carved initials and dates. Three examples are in the Titus Geesey Collection in the Philadelphia Museum of Art. One is marked "CY 1818"; another has carved into its back, "C.G. Weiss 1843 C.G.W."; the third is marked "SR". They may or may not be *aussteier* items.

After furniture, textiles were both the most highly valued and most abundant articles in young peoples' "outfittings." Certain textiles often had names or initials and sometimes dates sewn on them, bedding in particular. Numerous homespun sheets and pillowcases are found with their owners' initials and dates. They can represent male or female dowry since both were given bedding in their *aussteiers*. Quilts of both the Pennsylvania-German and English cultural groups frequently have single names and initials applied, stamped, or sewn on their tops or linings. Many of those names are those of the recipients who were unmarried when their quilt was made. Hundreds of examples of such named and/or dated quilts made for young males and females have been and continue to be sewn and put away for setting up one's household. This is probably the single largest body of extant "signed" or "marked" dowry objects, followed by blanket chests.

Another textile often executed before marriage and then stored away was the Pennsylvania-German decorated door panel, commonly called "show towel." Ellen Gehret's book *This is The Way I Pass My Time* (Birdsboro, PA.: The Pennsylvania German Society, 1985) documented hundreds of such towels. When she was able to trace the genealogy of the maker, it became clear that most were made by or for single young women before their marriage date.

Other textiles sometimes stamped with initials or name along with a date are the grainbags which were traditionally given to the males. A bag stamped "Samuel Meyer 1828 4" is one of two extant from a traditional set of six, twelve, or twenty-four, (see cover).

Some metal *aussteier* or dowry objects are marked for the recipient like these porringers (p. 81) marked the year of and year after David Townsend's marriage in Chester County. Another porringer in the same collection is marked "EH" for Elizabeth Hibberd who later married Chester countian Benjamin Bonsall. Pewter, along with earthenware, was the tableware most often mentioned in the eighteenth-century family dowry accounts.

Ironware, both forged, cast and later stamped, was always part of the female's kitchenware in her dowry. Items such as these illustrate just a small selection of what was given in an early period: hearth griddles (the one in upper left is marked "1765" on its strap handle), the basic utensil set of skimmer, ladle, flesh fork, and spatula, also tasters and spoons—some with copper or brass bowls, a handpress, a set of quilting screws or clamps, a Betty lamp and a dough scraper. Courtesy of William and Jeannette Lasansky, except inlaid "1839" fork, courtesy of Robert and Shirley Kuster.

Some forged iron kitchen utensils might have a stamped maker's mark or engraved owner's initials or name. Some pieces are dated. This unusual double-ended utensil has both an incuse stamp "WERMAN" as well as "•1785/•M•D•M•" engraved at the fork's end. Kitchen forks were mentioned in female accounts as were ladles and skimmers, but spatulas or cake turners are not although many exist and as part of such *sets*.

It is felt by this researcher that stamped names, struck with a single strike, were those of the maker while engraved or punched names or initials were those of the recipient. Also, that since females are well documented to have received these utensils as part of their outfitting or dowry, recipient names or initials therefore are most likely females'. Dates are often inscribed on such pieces. This utensil measures 21³⁄₈" l. x 3³⁄₄" w. Courtesy of Mr. and Mrs. Richard Flanders Smith.

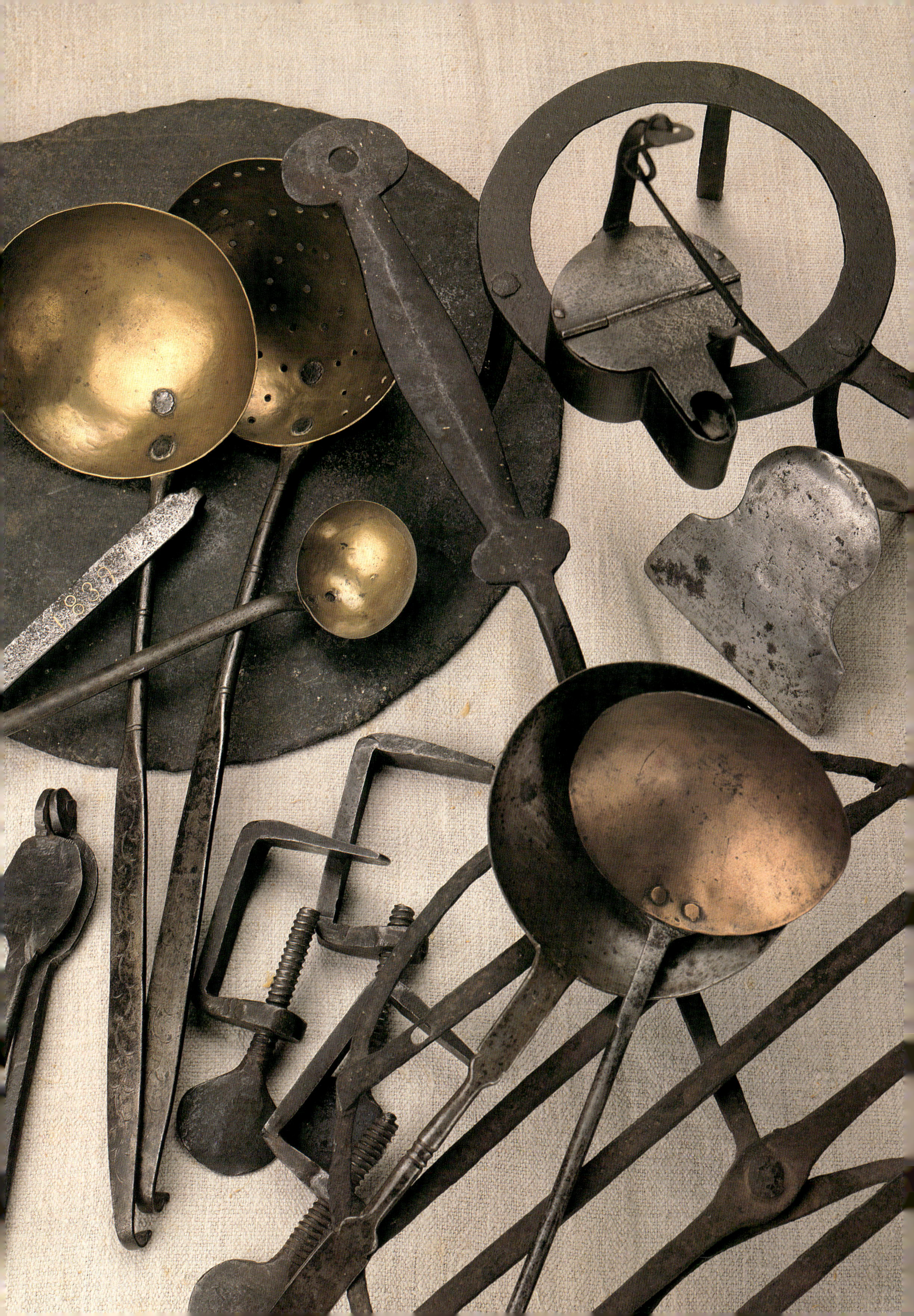

INITIALED AND DATED OBJECTS

Tinware, introduced as the major metalware in the nineteenth century, also is sometimes marked—almost exclusively on fancy punched tin coffeepots. Willoughby Shade (b.1820 and working in Marlborough and Towamensin townships, Montgomery County at least from 1842 to 1850 and in Philadelphia from 1864 to 1866); John B. Ketterer (b.1796 and working in Bucks County from before 1850 and to 1864) and Daniel Gilbert (working in Pottsgrove Township, Berks County at least around the 1830s) were three master tinsmiths who made such "marked" punch-decorated crookedneck coffeepots. Willoughby Shade not only elaborately punched motifs (below) but also the names of some recipients: a father, Jacob Rhoades, his wife Sarah Ann and their oldest daughter, Lucy Ann; also for a Catharenah Moyer. The coffeepots for two of the Rhoades (father and daughter) are also dated "January 10, 1845". The date of manufacture would have been around Lucy Ann Rhoades's fifteenth birthday. Three of five known Ketterer coffeepots, marked with initials or initials and a date, have initials of married couples. Whether the dates of their manufacture coincide with dates of marriage or well after is not known.

It is on ironware, however, particularly on some pieces from the housewife's basic set of utensils—skimmer, ladle, flesh fork, taster, and spatula—that one finds the greatest frequency of recipient initials and names; sometimes dates as well. From *aussteier* accounts it is known that women received these handforged utensils as part of their marriage portion from at least the 1740s through the mid-nineteenth century when mass-manufactured examples would have become readily available. A number of the iron utensils of that period, collected by Henry Francis DuPont, have engraved or inlaid initials or names. So it is in other major collections. Now separated from family provenance these pieces can only be assumed to have often been made by a local blacksmith for a young girl soon to be married or just married. Such is known to be the case with a set of forged iron utensils with brass inlay in a private collection: the set was made for Johanna "Hanna" Ditzler (b.1806, d.1891) who married Wilhelm Schmidt in Upper Northumberland County in the fall of 1832. Three of the remaining pieces—the fork, taster, and spatula—are inlaid in brass "HS 1832".

Another iron object that was frequently punched with dates and initials are flax hatchels which appeared in only one male *aussteier*. Most hatchels exhibit elaborate punched decoration and many are dated from the eighteenth century. One seen recently in an Amish household has "JP Reading 1801" on both sides in script. Another, at Winterthur Museum, is punched "MICHAEL ZIMMERMAN/1749". Whether the date of manufacture of these items coincides with the accumulation of a male or female's *aussteier* is conjecture because of lack of manuscript documentation. The dated objects themselves are numerous.

Lighting devices, in particular Betty lamps, were made by blacksmiths, anonymous as well as known: Peter Derr, the Schmidts, and the Sebastians who signed and often dated them in addition to their pie crimpers, spatulas and dough scrapers. All were items in a female's outfitting. The Betty lamp (on right) was made by John Long (b.c.1787) of Rapho Township, Lancaster County. It is inscribed on the hinged brass lid "Nancy Musser/made by me J. Long/1846." Another is similarly inscribed "Fanny M. Erisman/Manufactured By/ John Long/1848." Fanny Erisman is known to have married John Becker sometime after that date so it was most likely another example of a dowry or *aussteier* item.

Pennsylvania-German poplar butter print 12¼" h. x 11" w. x 2⅝" d. Courtesy of the Philadelphia Museum of Art, gift of Miss Frances Lichten. Accession number '60-91-3.

Montgomery County punched plain tin coffeepot by Willoughby Shade 11⅞" h. x 5⅞" d. and dated "1845". Courtesy of Mr. and Mrs. Richard Flanders Smith.

Finally, with locally-produced ceramics—mainly red earthenwares—there are quite a number of surviving examples with incised sayings, initials and/or dates. One might ask, "Were these 'marked' pieces always considered special or 'precious,' accumulated and kept apart on a mantel or in a corner cupboard much as the Amish do today with their favorite china or glass pieces?"

It is interesting to speculate on the possible reasons for the dating and initialing of some pieces rather the others. With certain metalware, textile and furniture forms, a link between dates of manufacture and dates of marriage cannot be considered insignificant. Family tradition and genealogical research has provided us with clues and answers some of the time.

*W*hile much of the dowry or *aussteier* was and is provided by parents for children, some items were made by the children for themselves. This is often the case with the females in many cultures and may be the reason why many people think of dowry as exclusively "female" when it is not. A rare example of a male making a dowry article for himself was the comb case made by Andrew E. Baer of Somerset County (p. 82). The articles made by women for their marriage portions were and are still exclusively textiles: functional bedding, table linens and clothing as well as purely decorative pieces. These textiles have traditionally been stored in chests of some sort. In the twentieth century these chests were labeled as the "dowry," "dower" (incorrect usage of word, see p. 23), or "hope chest."

A flax hatchel was specifically mentioned in only one dowry listing: a male's in the early nineteenth century. Many hatchels, as shown in this example, have fancy decorative punched work in their sheet iron. Often there are initials and dates which may commemorate the date of a male or female recipient's gift. This one is dated "1792". It measures 4³⁄₄" h. x 3⁷⁄₈" w. x 12¹⁄₄" l. Courtesy of William and Jeannette Lasansky.

Lighting devices were sometimes listed in female dowry outfittings but more often than not were lumped together with other things under the headings of "blacksmith work," "ironware," or "tinware." However, Jacob Clemens specifically listed an iron light for his daughter Magreda in 1773, and Michael Albrecht gave his three daughters oil lights as well as candleholders in the 1830s. Several brass and iron Betty (possibly a corruption of the German *besser* for better) lamps, are known to have been made by locksmith John Long (b. c. 1787) Rapho Township, Lancaster County. This one was made in 1846 for Nancy Musser and measures 9¹⁄₂" h. x 7³⁄₄" w. Detail. Courtesy of the Philadelphia Museum of Art, Titus C. Geesey Collection. Accession number '58-110-52.

Pewterware is sometimes listed generically in eighteenth-century family dowry accounts. These pewter porringers, 7" l. x 5¹⁄₄" w. x 2" h., are inscribed "David/Townsend/1816"and "1817" for Chester Countian David Townsend. Courtesy of the Chester County Historical Society, West Chester, PA. Photo by George J. Fistrovich. Accession numer 1983. 24.1, .2.

"We no longer make linen; but I have heard of one Dutch [Pennsylvania-German] girl who had a good supply of domestic linen made into shirts and trousers for the future spouse whose 'fair proportions' she had not yet seen," recorded Phebe Earle Gibbons in 1882 in her book *Pennsylvania Dutch and Other Essays*. Another chronicler of old ways remarked in his talk to the Pennsylvania German Society in October 1902: "While I have the same good woman in mind; perhaps I may interject that she is keeping alive another nearly lost art in Pennsylvania-Germany. She is proud of the fact that she has spun the thread for a complete outfit of bedlinen for each of her marriageable daughters. What a dower [dowry] it is!" (*The Pennsylvania German Society, Proceedings and Addresses* Vol. XIII, Published by Society 1904)

By the early twentieth century the concept of the dowry chest and the making of quilts for such a chest was part of the general public's "colonial revival" mentality. Many, whose families had neither old family quilts nor the heirloom piece to put them in, got caught up in the rage. Others, like Pennsylvania-German rural farm women, had never stopped being part of that tradition.

Nancy Roan and Ellen Gehret in their interviews with women in the Goschenhoppen Region of Montgomery, Lehigh, Bucks, and Berks counties recorded the dowry quilt-making traditions of some. A few remembered making their own like Elsie Rosenberger, b. 1901 near Quakertown, Bucks County: "When we got married Homer got the comforts and five quilts. And I had made two comforts and Mamma gave me one, and I made some quilts." But most recalled these

Family tradition has been that Andrew Baer made this oak comb case, 9¼" h. x 7¼" w., and a related match holder in anticipation of his impending marriage to Mary Belle Yutzy in October 1894. They were prized as being among the couple's first furnishings. Courtesy of Jane and John H. Ziegler.

Pennsylvania-German sgraffito red earthenware plates made by George Hübener of Upper Hanover Township, Montgomery County. On the left: (detail) the German around the rim translates to "1786 G. H From earth with sense the potter makes everything. Cadarina Raeder, her dish", 2⅛" h. x 12½" d., Accession number '00-21; on the right: (detail) the German inscription around the rim translates to "The dish is made of earth when it breaks the potter laughs. Therefore take care of it. Mathalena Jung, her dish. Painting flowers is common but giving it an odor is given to God alone. 1789", 2¼" h. x 12½" d. Courtesy of the Philadelphia Museum of Art, gifts of John T. Morris. Accession number '96-55.

Earthenware was listed in the earliest Pennsylvania female dowries. Most surviving earthenware is unmarked by either the maker or with the recipient's initials or names. Some rare pieces have initials and dates such as are on this glazed sugar bowl, 4¾" d. x 9⅛" h. (subsequently covered with a matte blue paint by its Amish owner). It was probably made by Joel "Potter" Zook for his sister Magdalena. The piece has written in slip, "MZ 1827 AP", for Abraham Z. Peachy (b. 1799, d. 1844) and Magdalena Zook (b. 1809, d. 1865) who married that year and lived in Union Township, Mifflin County in the area now known as Mechanicsville. Courtesy of Forest R. Kauffman.

bedcoverings as being made *for* a girl often by a mother or grandmother, rather than by the young girl herself. This corroborates what the Plain sects are doing now. As Katie Mininger Oelschlager recalled about her grandmother, Katie Lewis Willouer of Franconia Township, Montgomery County: "Grandmother made *Rising Sun* for all her namesakes. That date and everything is on them"; also Grace Keim John remembered of her grandmother, Amanda Nagel Erb of Sassamansville, Douglas Township, Montgomery County: "Her favorite was *The Double Irish Chain*. That's what she did for each one of the grandchildren. She made them all the same. In her family everyone got exactly the same thing. They never played any favorites." (*Just a Quilt or Juscht en Deppich*, Green Lane, PA, Goschenhoppen Historians, 1984, p. 23)

As mentioned earlier, the decorated door towel was frequently done by single young women—presumably to be stored away for use later on in their own households (on right). This textile tradition was carefully researched by Ellen Gehret who wrote *This Is The Way I Pass My Time*. These towels were often decorated with counted cross-stitch designs, initials or names, and dates as well as drawn work. They were traditionally hung first on the back of the *schtubb* or stove-room door in many Pennsylvania-German homes and later on the upstairs' bedroom door. They appear to have been made primarily by Franconia and Lancaster Conference Mennonites, Schwenkfelders, and much less frequently by members of the Lutheran and Reformed, the United Brethren, the Evangelicals or the Church of God (Gehret, p. 4). As Ellen Gehret points out: "This folk artifact was almost exclusively the work of adolescent women—those few towels with men's names no doubt the gift of brides and sisters—and that while there were a few professional seamstresses who made towels to order, most were done by amateurs, in the best sense of that word." (Gehret, p. 5) These were not done, she notes, outside of a small portion of the Pennsylvania-German community reaching the height of their popularity between 1820 and 1850 with some Amish women executing them as late as 1948. Most young women did not make more than one for themselves (Gehret, pp. 8, 9). Many have the young girl's name with the feminine suffix "-in." The dates on the towels are those of the date of manufacture. Sometimes that date corresponds to the date of marriage, as in the case of Rebecca Gerhart (Gehret, p. 172).

Most of the fabric on which designs were executed was made by male professional weavers before the advent of mass-manufactured goods. Women sometimes wove, but not the bulk of the textiles needed to set up and maintain an active household. They were involved primarily in the initial processing of flax or wool and in spinning; the fiber was usually woven elsewhere. Upon receipt of the finished yardage, women were again involved in the construction and the decoration of traditional textile items often destined to become part of their dowry.

Other textile items that were and still are made by young girls for *aussteier* are homemade pincushions (*schpella kisse*) in pieced work or needlepoint, and pillowcases and spreads decorated with embroidery. Family name registers are similarly decorated. Amish women, like Hannah Stoltzfoos, still pass down favorite needlework patterns within their families for use on such textiles.

Pennsylvania-German cotton towel with drawnwork and applied decorative needlework 23½" l. x 8¾" w. and dated "1815". Courtesy of the Henry Francis du Pont Winterthur Museum. Accession number 67.1266.

Bibliography

GENERAL

PRIMARY SOURCES

Abstracts of Wills. Berks County 1752-1825. Prepared by Jacob Martin and John Smith, 1898.

Abstracts of Wills. Chester County 1714-1825. Prepared by Jacob Martin, 1900.

Alcott, William A. *The Young Wife*. Boston: George W. Light, 1877.

The American Agriculturalist, 1848-1866.

The Bazar Book of Household. New York: Harper & Brothers, 1875.

Blacks Law Dictionary, 3rd ed. St. Paul, Minn.: West Publishing Co., 1891; 5th ed. St. Paul, Minn.: West Publishing Co., 1933.

The Century Dictionary & Encyclopedia, Vol. II 1889.

Charter to William Penn and Laws of the Province of Pennsylvania.

Endlich, Gustav A. and Louis Richards. *Rights and Liabilities of Married Women Concerning Property, Contracts and Torts Under the Common and Statute Law of Pennsylvania,* 1889.

Freeling, Arthur. *The Young Brides Book*. Wilson, 1845.

Godey's Lady's Magazine, 1830-1898.

How to Behave: A Pocket Manual of Republican Etiquette. New York: Fowler and Walls, 1866.

Indenture Collection. Thirty-seven eighteenth and nineteenth-century indentures. Bucks County Historical Society.

Messinger, C.S. and others. "Shall Our Daughters Have Dowries?" *The North American Review,* 1890 Vol. 151, pp. 747-769.

A New English Dictionary of Historical Principles Vol. III, Oxford, England, 1897.

Peterson's Magazine, 1842-1898.

The Plough, the Loom and the Anvil or *The American Farmer,* 1848-1857.

Statutes at Large of Pennsylvania 1682-1809, Vol. II-XVIII. State Printer of Pennsylvania: William Stanley Ray, 1899. Vendues. Lancaster County. 1820-1872. Lancaster County Historical Society.

Wright, Julia. *The Complete Home*. Philadelphia: J.C. McCurdy & Co., 1879.

SECONDARY SOURCES

Adam, Madame. "The Dowries of Women in France," *The North American Review,* 1891, Vol. 152, pp. 37-46.

Applebome, Peter. "Ancient Bequest Puts Some Profit in Wedding Vows," *New York Times,* September, 1987.

Arksey, Laura and Nancy Pries, Marcia Reed. *American Diaries Vol. 1 (1792-1844).* Detroit: Gale Research Co., 1983.

Benson, Mary Sumner. *Women in Eighteenth-Century America*. New York: Columbia University Press, 1935.

Berkin, Carol Ruth and Mary Beth Norton. *Women of America/A History*. Boston: Houghton Mifflin Company, 1979.

Briffault, Robert and Bronislaw Malinowski. *Marriage Past and Present*. Boston: Porter Sargent, 1956.

Calhoun, Arthur. *A Social History of the American Family/From Colonial Times to the Present*. Vol. I-III. Cleveland: The Arthur H. Clark Company, 1918.

Culley, Margo. *A Day at a Time. The Diary Literature of American Women from 1794 to the Present*. The Feminist Press, 1985.

Dewhurst, C. Kurt, Betty and Marsha MacDowell. *Artists in Aprons/Art by American Wives,* New York: E.P. Dutton, 1979.

Ditzion, Sidney. *Marriage, Morals and Sex in America*. New York: Bookman Associates, 1953.

Earle, Alice Morse. "Marriage Customs," *Journal of American Folklore,* 1893, pp. 104-105.

Fielding, William J. *Strange Customs of Courtship and Marriage,* New York: The New Home Library, 1942.

Fletcher, Stevenson. *Pennsylvania Agriculture and Country Life*. Harrisburg, PA: Pennsylvania Historical and Museum Commission, 1950.

Goode, William J. *World Revolution and Family Patterns*. New York: The Free Press, 1963.

Goody, Jack. *The Development of the Family and Marriage in Europe*. Cambridge: Cambridge University Press, 1983.

Gordon, Michael, ed. *The American Family in Social Perspective*. New York: St. Martins Press, 1978.

Grossberg, Michael. *Governing the Hearth/Law and Family in Nineteenth-Century America*. Chapel Hill, North Carolina: University of North Carolina Press, 1985.

Haines, Frank and Elizabeth. *Early American Brides. A Study of Costume & Tradition 1594-1820.* Cumberland, Maryland: Hobby House Press, Inc., 1982.

Hamilton, Cicely. *Marriage as a Trade*. London: Chapman and Ltd., 1912.

Hellerstein, Erna Olafson and Leslie Parker Hume and Karen M. Offer. *Victorian Women/A Documentary Account of Women's Lives in 19th Century England, France and the United States*. Stanford, California: Stanford University Press, 1981.

Hogeland, Ronald W. *Women and Womanhood in America*. Lexington, Mass.: D.C. Heath and Company, 1973.

Hughes, D.O. "From Bride Price to Dowry in Medieval Europe," *Journal of Family History,* Vol. 3, pp. 262-296.

Hutchinson, Reverend H. N. *Marriage Customs in Many Lands*. London: Seeley and Co. Limited, 1897.

Ironside, Charles Edward. *The Family in Colonial New York/A Socialized Study*. New York: Columbia University, 1942.

Kaplan, Marion, ed. *The Marriage Bargain/Women and Dowries in European History*. The Haworth Press, Inc. 1985.

Keim, C. Ray. "Primogeniture and Entail in Colonial Virginia," *William and Mary Quarterly.* October 1968, pp. 545-586.

Kirshner, Julius and Suzanne F. Wemple. *Women of the Medieval World.* New York: Basil Blackwell, Inc. 1985.

Lacy, Peter. *The Wedding.* New York: Grosset & Dunlap, 1969.

Leonard, Eugenia and Sophia Drinker and Miriam Holden. *The American Woman in Colonial and Revolutionary Times, 1565-1800.* Philadelphia: University of Pennsylvania Press, 1962.

"Marriage Celebration in the Colonies," *Atlantic* 1889, pp. 350-359, 527-530.

"Marriage Settlement," *Cornhill Magazine* 1863, pp. 666-677.

Mazer, Wendy. *Mary's Quilting.* East Stroudsburg, PA: Wendy Mazer, 1976.

Merrill, Francis. *Courtship and Marriage/A Study in Social Relationships.* New York: William Sloane Associates, Inc. 1949.

Rothman, Ellen K. *Hands and Hearts/A History of Courtship in America.* New York: Basic Books, Inc., Publishers, 1984.

Salmon, Mary Lynn. *Women and the Law of Property in Early America.* Chapel Hill: University of North Carolina Press, 1986.

Something Old, Something New/Ethnic Weddings in America. Philadelphia: Balch Institute for Ethnic Studies, 1987.

Stuard, Susan Mosher, ed. *Women In Medieval Society.* Philadelphia: University of Pennsylvania Press, 1976.

Swan, Susan Barrows. *Plain & Fancy/American Women and Their Needlework, 1700-1850.* Holt, Rinehart and Winston, 1977.

Waciega, Lisa Wilson. "A `Man of Business': The Widow of Means in Southeastern Pennsylvania, 1750-1850." *William & Mary Quarterly: A Magazine of Early American History and Culture.* Vol. 44, No. 1. January 1987, pp. 40-64.

Westermark, Edward. *The History of Human Marriage, Vol. II.* New York: The Allerton Book Company, 1922.

Zimmerman, Catherine S. *The Bride's Book/A Pictorial History of American Bridal Dress.* New York: Arbor House, 1985.

PENNSYLVANIA-GERMAN TRADITIONS

PRIMARY SOURCES

Account book. John and Jacob Bachman (joiners). Conestoga Township, Lancaster County. 1769-1828. Joseph Down's Manuscript Collection, Winterthur Museum.

Account book. Clemens family (farmers). Lower Salford Township, Montgomery County. 1749-1857. Private collection. Microfilm at Mennonite Historical Library of Eastern Pennsylvania, Lansdale; translated by Raymond E. Hollenbach. Edited by Alan G. Keyser, Breinigsville, PA: The Pennsylvania German Society, 1975.

Account book. Charles Daub (carpenter, cabinet maker, and undertaker). Franconia Township, Montgomery County. 1809-1887. Mennonite Historical Library of Eastern Pennsylvania, Lansdale.

Account book. Henry H. Dietz (farmer and carpenter). York County. 1854-1870. Historical Society of York County.

Account book. Jacob Gerhard (Justice of the Peace). Upper Hanover Township, Montgomery County. 1815-1840. Schwenkfelder Library, Pennsburg.

Account book. Charles Gotchell. Wakefield, Fulton Township, Lancaster County. 1865-1879. Lancaster Historical Society.

Account book. Johannes Helm (farmer). East Hanover Township, Lebanon County. 1792-1855. Lebanon County Historical Society.

Account book. Christian Howser (farmer). Lancaster County. 1799-1844. Private Collection.

Account book. Moses A. Kaufman. Walnut Creek Township, Holmes County, Ohio. 1857-1946. Private Collection.

Account books. Peter Knab (farmer). Oley, Berks County, 1793-1806, 1817-1831. Schwenkfelder Library, Pennsburg.

Account book. Benjamin Landis. Landis Valley, Lancaster, 1812-1834. Private Collection.

Account book. Jacob Leiby. Perry Township, Berks County. 1855-1884. Collection of Don Yoder.

Account books. Henry Moyer (carpenter and farmer). Hereford Township, Montgomery County. 1837-1847. Schwenkfelder Library, Pennsburg.

Account book. Abraham Overholt (farmer and joiner). Plumstead Township, Bucks County. 1790-1833. Private Collection. Translated by Alan G. Keyser, Breinigsville, PA: The Pennsylvania German Society, 1978.

Account book. Peter Ranck (joiner). Jonestown, Lebanon County. 1794- . Private Collection. Translated by Frederick S. Weiser and Larry M. Neff, Breinigsville, PA: The Pennsylvania German Society, 1978.

Account book. Erastus D. Rhoads (school teacher and organist). Unionville, Lehigh County. 1867-1870. Lehigh County Historical Society.

Account book. Jacob Scholl (potter). Upper Salford Township, Montgomery County. 1838. Private collection.

Account books. William and Samuel Schultz (farmers). Hereford Township, Montgomery County. 1812-1871. Schwenkfelder Library, Pennsburg.

Day book. Christian Myers (blacksmith). Central Bucks County. 1809-1845. Mennonite Historical Library of Eastern Pennsylvania, Lansdale.

Family book. Michael Albrecht (weaver and farmer). New Hanover Township, Montgomery County. 1780-1857. Private Collection.

Family book. Christian Bomberger (farmer and Mennonite bishop). Warwick Township, Lancaster County. 1860-1909. Lancaster County Mennonite Historical Society.

Family book. Johan Bomberger (farmer). Warwick Township, Lancaster County. 1832-1861. Lancaster Mennonite Historical Library.

Family book. Daniel S. Burkholder (farmer). Earl Township, Lancaster County. 1858-1902. Muddy Creek Farm Library.

Family book. Abram F. Derstein, Sr. (blacksmith and farmer). Franconia Township, Montgomery County. 1883-1888. Private Collection.

Family book. Jacob Krob (weaver, farmer, and blue dyer). Lower Salford Township, Montgomery County. 1764-1782. Mennonite Historical Library of Eastern Pennsylvania, Lansdale.

Family books. Abraham Wismer, Sr. and Abraham Wismer, Jr. (weaver and distiller). Bedminster Township, Bucks County. 1794-1830. Mennonite Historical Library of Eastern Pennsylvania, Lansdale.

Family book. Peter Zimmerman (farmer). Earl Township, Lancaster County. 1862-1885. Muddy Creek Farm Library.

BIBLIOGRAPHY

Gehman family records. Upper Hanover Township, Berks County. 1804-1879. Private collection. Translated by Raymond E. Hollenbach. Mennonite Historical Library of Eastern Pennsylvania, Lansdale.

Lederach Store records. 1828. Private collection: Translated by Raymond E. Hollenbach. Mennonite Historical Library of Eastern Pennsylvania, Lansdale.

Leiby, Jacob. Court case materials. Collection of Don Yoder.

Miller, Lewis. *Sketches and Chronicles.* 1799-1870. (reprinted with introduction), York: Historical Society of York, 1966.

Rush, Benjamin. "An Account of the Manners of the German Inhabitants of Pennsylvania" (1789). Reprinted in the *Proceedings and Addresses of the Pennsylvania German Society, Vol. XIX.* Lancaster: Pennsylvania German Society, 1909.

Will. Jonathan Kolb. (b. 1827, d. 1897) East Vincent Township, Chester County. Translation. Mennonite Historical Library, of Eastern Pennsylvania, Lansdale.

Will. Peter Yerger. (2WZ450). Register of Wills, Montgomery County.

Wills. 1792-1862. Thirty translations of Pennsylvania-German wills from Berks, Lehigh, and Northampton counties by Lewis W. Donat, Allentown, 1986 at Lehigh County Historical Society.

SECONDARY SOURCES

Bachman, Calvin George. "The Old Order Amish of Lancaster County," *The Pennsylvania German Society, Vol. 60,* 1961.

Burkholder, Anna. *Daniel S. Burkholder Family History.* Denver, PA: Amos B. Hoover, 1981.

Buzelius, Margaret. "Amish Surprises/Handknit Socks with Colors and Frills." *Vogue Knitting.* Fall/Winter 1987, p.10.

Cummings, John and Martha S. "John Drissel and His Boxes," *Pennsylvania Folklife*, Vol. 9, #4, Fall, 1958, pp. 28-31.

"Extract From an Old Will," *Lancaster Historical Proceedings,* Vol. X, No. 1, January 1906, pp. 120-122.

Fabian, Monroe. *The Pennsylvania-German Decorated Chest.* New York: Main Street Press, 1978.

Fegley, H. Winslow. "Among Some of the Older Mills in Eastern Pennsylvania," *Proceedings of the Pennsylvania German Society, Vol. XXXIX,* 1928.

Fryer, Judith E. *25 Year Index to Pennsylvania Folklife 1949-1976.* Collegeville, PA: Folklife Society, 1980.

Garvin, Beatrice B. *The Pennsylvania-German Collection.* Philadelphia: the Philadelphia Museum of Art, 1982.

Gehret, Ellen J. *This is the Way I Pass My Time.* Birdsboro, PA: Pennsylvania German Society, 1985.

"George Erion, the Ragman." *The Quarterly of the Pennsylvania German Society, 1975. Vol. X, No. 1,* 1976, pp. 3-16.

German-American Relations and German Culture in America/A Select Bibliography 1941-1980. Millward, NY: Knauss International Publications, 1984.

Gibbons, Phebe Earle. *Pennsylvania Dutch and Other Essays* rev. ed., Philadelphia: J.B. Lippincott & Co. 1882.

Gilbert, Russell. "Pennsylvania German Wills." *Pennsylvania German Folklife Society.Vol. 15,* 1951.

_____. "Pennsylvania German Wills in Berks County," *Historical Review of Berks County, Vol. XXI, No. 1,* October/December 1955, pp. 8-12.

"Gottshalk Gottshalk An Old-time Weaver/S. Pennsylvania Deitsch Eck," *The Allentown Morning Call,* March 16, 1968.

Granick, Eve. *The Amish Quilt.* Intercourse, PA: Good Books, 1989.

Gunn, Virginia and Stephanie Tan and Ricky Clark. *Treasures from Trunks,* Wooster, Ohio: The College at Wooster, 1987.

Hollenbach, Raymond E. "Ausstever — Dowries. Parts I-III./S. Pennsylvania Deitsch Eck," *The Allentown Morning Call,* March 23-April 6, 1968.

Hostetler, John A. *Amish Society.* Baltimore: Johns Hopkins University Press, (third edition) 1980.

Keyser, Alan G. "Beds, Bedding, Bedsteads and Sleep" *Der Reggeboge, The Quarterly of the Pennsylvania German Society Vol. 12 No. 4,* October 1978.

Knauss, James Owen, Jr. "Social Conditions Among the Pennsylvania-Germans in the Eighteenth Century as Revealed in the German Newspapers Published in `Pennsylvania German Diaries/S. Pennsylvania Deitsch Eck,' *The Allentown Morning Call,* April 8, 1967.

Kriebel, Howard Wagner. "A Narrative and Critical History of the Schwenkfelders in Pennsylvania," *The Proceedings of the Pennsylvania German Society, Vol. XIII,* 1904.

The Life and Times of Amos Schultz 1809-1895. n.p.: Amos Schultz Family Union, 1953.

McCauley, Daniel and Kathryn. *The Decorative Arts of the Amish of Lancaster County.* Intercourse, PA: Good Books, 1988.

Moyer Family History Vol. III. Elmer, N.J.: Fretz Family Association, 1987.

Parsons, Phyllis Vibbard "Indentured Servants in Montgomery County," *Bulletin of the Historical Society of Montgomery County, Vol. XXV, No. 1,* Fall 1985, pp. 43-50.

Parsons, William T. "Schwenkfelder Indentures, 1754-1846," *Schwenkfelders in America* ed. Peter C. Erb, Pennsburg, PA: Schwenkfelder Library, 1987.

Reed, Henry M. *Decorated Furniture of the Mahantongo Valley.* Lewisburg, PA: The Center Gallery, Bucknell University, 1987.

Roan, Nancy and Ellen Gehret. *Just a Quilt, Juscht en Deppich.* Green Lane, PA: Goschenhoppen Historians, 1984.

Scott, Stephen. *The Amish Wedding and Other Special Occasions of the Old Order Communities.* Intercourse, PA: Good Books, 1988.

Seidel, John. "Dowry and Inheritance in Rural Pennsylvania German Society." Unpublished paper for Don Yoder's seminar on Pennsylvania-German ethnography at the University of Pennsylvania, 1980-1981.

Swank, Scott. *The Arts of the Pennsylvania Germans.* New York: W.W. Norton & Co., 1983.

Tortora, Vincent. "The Courtship and Wedding Practices of the Old Order Amish," *Pennsylvania Folklife, Vol. 9, No. 2,* Spring, 1958, pp. 12-21.

"Where There's a Will," *Lancaster County Connections,* Vol. 1, Nov. 4, pp. 71-73 and Vol. 4, No. 2, pp. 72-75.

ANGLO-SAXON TRADITIONS

PRIMARY SOURCES

Account book. William Canby Biddle. Philadelphia Meeting. Friends Historical Library of Swarthmore College.

Account book. Jacob Cassat (farmer, tanner, and surveyor). Near Gettysburg, Adams County. 1801-1879. Bucks County Historical Society.

Account books. Amos Darlington, Jr. (cabinetmaker). West Chester, Chester County. 1819-1836, 1823-1853, MS # 3185, 3184. Chester County Historical Society.

Account book. Amos Darlington Sr. (cabinetmaker). West Chester, Chester County. 1764-1828. MS #3186. Chester County Historical Society.

Account book. Mathias Foy (cabinetmaker). East Bradford Township, Chester County. 1812-1826. MS #77050. Chester County Historical Society.

Account book. William and James Gibbons (farmers). East Bradford Township, Chester County. 1789-1803, 1822-1839. MS #76850. Chester County Historical Society.

Account book. Jonathan D. Larkin (furniture, coffinmaker, and gravedigger). Chester County. 1827-1841. Friends Historical Library of Swarthmore College.

Account book. Agnes Salkeld Minshall. Middletown, Chester County. 1783-1810. Painter collection. Friends Historical Library of Swarthmore College.

Account book. Jacob Minshall. Middletown, Chester County. 1783-1800. Painter collection. Friends Historical Library of Swarthmore College.

Account book. Thomas Montague (farmer). 1816-1828. Hartsville, Bucks County, Bucks County Historical Society.

Account book. Samuel Pennock. West Marlborough Township, Chester County. 1810-1831. MS #10723. Chester County Historical Society.

Account book. Enos Thomas (cabinetmaker. sawyer and farmer). East Goshen Township, Chester County. 1791-1804. Chester County Historical Society.

Account book. Jasper Yeates (attorney). Lancaster, Lancaster County. 1764-1817. Lancaster County Historical Society.

Contract. Ruth Pennock. January 2, 1822. MS #10788. Chester County Historical Society.

Diaries. Eighty-seven from 1759-1869. Chester County Historical Society.

Diary. Mary Asheton Henry Beatty. #A-201. Bucks County Historical Society.

Dowry listing. Levis Pennock to Mary Pennock Passmore. May 7, 1777. MS #10549. Chester County Historical Society.

Estate papers. William and Jane Gibbons. 1804-1805. Chester County Archives.

Inventory. Mary Pennock. May 5, 1777. MS #10549. Chester County Historical Society.

Letter. Jane Ashbridge to cousin Rebecca. December 30, 1850. MS #10222. Chester County Historical Society.

Marriage certificate. William Lunnard and Mary Miers. MS #3/23/88.Friends Historical Library of Swarthmore College.

Marriage contracts. Twenty-nine from 1700-1800. Chester County Archives.

Marriage settlement. Robert Plumstead and Hannah Lunn. June 1, 1748. MS #3/23/88. Friends Historical Library of Swarthmore College.

Receipt book. Caleb and Robert Johnson family. Possibly Chester County. 1766-1797. MS #76509. Chester County Historical Society.

Rules of Discipline of the Religious Society of Friends. London: Darton and Harvy, 1834.

Will. Ziba Darlington. West Chester, Chester County. April 6, 1874. MS #2312. Chester County Historical Society.

Will. Abraham Marshall. West Bradford Township, Chester County. January 4, 1865. MS #635. Chester County Historical Society.

Will. Humphrey Marshall. West Bradford Township, Chester County. Chester County Historical Society.

Will. James Miles. Kennett Square, Chester County. December 11, 1852. MS #9179. Chester County Historical Society.

Will. Levis Pennock. West Marlborough Township, Chester County. August 28, 1815. MS #10772. Chester County Historical Society.

Wills. Ruth Pennock. West Marlborough Township, Chester County. July 28, 1822. MS #10782; March 23, 1826. MS #10803. Chester County Historical Society.

SECONDARY SOURCES

Brey, Jane W.T. *A Quaker Saga*. Philadelphia: Dorrance & Company, n.d. (c.1967).

Frost, Jerry William. *The Quaker Family in Colonial America*. New York: St. Martin's Press, 1973.

Gillis, John R. *For Better or Worse; British Marriage 1600- Present*, 1985.

Griffth, Lee Ellen. *Line and Berry and Inlaid Furniture: A Regional Craft Tradition in Pennsylvania, 1682-1790*. University of Pennsylvania, Ph.D. Thesis, 1988.

_____. "The Line-and-Berry Inlaid Furniture of Eighteenth Century Pennsylvania" *Antiques*. May 1989, pp. 1202-1211.

_____. *The Pennsylvania Spice Box*. West Chester: Chester County Historical Society, 1986. Levy, Barry John. *The Light in the Valley: The Chester and Welsh Tract Quaker Communities and the Delaware Valley, 1681-1750*. University of Pennsylvania, Ph. D. Thesis, 1976.

_____. *Quakers and the American Family/British Settlement in the Delaware Valley*. Oxford, England: Oxford University Press, 1988.

Massey, George Valentine II. *The Pennocks of Primitive Hall*. West Chester, PA: Chester County Historical Society, 1951.

Parsons, William. "The Brief Married Life of Isaac and Sarah Norris," *Quaker History/The Bulletin of Friends Historical Association,Vol. 57, No. 2*, Autumn 1968. pp, 67-81.

Schiffer, Margaret B. *Chester County Inventories 1684-1850*. Exton, PA: Schiffer Publishing Ltd., 1974.

Soderland, Jean R. "Women's Authority in Pennsylvania and New Jersey Quaker Meetings, 1680-1760, "*William and Mary Quarterly/A Magazine of Early American History and Culture Vol. 44, No. 4*, October 1987, pp. 722-749.

Stone, Lawrence. *Family, Sex and Marriage in England 1500-1800*. London: Weidenfeld and Nicolson, 1977.

Correspondence with Joel Alderfer, Mennonite Historians of Eastern Pennsylvania, Lansdale; Gloria Braun, State College; Rodney G. Cavernough, Scottdale; Dr. Paul M. Corman, Bellefonte; Frances K. Faile, Bethlehem; Holly K. Green, Boyerstown; June Griffith, Lehigh County Historical Society's Library, Allentown; Patricia Herr,Lancaster; Tandy Hersh, Carlisle; Amos B. Hoover, Denver; Lois Huffines, Professor of Linguistics and German, Bucknell University, Lewisburg; Alan G. Keyser, East Greenville; Vertie Knapp, Stroudsburg; Lane Furniture Company, Altavista, Virginia; Nancy Spears, Swarthmore; Gail Stern, Balch Institute, Philadelphia; William Woys Weaver, Paoli; Don Yoder, Devon; and John Zeigler, State College.

Index

Albrecht, Michael 58, 64, 66, 81
affluence 25, 27, 28, 43, 48, 50
Amish customs 4, 7, 8, 15, 30-41, 71, 77, 78, 82, 83
Anglicans 27, 28
Anglo-Saxon 4, 5, 24-28, 43-50, 74-77, 80, 81
approval 4, 15, 17
assimilation 4, 41, 43, 72
ausbehalt 8, 20-24
aussteier components 8, 30, 71

Bachman, John and Jacob 56
baskets 5, 41
bedding traditions 32, 34, 39, 41-43, 60, 61
Biddle, William 50
Bomberger, Christian 62, 65, 67, 69
Bomberger, Johan 59, 64, 66, 76
Burkholder, Daniel 63, 65, 67, 69, 71, 76

cabinetmakers' accounts 32, 35, 47, 48, 50, 56, 57, 61, 63
cash 37, 39, 41, 43
Cassett, Jacob 46, 50
ceramics 28, 29, 33, 35-37, 39, 41, 72, 82
charts 46, 51, 52, 54, 55, 64-69
Chester County 5, 24, 25, 74, 75, 77, 80
Clemens family 4, 5, 52-55, 72, 81
clothing 35, 36
colonial revival 75, 83
cost of dowry 38

Darlington, Amos, Jr. and Sr. 47, 48
dated objects 24, 72-83
Daub, Charles 63
debt 17
definitions 4, 6-9, 11-13, 15, 36
Dietz, Henry 63
Derstein, Abraham 65, 67, 69, 71
dower 8, 9, 11, 20-23, 74, 82

economic considerations 4, 9, 30, 32, 33
English traditions 8, 9, 24-28, 43-50
equity 17, 18, 22, 24, 27, 28, 32, 33, 37, 38, 43
evolution of goods 28, 38, 41, 43, 52, 54, 55, 64-70

family books inside cover, 4, 17, 30, 33, 35, 37, 38, 43, 44-48, 50-59, 61-69, 71
farm equipment 31-34, 41, 43, 46, 54, 55, 64-69
farming 28, 32, 33, 36-39, 41
food 36-41, 46, 54, 55, 64-69
Foy, Mathias 48
furniture forms 18, 19, 30, 31, 38, 39, 42, 45, 46, 51, 54, 55, 64-69, 72-77, 80

garden tools 46, 54, 55, 64-69
Gehman, Johannes 59, 65, 67, 69, 76
German traditions 7, 9
Gibbons, William and James 45, 46
gifts from home 4, 8
glassware 32, 35-37, 39-41, 46, 54, 55, 64-69
grain cover, 36, 39, 46, 54, 55, 64-69

haussteier 8, 36, 40, 41
Helm, Johannes 59
"hope" chest 6, 12, 13, 34, 35, 74, 82
Howser, Christian 58, 64

indentures 14-17
inheritance 4, 15-18, 19-28
initialed objects 72-83
inventories 23-24, 77

Johnson, Caleb and Robert inside cover, 44, 46

Kaufman, Moses 65, 67, 69, 71, 76
Knab, Peter 57, 64
Krob, Jacob 53, 56, 64

land 17, 22-25, 28, 33, 37
Lane cedar chest 4, 43
Larkin, Jonathan 50
Leiby, Jacob 4, 17, 18, 61, 62, 65, 67, 69
livestock 32, 33, 36-39, 41, 43, 46, 54, 55, 64-69

mainstream culture 4, 6, 7, 12, 13
marriage contracts 11, 27
marriage portion 15, 17, 25, 27, 28, 30, 82
Mennonite 4, 7, 8, 23, 32, 36-38, 52, 53, 56, 57, 59, 62, 63, 71, 83
metalware 32, 37, 39-41, 48, 49, 78-82
Minsall, Jacob 44
Montague, Thomas 50
Moyer, Henry 61
mutual obligations 20, 22, 23, 27, 28
Myers, Christian 57, 58, 64, 66

needlework 7, 32, 36, 37, 39, 41, 43, 78, 80, 82, 83

outfitting 4

Overholt, Abraham 56, 57

parental control 4, 15, 17, 25, 27
patterns of giving 30-71
Pennock family 16, 18, 20, 21, 25, 46, 48, 50
Pennsylvania German 4, 15-18, 20-24, 26-28, 30-43, 72-76, 78-83
pewter 31, 41, 77, 81
Plain people 14, 23, 27, 30-41
"precious" items 34, 35, 72, 78
primogeniture 9, 11, 27, 28

Quaker traditions 24-28, 44, 47, 48, 50, 74-78, 80, 81
quiltmaking 32, 34-37, 39-41, 43, 80, 83

Ranck, Peter 57
revolving fund concept 20, 22, 23, 27, 28
rite of passage 4, 6, 7
Rhoads, Erastus 63
rugs 32-36, 39-41

Scholl, Jacob 61
Schultz, William and Samuel 57
sex-linked objects 38, 39, 41, 43, 46, 54, 55, 64-69
social mobility 4
spousal control 20-23
store accounts 59, 61

terminology 37
textiles 7, 32, 36, 37, 39, 41, 43, 78, 80, 82, 83
tools 33, 36-39, 41, 46, 54, 55, 64-69

vehicles 32, 33, 37, 39, 41, 43

wages 17, 33, 37, 38
widow's share 9, 20-23, 44
wills 17, 18, 20-23, 77
Wismer, Abraham 57, 64

Yeates, Jasper 45, 47

Zimmerman, Peter 62, 63, 65, 67, 69